SMITH'S GUIDE™ TO SECOND OR SUCCESSIVE FEDERAL
HABEAS CORPUS RELIEF

FOR STATE AND FEDERAL PRISONERS

Also by Zachary A. Smith

SMITH'S GUIDE to Habeas Corpus Relief
for State Prisoners Under 28 U.S.C. §2254

SMITH'S GUIDE to Executive Clemency
for State and Federal Prisoners

SMITH'S GUIDE to Chapter 7 Bankruptcy
for Prisoners

SMITH'S GUIDE to State Habeas Corpus Relief
for State Prisoners

*Available through Amazon.com
and distributed by Ingram*

SMITH'S GUIDE™
to
Second or Successive Federal Habeas Corpus Relief

for
State and Federal Prisoners

By
Zachary A. Smith

redbat books
2017

First Edition, August 15, 2017

Copyright © 2017 by Zachary A. Smith
All rights reserved

No part of this book may reproduced in any form whatsoever, whether by graphic, visual, electronic, film, microfilm, tape recording, or any other means, without prior written permission of the author, except in the case of brief passages embodied in critical reviews or articles.

ISBN-10: 1-946970-90-5
ISBN-13: 978-1-946970-90-9
    Library of Congress Control Number: 2017950507

Published by
redbat books
2901 Gekeler Lane
La Grande, OR 97850
www.redbatbooks.com

Text set in Chaparral Pro.

Book design by Kristin Summers, redbat design | www.redbatdesign.com

DISCLAIMER

This book is not an alternative to professional assistance by an attorney. This book does not provide licensed, professional legal advice. Its author is a paralegal, not a lawyer; its text is for informational purposes only. The material contained herein is not intended to substitute for professional legal advice by an attorney. Never disregard professional legal advice, and never delay in seeking it or hiring an attorney to represent you because of anything you read in this book. It is the responsibility of you, the reader, to seek out and secure legal advice on how to proceed within the federal judicial system.

The information in this book has been carefully researched, and all efforts have been made to ensure accuracy. The author and publisher assume no responsibility for any damages or losses incurred during, or as a result of, the application of the information presented here. All information should be carefully studied and clearly understood before taking any action based on the contents of this book. The reader assumes full responsibility for the consequences of his or her own actions, filing, and strategic decisions.

INTRODUCTION

When I was writing *Smith's Guide™ to State Habeas Corpus Relief for State Prisoners*, there was a lot of prison talk surrounding the retroactive effect of *Miller v. Alabama*, 132 S.Ct. 2455 (2012), which held that a juvenile offender convicted of a homicide offense cannot be sentenced to life in prison without parole, absent consideration of the juvenile's special circumstances in light of the principles and purposes of juvenile sentencing.

The state courts were in conflict as to whether *Miller* had retroactive effect, and which standard of review, *Teague* or *Linkletter-Stovall*, was applicable. Several state courts refused to apply *Miller* retroactively to juvenile offenders, denying them relief, thus leaving the issue for federal courts to sort out.

Missouri juvenile offenders were appointed attorneys to represent them, but instead of litigating each offender's case individually, the attorneys waited for the United States Supreme Court to issue a decision in *Montgomery v. Louisiana*, 136 S.Ct. 718 (2016). In that decision, the Court held that when a new substantial rule of constitutional law controls the outcome of a case, the Constitution requires state collateral review courts to give retroactive effect to that rule. *Miller* was made retroactive. At the end of its opinion, however, the Court threw the states a bone, suggesting that a state may remedy a *Miller* violation by permitting juvenile homicide offenders to be considered for parole, rather than by resentencing them.

On July 13, 2016, then-governor of Missouri Jeremiah W. Nixon signed Senate Bill 590, enacting into law Revised Missouri Annotated Statute 558.047 RSMo (2016), which states, among other things, that "[a]ny person sentenced to a term of imprisonment for life without eligibility for parole before August 28, 2016, who was under eighteen years of age at the time of the commission of the offense or offenses, may submit to the parole board a petition for a review of his or her sentence, regardless of whether the case is final for purposes of appeal, after serving twenty-five years of incarceration on the sentence of life without parole."

For those sentenced after August 28, 2016, according to 565.033 RSMo (2016), "[a]ny person found guilty of murder in the first degree who was under the age of eighteen at the time of the commission of the offense shall be sentenced to a term of life without eligibility for probation or parole as provided in section 565.034, life imprisonment with eligibility for parole, or not less then thirty years and not to exceed forty years imprisonment."

As of the time of this book's writing, litigation continues for juvenile offenders' resentencing, with the federal courts flooded by applications for filing second or successive habeas corpus petitions. On July 11, 2017, the Missouri Supreme Court held, in *State ex rel. Jason Clay Carr v. Wallace*, SC93487—S.W.3d—(Mo. banc July 11, 2017), that juvenile offenders sentenced to life without parole are entitled to resentencing under *Miller*. The Court also concluded in two separate cases that imposing consecutive sentences in juvenile cases does no violate *Miller v. Alabama* or *Graham v. Florida*. See *Willbanks v. Missouri Department of Corrections*, SC95395, —S.W.3d—(Mo. banc July 11, 2017) and *State v. Nathan*, SC95473,—S.W.3d—(Mo. banc July 11, 2017). This issue is ripe for review by the United States Supreme Court.

This book was written to fill prisoners' need for a guide in their fight for their rights, in the event that the United States Supreme Court issues a decision of questionable retroactivity, as well as instances when new evidence establishes actual innocence after all a prisoner's appeals have been exhausted.

Here I have laid out the process, step by step, for filing an application for leave to file a second or successive § 2254 or § 2255 habeas corpus petition. If you are familiar with my other *Smith's Guides*, no further introductory information is necessary. If not, start reading; you will quickly realize that your purchase of a *Smith's Guide* was a wise decision.

Z.A. Smith

—Zachary A. Smith

TABLE OF CONTENTS

Disclaimer 5

Introduction 7

<1> Overview of Second or Successive Habeas Corpus Application 13
    Statutory Authority 13
    Statutory Grounds for Authorization 15
    Standard of Review for Authorization 15
    Thirty-Day Time Limit for Court's Decision 16
    The Grant or Denial of Application Is Not Appealable 16
    Standard of Review in District Court after Authorization Is Granted 16
    (State Prisoner) Statute of Limitations for Filing Application 17
    (Federal Prisoner) Statute of Limitations for Filing Application 17
    Equitable Tolling of the One-Year Requirement 17

<2> Statutory Requirements for Authorization 19
    New Rule of Constitutional Law 19
    Newly Discovered Evidence 21

<3> One-Year Statute of Limitations 23
    Exhaustion of State Remedies 23
    One-Year Limitation Period for Federal Prisoners 24
    Equitable Tolling 25

<4> Legal Research, Investigative Methods, and Legal Writing 27
    Legal Research 27
    Investigative Methods 28
        Case File 28
        Public Records 29
        Records Open to Public 29
        State, County, and Federal Records 29
        Records Available Only Upon Proof of a Legal Need 30
        Records Available Only Upon Written Request 30
        Freedom of Information Act 30
        Finding Potential Witnesses 31
        Finding Expert Witnesses 31
    Legal Writing 32

<5> Application to File Second or Successive Habeas Corpus Petition 33

Preparation of Application 33
Application to File Second or Successive Habeas Corpus Petition 33
   Caption 33
   Jurisdictional Statement 34
   Statement of the Case 34
   Reason for Granting Application 34
   Conclusion 34
   Verification of Application 34
   Certificate of Service 34
Example Applications 35
   Example Application #1—Robert James Campbell 35
   Example Application #2—Dewitt McDonald, Jr. 84
   Example Application #3—Leslie A. Parker 139
   Example Application #4—Jasper Moore 159

<6> Preparation of Appendix for Accompanying Exhibits 191

Organization of Appendix 191
Page Numbering (Optional) 191
Binding 191
Affidavits 191
Examples 195
   Appendix for Exhibits in Support of Application 195
   Affidavit of Zachary A. Smith 198
   Affidavit of Jim Miller 201
   Affidavit of George A. Halterman, III 204
   Affidavit of Steven J. Pietroforte 206

<7> Filing Application and Accompanying Exhibits with the Court 209

Filing Requirements 209
Filing Fee 209
Mailing Application and Exhibits 209
Example 210
   Letter from Clerk for the Eighth Circuit 210

<8> Respondent's Response to Petitioner's Application 211

Respondent's Response 211
Petitioner's Reply 212
Case Submission 212
Example 213
   Petitioner's Reply—Robert James Campbell 213

<9> Court of Appeals' Decision **245**
    Grant or Denial of Leave to File Second or Successive Habeas Corpus Petition 245
    Court of Appeals' Decision 245
    Conclusion 245
    Examples 246
        Decision Granting Application (In Re: Jackson Stallings) 246
        Decision Granting Application (In Re: Ralph Brazel, Jr.) 240
        Decision Granting Application (In Re: Jasper Moore) 254
        Judgment and Mandate Denying Application (In Re: Zachary A. Smith) 262

Appendix A: Application Process **265**
    District of Columbia Circuit Court of Appeals 266
    First Circuit Court of Appeals (ME, MA, NH, RI, PR) 267
    Second Circuit Court of Appeals (CT, NY, VT) 269
    Third Circuit Court of Appeals (DE, NJ, PA, VI) 271
    Fourth Circuit Court of Appeals (MD, NC, SC, VA, WV) 273
    Fifth Circuit Court of Appeals (LA, MS, TX) 275
    Sixth Circuit Court of Appeals (KY, MI, OH, TN) 277
    Seventh Circuit Court of Appeals (IL, IN, WI) 279
    Eighth Circuit Court of Appeals (AR, IA, MN, MO, NE, ND, SD) 281
    Ninth Circuit Court of Appeals (AK, AZ, CA, GU, HI, ID, MT, NV, MP, OR, WA) 283
    Tenth Circuit Court of Appeals (CO, KS, NM, OK, UT, WY) 285
    Eleventh Circuit Court of Appeals (AL, FL, GA) 287

Appendix B: Attorneys General Offices **289**
    State Attorneys General Offices 289
    United States Attorneys Offices 296

Appendix C: Blank Application Form **329**

Appendix D : Glossary of Terms **343**

Acknowledgments **347**

<1> OVERVIEW OF SECOND OR SUCCESSIVE HABEAS CORPUS APPLICATION

Statutory Authority

No state prisoner under *28 USCS § 2244(b)(3)(A)*, nor federal prisoner under *28 USCS § 2255(h)*, will be permitted to file a second or successive application for a writ of habeas corpus in a United States district court without first obtaining permission from the appropriate United States court of appeals. The statutory authority of 28 USCS § 2244 states:

(a) No circuit court or district judge shall be required to entertain an application for a writ of habeas corpus to inquire into the detention of a person pursuant to a judgment of a court of the United States if it appears that the legality of such detention has been determined by a judge or court of the United States on a prior application for a writ of habeas corpus, except as provided in section 2255 [28 USCS § 2255].

(b) (1) A claim presented in a second or successive habeas corpus application under section 2254 [28 USCS § 2254] that was presented in a prior application shall be dismissed.

(2) A claim presented in a second or successive habeas corpus application under section 2254 [28 USCS § 2254] that was not presented in a prior application shall be dismissed unless—

(A) the applicant shows that the claim relies on a new rule of constitutional law, made retroactive to cases on collateral review by the Supreme Court, that was previously unavailable; or

(B) (i) the factual predicate for the claim could not have been discovered previously through the exercise of due diligence; and

(ii) the facts underlying the claim, if proven and viewed in light of the evidence as a whole, would be sufficient to establish by clear and convincing evidence that, but for constitutional error, no reasonable factfinder would have found the applicant guilty of the underlying offense.

(3) (A) Before a second or successive application permitted by this section is filed in the district court, the applicant shall move in the appropriate court of appeals for an order authorizing the district court to consider the application.

(B) A motion in the court of appeals for an order authorizing the district court to consider a second or successive application shall be determined by a three-judge panel of the court of appeals.

(C) The court of appeals may authorize the filing of a second or successive application only if it determines that the application makes a prima facie showing that the application satisfies the requirements of this subsection.

(D) The court of appeals shall grant or deny the authorization to file a second or successive application not later then 30 days after the filing of the motion.

(E) The grant or denial of an authorization by a court of appeals to file a second or successive application shall not be appealable and shall not be the subject of a petition for rehearing or for a writ of certiorari.

(4) A district court shall dismiss any claim presented in a second or successive application that the court of appeals has authorized to be filed unless the applicant shows that the claim satisfies the requirements of this section.

(c) In a habeas corpus proceeding brought in behalf of a person in custody pursuant to the judgment of a State court, a prior judgment of the Supreme Court of the United States on an appeal or review by a writ of certiorari at the instance of the prisoner of the decision of such State court, shall be conclusive as to all issues of fact or law with respect to an asserted denial of a Federal right which constitutes ground for discharge in a habeas corpus proceeding, actually adjudicated by the Supreme Court therein, unless the applicant for the writ of habeas corpus shall plead and the court shall find the existence of a material and controlling fact which did not appear in the record of the proceeding in the Supreme Court and the court shall further find that the applicant for the writ of habeas corpus could not have caused such fact to appear in such record by the exercise of reasonable diligence.

(d) (1) A 1-year period of limitation shall apply to an application for a writ of habeas corpus by a person in custody pursuant to the judgment of a State court. The limitation period shall run from the latest of—

(A) the date on which the judgment became final by the conclusion of direct review or the expiration of the time for seeking such review;

(B) the date on which the impediment to filing an application created by State action in violation of the Constitution or laws of the United States is removed, if the applicant was prevented from filing by such State action;

(C) the date on which the constitutional right asserted was initially recognized by the Supreme Court, if the right has been newly recognized by the Supreme Court and made retroactively applicable to cases on collateral review; or

(D) the date on which the factual predicate of the claim or claims presented could have been discovered through the exercise of due diligence.

(2) The time during which a properly filed application for State post-conviction or other collateral review with respect to the pertinent judgment or claim is pending shall not be counted toward any period of limitation under this subsection.

The statutory authority for authorizing a federal prisoner to file a second or successive application under 28 USCS § 2255, in connection with the provisions of 28 USCS § 2244, is similar to that for a state prisoner:

(h) A second or successive motion must be certified as provided in section 2244 [28 USCS § 2244] by a panel of the appropriate court of appeals to contain—

(1) newly discovered evidence that, if proven and viewed in light of the evidence as a whole, would be sufficient to establish by clear and convincing evidence that no reasonable factfinder would have found the movant guilty of the offense; or

(2) a new rule of constitutional law, made retroactive to cases on collateral review by the Supreme Court, that was previously unavailable.

Statutory Grounds for Authorization

The statutory grounds for authorizing a state or federal prisoner to file a second or successive application for a writ of habeas corpus are extremely narrow, requiring that:

(1) the claim relies on a new rule of constitutional law, made retroactive to cases on collateral review by the United States Supreme Court, and was previously unavailable; or

(2) the claim is newly discovered, meaning the factual predicate for the claim could not have been discovered previously through the exercise of due diligence, and the facts underlying the claim, if proven and viewed in the light of the evidence as a whole, would be sufficient to establish by clear and convincing evidence that, but for the constitutional error, no reasonable factfinder would have found the petitioner guilty of the offense.

Each of these statutory requirements will be discussed in detail in the next chapter.

Standard of Review for Authorization

A United States court of appeals may only grant leave for a prisoner (state or federal) to file a second or successive application for a writ of habeas corpus if the prisoner makes a *prima facie* showing that the application satisfies the requirements of § 2244(b)(2) or § 2255(h). "'Prima facie' in this context means simply sufficient allegations of fact together with some documentation that would 'warrant a fuller exploration in the district court.'" *Bennett v. United States, 119 F.3d 468, 569 (7th Cir. 1997)*.

If it appears reasonably likely from a prisoner's application that the application satisfies the stringent statutory requirements then the court of appeals is required to grant it. See *In re Morris, 328 F.3d 739 (5th Cir. 2003)*. See also *In re Williams, 330 F.3d 277 (4th Cir. 2003)*.

For example, the court in *In re McDonald, 514 F.3d 539 (6th Cir. 2008)* granted the petitioner leave to file a second or successive petition, where a key witness provided an affidavit stating she was coerced by the prosecutor into giving perjured testimony against the petitioner, and that evidence was unavailable to him at time of filing his first habeas petition. See also *In re LeGrone, 2010 U.S. App. LEXIS 27789 (6th Cir. 2010)*, and *In re Bell, 2009 U.S. App. LEXIS 29784 (6th Cir. 2009)*.

Thirty-Day Time Limit for Court's Decision

Although 28 USCS § 2244(b)(3)(C) states that "the court of appeals shall grant or deny the authorization to file a second or successive application not later then 30 days after the filing of the motion," the courts differ with respect to how the thirty-day period should be applied. Some circuits have concluded that § 2244(b)(3)(C) is advisory or hortatory rather than mandatory. See *In re Siggers, 132 F.3d 333 (6th Cir. 1997)*, and *Ezell v. United States, 778 F.3d 762 (9th Cir. 2015), cert. denied at 136 S.Ct. 256, 193 L.Ed.2d 212 (US 2015)*.

Nevertheless, courts of appeal adjudicate applications to file second or successive petitions for habeas corpus relief expediently unless the application presents a complex issue. See *In Re Williams, 330 F.3d 277 (4th Cir. 2003)*.

The Grant or Denial of Application is not Appealable

Once a panel of the United States court of appeals grants or denies a prisoner permission to file a second or successive petition in the district court, 28 USCS § 2244(b)(3)(E) prohibits any party (petitioner or respondent) from seeking further review of that court's decision, whether from the original panel, from the court en banc, or from the United States Supreme Court. See *In re King, 190 F.3d 479 (6th Cir. 1999), cert. denied at 120 S.Ct. 1538, 157 L.Ed.2d 352 (US 2000)*.

Standard of Review in District Court After Authorization Is Granted

A district court must dismiss the petition that the court of appeals granted leave to file, without reaching the merits of the petition, if the district court finds that the prisoner has not satisfied the requirements for filing the petition under § 2254 or § 2255. Such failures could include: that a petition contains exhausted and unexhausted claims; that the claim could have been presented and considered in a prior petition; that the claim does not rely on a new rule of constitutional law; or that the claim fails to show that no reasonable fact-finder could have found the petitioner guilty.

A prisoner must get through the statutory requirements before the merits of his or her petition will be considered. See *Bennett v. United States, 119 F.3d 468 (7th Cir. 1997)*. See also *Tyler v. Cain, 121 S.Ct. 2478 (US 2001)*.

(State Prisoner) Statute of Limitations for Filing Application

The failure to file a habeas corpus petition within the one-year limitation period is an affirmative defense against any claim pleaded by a petitioner who is a state prisoner. Although United States courts of appeal do not consider the one-year limitation period, under 28 USCS § 2244(d), the United States district courts do and are permitted to consider, *sua sponte*, the timeliness of prisoners' habeas petitions. See *Day v. McDonough*, 126 S.Ct. 1675, 164 L.Ed.2d 376 (US 2006).

(Federal Prisoner) Statute of Limitations for Filing Application

For federal prisoners, the one-year statute of limitation period is governed by 28 USCS § 2255(f), which states:

A 1-year period of limitation shall apply to a motion under this section. The limitation period shall run from the latest of—

(1) the date on which the judgment of conviction becomes final;

(2) the date on which the impediment to making a motion created by governmental action in violation of the Constitution or laws of the United States is removed, if the movant was prevented from making a motion by such governmental action;

(3) the date on which the right asserted was initially recognized by the Supreme Court and made retroactively applicable to cases on collateral review; or

(4) the date on which the facts supporting the claim or claims presented could have been discovered through the exercise of due diligence.

Equitable Tolling of the One-Year Requirement

The United States Supreme Court held, in *Pace v. DiGugielmo, 125 S.Ct. 1807, 161 L.Ed.2d 669 (2005)*, that equitable tolling is available when the prisoner can demonstrate "(1) that he has been pursuing his rights diligently, and (2) that some extraordinary circumstance stood in his way," or on what date the prisoner was able to discover the evidence in question through due diligence.

When considering an application to file a second or successive habeas corpus petition, a United States court of appeals does not have a developed record because the new petition has not been considered by a district court. Therefore, a court of appeals cannot determine whether the one-year statute of limitations should be equitably tolled and the issue must be decided by a district court after leave is granted.

The issues concerning the one-year requirement and equitable tolling will be discussed in Chapter Three.

<2> STATUTORY REQUIREMENTS FOR AUTHORIZATION

New Rule of Constitutional Law

When the United States Supreme Court decides a criminal case and announces a new constitutional rule, the rule must be applied retroactively to all cases, state or federal, that are still pending on direct review. See *Griffith v. Kentucky, 479 U.S. 314, 107 S.Ct. 708 (1987)*. "As to convictions that are already final, however, the rule applies only in limited circumstances." *Schriro v. Summerlin, 542 U.S. 348, at 351, 124 S.Ct. 2519, 2522 (2004)*.

Oftentimes its difficult to determine whether the United States Supreme Court has announced a new rule. "In general [...] a case announces a new rule when it breaks new ground or imposes a new obligation on the States or the Federal Government." *Teague v. Lane, 498 U.S. 288, 301 (1989)*. "To put it differently, a case announces a new rule if the result was not dictated by precedent existing at the time the defendant's conviction became final." *Ibid*.

The meaning of *final* is when a judgment of conviction has been rendered and one full round of appeals has been exhausted, including the filing of a petition with the United States Supreme Court for a writ of certiorari, either considered and denied or for which the ninety-day filing limitation has elapsed. See *United States v. Johnson, 457 U.S. 537 (1982)*.

A new rule of constitutional law satisfies 28 U.S.C. § 2244(b)(2)(A), or 28 U.S.C. § 2255(h)(2), when the United States Supreme Court states that the new rule is retroactively applicable to cases on collateral review. A new rule can also be made retroactive with the right combination of United States Supreme Court holdings. See *Tyler v. Cain, 533 U.S. 656, 121 S.Ct. 2478 (2001)*, and, for an example, see *In re Holladay, 331 F.3d 1169 (11th Cir. 2003)*.

A new rule will not be applied or announced in cases on collateral review unless it falls into one of two exceptions. Under the framework of *Teague v. Lane, 489 U.S. 288, 109 S.Ct. 1060 (1989)*, a new rule will only apply in a collateral proceeding if the rule is a matter of substantive law, or is a procedural rule that implicates the fundamental fairness and accuracy of the criminal proceeding (referred to as a *watershed procedural rule*).

The United States Supreme Court determines whether a new rule is substantive or procedural by considering the function of the rule and not its underlying constitutional source. *Teague's* framework creates a balance between the need for finality in criminal cases and the countervailing need to ensure that criminal punishment is imposed only when authorized by law. Therefore, the balance turns on the function of the rule at issue and not the constitutional guarantee from which the rule originated.

If a new rule only regulates the procedures for determining a defendant's culpability, the *Teague* balance will usually tip in favor of finality. "The possibility of a more accurate outcome under the new procedure normally does not justify the cost of vacating a conviction whose only flaw is that its procedures 'conformed to then-existing constitutional standards.'" *Teague, 489 U.S., at 310.*

On the other hand, if a new rule changes the scope of the underlying criminal proscription, the balance is different. According to *Bousley v. United States, 523 U.S. 614, 620, 118 S.Ct. 1604 (1998) (quoting Davis v. United States, 417 U.S. 333, 346, 94 S.Ct. 2298 (1973)*, a change of that character will "necessarily carry a significant risk that a defendant stands convicted of 'an act that the law does not make criminal.'"

Under the first *Teague* exception to retroactivity, a rule is substantive "if it alters the range of conduct or the class of persons that the law punishes." *Schriro, 542 U.S., at 353.* "This includes decisions that narrow the scope of a criminal statute by interpreting its terms, as well as constitutional determinations that place particular conduct or persons covered by the statute beyond the State's power to punish." *Id., at 351-252.*

To put it another way, a new rule of constitutional law is a rule that forbids criminal punishment of certain conduct or prohibits a certain category of punishment for a class of defendants because of their status or the type of offense committed. See *Penry v. Lynaugh, 492 U.S. 302, 109 S.Ct. 2934 (1989).*

For example, the United States Supreme Court has announced new rules that categorically ban sentencing practices on certain classes of defendants: in *Atkins v. Virginia, 526 U.S. 302 (2002)*, the Court held that imposing the death penalty on mentally retarded defendants violates the Eighth Amendment; in *Roper v. Simmons, 543 U.S. 551 (2005)*, the Court held that the Eighth Amendment bars capital punishment for juvenile offenders; in *Graham v. Florida, 560 U.S. 48 (2010)*, the Court held that the Eighth Amendment prohibits a sentence of life without the possibility of parole for a juvenile offender who commits a non-homicide offense; in *Miller v. Alabama, 132 S.Ct. 2455 (2012)*, the Court held that "[b]y removing youth from the balance—by subjecting a juvenile to the same life-without-parole sentence applicable to an adult—these [mandatory sentencing schemes] prohibit a sentencing authority from assessing whether the law's harshest term of imprisonment proportionately punishes a juvenile offender." *Id., at 2466.*

"New substantive rules apply retroactively because they necessarily carry a significant risk that a defendant stands convicted of an act that the law does not make criminal or faces a punishment that the law cannot impose on him because of his status or offense." *Schriro, at 352.* Where a new constitutional rule restricts imposition of a punishment for a particular class of defendants, that rule is substantive. See *Montgomery v. Louisiana, 136 S.Ct. 718 (2016)*, in which the Court held that *Miller v. Alabama* announced a substantive rule of constitutional law, giving it retroactive effect to cases on state collateral review. See also *Welch v. United States, 136 S.Ct. 1257 (2016)*, holding that the new rule announced in *Johnson v. United States, 135 S.Ct. 2551 (2015)* (which voided the residual clause of the Armed Career Criminal Act of 1984 because of its vagueness) was a substantive decision that applied retroactively to federal prisoners on collateral review.

Under the second *Teague* retroactivity exception, a new rule must meet two requirements: 1) infringement of the rule must have "seriously diminished the likelihood of obtaining an accurate conviction," and 2) it must have "altered the court's understanding of the bedrock procedural elements" essential to the fairness of the proceeding. See *Sawyer v. Smith*, 497 U.S. 227, at 242 (1990). "New 'watershed rules of criminal procedure,' which are procedural rules 'implicating the fundamental fairness and accuracy of the criminal proceeding,' will also have retroactive effect." *Saffle v. Parks*, 494 U.S. 484, at 495, (1990).

Procedural rules regulate only the manner of determining a defendant's culpability. Such rules alter the range of permissible methods for determining whether a defendant's conduct is punishable. "They do not produce a class of persons convicted of conduct the law does not make criminal, but merely raise the possibility that someone convicted with use of the invalidated procedure might have been acquitted otherwise. Because of this more speculative connection to innocence, the United States Supreme Court gives retroactive effect to only a small set of 'watershed rules of criminal procedure' implicating the fundamental fairness and accuracy of the criminal proceeding. That a new procedural rule is 'fundamental' in some abstract sense is not enough; the rule must be one without which the likelihood of an accurate conviction is seriously diminished. This class of rules is extremely narrow, and it is unlikely that any has yet to emerge." *Schriro*, 542 U.S. 348, at 352.

The United States Supreme Court case *Gideon v. Wainwright*, 372 U.S. 335 (1963), holding that a defendant has the right to be represented by counsel in all criminal trials for serious offenses, demonstrates the type of rule which would meet the second retroactivity exception. *Gideon* established an affirmative right to counsel in all felony cases, altering the Supreme Court's understanding of the bedrock procedural elements essential to the fairness and accuracy of a criminal proceeding.

A United States court of appeals' inquiry of whether you should be permitted to file a second or successive § 2254 or § 2255 habeas petition consists of three conditions: 1) that the claim relies on a new rule of constitutional law, 2) that it was made retroactive to cases on collateral review by the United States Supreme Court, and 3) that the rule was previously unavailable (meaning the rule of constitutional law was not in effect at the time you filed your first habeas petition).

If you make a prima facie showing of all three conditions, you should be granted leave to file a second or successive habeas petition with the United States district court.

Newly Discovered Evidence

28 U.S.C. § 2244(b)(2)(B) and 28 U.S.C. § 2255(h)(1) prescribe that a second or successive habeas petition based on newly discovered evidence be dismissed unless: 1) the factual predicate for the claim could not have been discovered previously through the exercise of due diligence; and 2) the facts underlying the claim, if proven and viewed in light of the evidence as a whole, would be sufficient to establish by clear and convincing evidence that, but for constitutional error, no reasonable factfinder would have found the petitioner guilty of the underlying offense.

When preparing your application to file a second or successive habeas petition, consider *Felker v. Turpin, 101 F.3d 657, 662 (11th Cir. 1996)*, in which the court denied his application because the petitioner "has not suggested any reason why [the means for discovering the facts underlying the application] would not have been just as available before he filed his first habeas petition as it was after he had unsuccessfully litigated the petition."

If your application simply states that the factual predicate for the claim could not have been discovered earlier, then the "previously discovered" requirement of § 2244(b)(2)(B)(i), or § 2255(h)(1), is not satisfied. You must detail a factual account, supported by evidence, showing how the factual predicate of the claim was discovered and why it could not have been discovered previously despite the exercise of due diligence. (Criminal defendants are presumed to have conducted a reasonable investigation of all facts surrounding their prosecution, according to *McClerkey v. Zant, 499 U.S. 467, 498, 111 S.Ct. (1991)*, which recognized the principle that a petitioner must conduct a reasonable and diligent investigation aimed at including all relevant claims and grounds for relief in his or her first federal habeas petition.)

In review of an application under § 2244(b)(2)(B), or § 2255(h)(1), a United States court of appeals considers whether a reasonable investigation conducted prior to an initial habeas petition filing would have uncovered the facts the petitioner alleges are newly discovered. Compare *Felker v. Turpin, 83 F.3d 1303, 1306 (11th Cir. 1996)*, in which the court held that a United States Supreme Court case establishing a new constitutional rule, made retroactive to cases on collateral review by the United States Supreme Court, was not "previously unavailable" under § 2244(b)(2)(A) because the case was decided a day before the previous petition had been filed.

A United States court of appeals' inquiry will consist of three steps. First, the court must identify the facts underlying your claim and accept them as true, for the purposes of reviewing your application. Next, the court must determine if these facts establish a constitutional error (e.g., prosecutorial misconduct, use of perjured testimony, Brady violation, juror misconduct, tainted forensic testing, etc.). Finally, the court must review these facts in light of the evidence as a whole, to determine whether or not your application, had you known these facts at the time of your trial, clearly proves that no reasonable fact-finder would have found you guilty of the underlying offense.

This is an extremely difficult standard to satisfy, but for a few examples of petitioners that have done so, see the following cases: *In re Austin, 2013 U.S. App. LEXIS 26400 (3rd Cir. 2013)*; *In re Campbell, 750 F.3d 523 (5th Cir. 2014)*; *In re Wilson, 442 F.3d 872 (5th Cir. 2004)*; *In re McDonald, 514 F.3d 539 (6th Cir. 2008)*; *In re Bell, 2009 U.S. App. LEXIS 29784 (6th Cir. 2009)*; and *In re LeGrone, 2010 U.S. App. LEXIS 27789 (6th Cir. 2010)*.

<3> ONE-YEAR STATUTE OF LIMITATIONS

Exhaustion of State Remedies

A state prisoner must exhaust all available state-court remedies, by any available procedure, before a federal court may grant habeas relief. See *O'Sullivan v. Boerckel, 526 U.S. 838 (1999)*. The Antiterrorism and Effective Death Penalty Act of 1996 (AEDPA) provides a one-year limitation period for filing a habeas application. 28 U.S.C. § 2244(d)(1) states:

> (d) (1) A 1-year period of limitation shall apply to an application for a writ of habeas corpus by a person in custody pursuant to the judgment of a State court. The limitation period shall run from the latest of—
>
>> (A) the date on which the judgment became final by the conclusion of direct review or the expiration of the time for seeking such review;
>>
>> (B) the date on which the impediment to filing an application created by State action in violation of the Constitution or laws of the United States is removed, if the applicant was prevented from filing by such State action;
>>
>> (C) the date on which the constitutional right asserted was initially recognized by the Supreme Court, if the right has been newly recognized by the Supreme Court and made retroactively applicable to cases on collateral review; or
>>
>> (D) the date on which the factual predicate of the claim or claims presented could have been discovered through the exercise of due diligence.
>
> (2) The time during which a properly filed application for State post-conviction or other collateral review with respect to the pertinent judgment or claim is pending shall not be counted toward any period of limitation under this subsection.

The mandatory exhaustion requirement applies with equal force to second or successive habeas petitions. A state prisoner must exhaust any available state-court remedies before seeking permission to file a second or successive habeas petition from a United States court of appeals.

Most state courts have a collateral review process for correcting an illegal sentence when the United States Supreme Court announces a new rule and makes it retroactive to cases on collateral review. Most states also have a state habeas process for correcting wrongful convictions based on newly discovered evidence of actual innocence. (See *Smith's Guide to State Habeas Corpus Relief for State Prisoners*.)

The exhaustion doctrine requires a federal district court to look into what procedures are available under state law, in order to determine whether a prisoner's claim has been fully exhausted. The United States Supreme Court, in *O'Sullivan v. Boerckel, 526 U.S. 838, 119 S.Ct. 1728 (1999)*, held:

> In order to satisfy the exhaustion requirement, a state prisoner must present his claims to a state supreme court in a petition for discretionary review when the review is part of the state's ordinary appellate review procedure. As a matter of comity § 2254(c)—which provides that a habeas petitioner "shall not be deemed to have exhausted [state court] remedies ... if he has the right under [state] law ... to raise, by any available procedure, the question presented"—requires that state prisoners give state courts a full and fair opportunity to resolve federal constitutional claims before those claims are presented to the federal courts. See e.g., *Castille v. Peoples, 489 U.S. 346, 351, 103 L.Ed.2d 380, 109 S.Ct. 1056*. State prisoners must give the state courts one full opportunity to resolve any constitutional issues by invoking one complete round of the state's established appellate review process.

For purposes of exhausting state-court remedies and tolling the one-year limitation period under § 2244(d)(2), the United States Supreme Court held, in *Artuz v. Bennett, 531 U.S. 4, 121 S.Ct. 361 (2000)*, that an application for state relief is "properly filed" where an application complies with the state's procedural requirements, such as rules governing time and place of filing. Time limits on post-conviction petitions are conditions to filing, therefore an untimely petition would not be considered "properly filed."

Federal courts are required to recognize and defer to any final state-court finding that an application was not "properly filed" under state procedural rules establishing requirements for such applications, including findings that a state application is time-barred, procedurally defaulted, or violates limits on second or successive petitions. See, e.g., *Rouse v. Iowa, 110 F. Supp. 2d 1117 (Iowa ND 2000)*. However, state rules governing filings must be "firmly established and regularly followed" before noncompliance will render a state petition improperly filed for purposes of the tolling provision in § 2244(d)(2).

When exhausting state-court remedies, a prisoner should use certified mail or return-receipt-requested postal services to avoid any filing or timeliness disputes. Furthermore, most states do not recognize the prison mailbox rule, making such services worth the extra expense.

One-Year Limitation Period for Federal Prisoners

A federal prisoner is not required to exhaust procedural remedies before seeking permission to file a second or successive habeas petition from a United States court of appeals. For a federal prisoner, the one-year limitation period is governed by 28 U.S.C. § 2255(f), which states:

> (f) A 1-year period of limitation shall apply to a motion under this section. The limitation period shall run from the latest of—

(1) the date on which the judgment of conviction becomes final;

(2) the date on which the impediment to making a motion created by governmental action in violation of the Constitution or laws of the United states is removed, if the movant was prevented from making a motion by such governmental action;

(3) the date on which the right asserted was initially recognized by the Supreme Court and made retroactively applicable to cases on collateral review; or

(4) the date on which the facts supporting the claim or claims presented could have been discovered through the exercise of due diligence.

Equitable Tolling

The United States Supreme Court reaffirmed, in *Holland v. Florida, 560 U.S. 631, 130 S.Ct. 2549 (2010)*, that a prisoner, state or federal, is entitled to equitable tolling if he or she shows (1) that he has been pursuing his rights diligently, and (2) that some extraordinary circumstance stood in the way and prevented timely filing, or on what date the prisoner was able to discover the evidence in question through due diligence. See also *Pace v. DiGugielmo, 125 S.Ct. 1807 (2005)* and *In re Wilson, 442 F.3d 872 (5th Cir. 2006)*.

A state prisoner has one year to file an application seeking permission to file a second or successive habeas petition, from the exact date the United States Supreme Court announces a new rule that is retroactively applicable to cases on collateral review. However, the one-year limitation period is equitably tolled while the prisoner is diligently pursuing collateral relief in state court, exhausting all state-court remedies, by any available state-court procedure.

As for a federal prisoner, the one-year limitation period begins to run from the date the United States Supreme Court hands down its decision announcing a new rule which was made retroactively applicable to cases on collateral review.

§ 2244(d)(1)(D) and § 2255(f)(4) both regard the date from which the facts supporting the claim or claims presented could have been discovered through the exercise of due diligence as the date when that evidence was discovered. For example, if a witness recants his or her testimony in an affidavit, that evidence should be considered discovered on the date the affidavit was made. See *Granger v. Hurt, 90 Appx. 97 (6th Cir. 2004)* as well as *Souter v. Jones, 395 F.3d 577 (6th Cir. 2005)*. Of course, some circuits differ on how to interpret the "previously discovered" requirement. See *In re McDonald, 514 F.3d 539 (6th Cir. 2008)*.

A state prisoner is still required to exhaust state-court remedies and, while doing so, is entitled to equitable tolling. A federal prisoner, on the other hand, has one year from the date the evidence was discovered, unless he or she can meet the requirements set forth in *Holland v. Florida, 560 U.S. 631, 130 S.Ct. 2549 (2010)*.

ONE-YEAR STATUTE OF LIMITATIONS

<4> LEGAL RESEARCH, INVESTIGATIVE METHODS, AND LEGAL WRITING

Legal Research

Depending upon the circumstances, conducting legal research can pose a challenge, especially for prisoners serving time in administration segregation, or at a prison without an adequate law library. This chapter will provide information with these conditions in mind. With exception to filing a second or successive habeas petition predicated on the United States Supreme Court's announcement of a new rule, a prisoner filing under the newly discovered evidence requirement can, if necessary, prepare an application without the benefit of case law to support his or her position. This is because there are only a few constitutional errors that are applicable under the newly discovered evidence requirement. A prisoner only needs the United States Supreme Court's legal standard for the constitutional error he or she is arguing, so that the newly discovered underlying facts can then be applied to that legal standard.

By exercising due diligence, you can learn of new United States Supreme Court decisions from newspapers, magazines, prison-interest publications e.g., (*Prison Legal News*, California Lifer Newsletter, or the CURE newsletter), and even word of mouth. You can also write to the address below and ask for a list of cases heard or to be heard, along with the question(s) presented, during the United States Supreme Court's current term.

The Public Information Office
United States Supreme Court
#1 First Street NE
Washington, DC 20543
Phone: (202) 479-3211

The United States Supreme Court hears and decides cases during an annual term, starting on the first Monday in October and ending on the day before the first Monday in October of the following year, as prescribed by 28 U.S.C. § 2. At the end of each term, all cases pending on the Court's docket are continued to their next term. (See *United States Supreme Court Rule 3*.) If you have case names, the Public Information Office will provide up to five opinions per request, at no charge.

Investigative Methods

A United States court of appeals will consider whether a reasonable investigation conducted prior to an initial habeas petition filing would have uncovered the facts a petitioner alleges are newly discovered. (See the Newly Discovered Evidence section of Chapter Two.)

There are an unlimited number of cases in which new evidence, discovered decades later, exonerated the prisoner—especially death penalty cases. Most of these cases concerned prosecutors withholding favorable evidence from the defendants, such as: DNA evidence, forensic evidence, witness statements, evidence of other suspects, etc. The following sections will assist you in locating information that could help to exonerate you.

Case File

When a trial attorney is retained or assigned to a new case, he or she will prepare a case file (typically called *trial counsel's file* or *trial file*). This file will consist of a copy of the discovery, which should include items such as police reports, witness statements, crime scene photos and diagrams, forensic reports, investigator notes, and attorney trial notes.

After the case is disposed of, either through trial or a guilty plea, the attorney will keep the file unless it is requested by one of the attorneys perfecting an appeal or a motion for postconviction relief (PCR).

At the conclusion of a direct appeal, the appellate attorney usually keeps the trial file and combines it with the appellate file.

In cases where a PCR motion is initiated, the PCR attorney will prepare a PCR file. He or she will also make requests for case files from the trial and appellate attorneys.

Upon the completion of the PCR proceedings, the PCR attorney usually keeps possession of the trial, direct appeal, and PCR case files—that is, unless the prior attorneys ask for the return of their case files.

You are entitled to everything contained in the case files; they belong to you, not to the attorneys. To obtain these files yourself, make a written request for them from each attorney who represented you. Most attorneys will first send an acknowledgment for you to sign, stating that once they are sent to you, the attorney or public defender's office is no longer responsible for storing the case files.

Some attorneys prefer to send clients copies of the case file while retaining custody of the original file. This is done to preserve the integrity of the files' contents. This can be beneficial to you, especially if a Brady claim is made. The attorney's testimony or affidavit, along with the original case file, can then be used to prove that the Brady material was never disclosed during discovery.

Oftentimes when an attorney is called to testify at a hearing, he or she will not remember whether a particular police report, witness's statement, etc., was in the case file. The issue then quickly becomes a question of credibility: prosecutor versus prisoner. In such instances, the court will more often than not make a factual finding that the prosecutor provided the discovery and deny the petitioner's Brady claim on that basis. It is nearly impossible to overcome a court's factual finding.

Public Records

There are different kinds of public records: records you can look up online; records that are only attainable upon proof of a legal need, such as birth certificates, death certificates, and marriage licenses; and records that are not made public but must be disclosed upon request.

Everyone leaves behind a trail of records throughout his or her lifetime: a birth certificate, school records, addresses and phone numbers in the White Pages, driver's licenses, utility records, marriage certificates, property records, liens, transcripts of court proceedings, tickets for traffic offenses and city ordinance violations, criminal conviction records, inmate locator records, sex offender registry listings, bankruptcy filings and discharges, divorce degrees, custody degrees, and a death certificate.

Records Open to Public

There are documents and databases open to the public online. This is problematic for prisoners, due to the lack of Internet access. The incarcerated must have someone look up the desired information online, or make a request for the information in writing. Occasionally the requested information will be sent to you free of charge; sometimes you will have to pay for the copies.

State, County, and Federal Records

You may be doing an investigation to see if a witness was given a lesser sentence in exchange for providing testimony against you. If this is your aim, write a letter to the court clerk where the witness was sentenced, requesting copies of the presentencing report and sentencing transcripts. (Courts usually charge for copies of these documents.)

This situation arises frequently. Most prosecutors will postpone such witnesses' cases to delay sentencing until after said witnesses have testified in other cases. Later on, a prosecutor will provide a letter on a witness's behalf, stating that a conviction wouldn't have been possible without the witness's testimony and asking the sentencing court to take his or her cooperation into consideration when imposing sentence.

(Note: newly discovered evidence that merely demonstrates a key prosecution witness lied about an expectation of receiving a deal or consideration for a lesser sentence may be sufficient to overturn a conviction in state court, but such evidence would not be enough to satisfy the requirements of § 2244(b)(2)(B) or § 2255(h)(1). Nonetheless, evidence that a key witness committed perjury may be used to persuade the witness to recant previous testimony and provide an affidavit to that effect. Thus, the requirements could be met.)

Records Available Only upon Proof of a Legal Need

Records that can only be reviewed upon proof of a legal need consist of birth certificates, death certificates, and marriage licenses. Despite the restrictions, most information contained in these records can be found in other documents. For example, if a person filed for bankruptcy or divorce, or probated a will upon the death of a family member, that is public information and, as such, documentation of those actions is available from the state or federal courts, containing all the information you may be looking for.

Records Available Only upon Written Request

State and federal agencies retain documents and other records that are only made available upon written request. If a Freedom of Information Act (FOIA) letter is received, these agencies must produce whatever requested information is not privileged or protected by law. This is usually done by sending you documents with any privileged or protected information redacted or blotted out.

Freedom of Information Act

The Freedom of Information Act establishes your rights to obtain information from federal government agencies.

If your request is denied, it is the government's burden to explain why the record should not be provided to you. There are nine types of records the FOIA protects:

- Classified matters of national defense or foreign policy
- Internal personnel rules and practices
- Trade secrets and commercial or financial information
- Investigatory records compiled for law enforcement purposes
- Records of financial institutions
- Information specifically exempted by other statutes
- Privileged inter- or intra-agency memoranda or letters
- Geographical and geophysical information concerning wells
- Personal information affecting an individual's privacy

The Department of Justice provides a guide, explaining what the FOIA can and cannot provide to you. A copy may be requested by writing to:

United States Department of Justice
Civil Division
Freedom of Information/Privacy Act Officer, Room 808
901 E Street NW
Washington, DC 20530-0001

Each state has its own version of the FOIA. Before making a request, you should thoroughly review your state's statutes.

Finding Potential Witnesses

Not having access to the Internet is a disadvantage. Finding potential witnesses from prison can be difficult, but it is not impossible. You may have friends and family members who can access the Internet for you.

The quickest and easiest way to find someone is through social media—Facebook, Linkedin, Twitter, etc. If you know the person's full name and city he or she lives in, then the person can likely be found online.

Of course, if the person doesn't want to get involved with your case, it would be better to find out his or her address so that you can send a letter or have someone talk with them on your behalf. However, learning someone's address is a little trickier than finding them on a social media site. Your computer-savvy friend or family member may be able to find the person's address by searching an online directory, such as Anywho, WhoWhere, or 411.com.

Finding Expert Witnesses

Whether you are looking for information that discredits the state's or federal government's expert witness, or trying to find an expert of your own, you can have Google searched for the expert's name and area of expertise. Professionals (e.g., doctors, forensic pathologists, or ballistics experts) advertise their services.

If you are a lone wolf and have to do everything yourself, you can write to any public library's reference librarian, explaining your situation, and ask for help finding an expert in a certain scientific field or specific information from such an expert. Be sure to send a self-addressed, stamped envelope for their reply. Also, writing to more than one public library improves your chances of receiving what you're searching for.

You might be able to find an expert through a search on your law library's computer. Doing so will also show you whether or not the scientific method has been used in other cases.

When doing research and investigating anything or anyone, you have to think "outside the box" and get creative. Sometimes the person or piece of information you need will be found by someone not known to you, from a place least expected. The effort you put into investigating your case, collecting information, could make the difference between overturning your conviction or losing more years of your life to prison.

Legal Writing

When drafting a pleading to be filed with a court, the pleading should be brief, concise, and to the point. There are two simple formats: 1) state the material facts, then state the legal standard, then apply that standard to the facts; or 2) state the legal standard, then state the material facts, then apply the legal standard to the facts. By using either of these formats, you will not need to decide how to start your pleading, wasting time and losing confidence in your ability to draft the pleading without assistance.

You should look at the first draft as an outline, and not be concerned with grammar, spelling, or punctuation. Just get something down on paper that you can work with. You should also avoid using "legalese"; plain, everyday words will suffice. If you have a rich vocabulary, by all means use it to succinctly state your claim.

In the second draft, cut any facts that are not germane to your claim and add any facts that are. When you're finished, read the pleading aloud. If any sentence sounds unclear or causes you to pause during the reading, rework it until it is coherent and sensible.

In the third draft, correct any errors in grammar, spelling, and punctuation. Also, polish your sentences by exchanging clunky, awkward words for simpler or more specific synonyms that make your meanings perfectly apparent.

Reread your pleading aloud one last time before typing or writing the final draft.

<5> APPLICATION TO FILE SECOND OR SUCCESSIVE HABEAS CORPUS PETITION

Preparation of Application

This chapter will provide information to assist you in preparing an application to file a second or successive habeas corpus petition. As in all *Smith's Guide* titles, you will find, at the end of this chapter, example applications to guide you when preparing your application.

First, turn to Appendix A of this book and read the application process for the United States court of appeals in your circuit. Each circuit has a specific application process in which prisoners are required to use the application forms provided by the court clerk. Three circuits, however, do not provide application forms—the District of Columbia, the Seventh Circuit, and the Eighth Circuit. If you are in one of these circuits, you may use the blank application form provided in Appendix C, or you may draft your own application.

Application to File Second or Successive Habeas Corpus Petition

You should answer completely all the questions on the appropriate application form provided by the court clerk of your circuit. If, as a prisoner in the District of Columbia, the Seventh Circuit, or the Eighth Circuit, you prefer to draft your own application, it should consist of the following.

Caption

Your application should start with a caption, a title such as "PETITIONER'S APPLICATION TO FILE SECOND OR SUCCESSIVE PETITION FOR A WRIT OF HABEAS CORPUS WITH SUGGESTIONS IN SUPPORT," and an introduction. The introduction should be brief, such as "COMES NOW the Petitioner, [your name], and requests this Court to enter its order permitting him [or her] to file a second or successive petition for a writ of habeas corpus, pursuant to 28 U.S.C. [§ 2244 or § 2255]. In support of application, Petitioner states the following."

Jurisdictional Statement

The jurisdictional statement should state your name and the address of your place of confinement, the name and address of the warden, the case citation and case number for any other federal habeas corpus filing, and a brief description of your illegal confinement, such as the announcement of a new rule by the United States Supreme Court, or newly discovered evidence.

APPLICATION TO FILE SECOND OR SUCCESSIVE HABEAS CORPUS PETITION

Statement of the Case

The statement of the case should have two sections, "A. Procedural History" and "B. Statement of Facts." The first should succinctly state the procedural history of your case, including conviction(s), sentence(s), appellate direct appeals, and any post-conviction proceedings. The procedural history should show the steps you took to exhaust all available state-court remedies, and provide dates showing that your application is timely filed, in accordance with § 2244(d)(1).

The statement of facts should supply all the necessary information to your claim(s) for relief. Each material fact should be followed by a citation—a reference to the trial transcript, appendix of accompanying exhibits, affidavit(s), or other documentation where the fact comes from.

Reason for Granting Application

Here you will state your claim(s), showing exactly why you should be granted permission to file a second or successive habeas corpus petition. Your claim(s) should include the facts of the claim(s), the controlling precedent, and an application of that legal precedent to the facts. (As stated in Chapter Four, you may, alternatively, state the law first, then apply it to the facts of your claim(s). By following either format, you will present concise and convincing arguments for the court's consideration.)

Conclusion

Your conclusion should be brief, such as "Based upon the foregoing, Petitioner prays for an order permitting him [or her] to file a second or successive petition for a writ of habeas corpus because he [or she] has made a prima facie showing that the application satisfies the statutory requirements as prescribed in 28 U.S.C. § 2244(b) [or § 2255(h)]." This is not a place to rehash the facts of your claim(s).

Verification of Application

You should verify your application with a statement, such as "I declare under Penalty of Perjury that the facts contained in this application are true and correct." Sign and date the verification thereafter.

Certificate of Service

The certificate of service should state that your application was mailed, postage prepaid, on a certain date, and that a copy was sent to the court and the State attorneys general office, or the United States Attorney's Office, in the district in which you were convicted. (See Appendix B for attorneys general addresses.)

APPLICATION TO FILE SECOND OR SUCCESSIVE HABEAS CORPUS PETITION

Example Application #1—Robert James Campbell

No. 03-20700

IN THE
UNITED STATES COURT OF APPEALS
FOR THE FIFTH CIRCUIT

———————————

In re ROBERT JAMES CAMPBELL,

Movant.

———————————

MOTION FOR AN ORDER AUTHORIZING
CONSIDERATION OF SECOND PETITION FOR
WRIT OF HABEAS CORPUS UNDER 28 U.S.C. § 2254

THIS IS A DEATH PENALTY CASE

ROBERT C. OWEN	**RAOUL D. SCHONEMANN**
Texas Bar No. 15371950	Texas Bar No. 00786233
BLUHM LEGAL CLINIC	**CAPITAL PUNISHMENT CLINIC**
Northwestern University School of Law	The University of Texas at Austin School of Law
375 East Chicago Ave.	727 East Dean Keeton St.
Chicago, IL 60611	Austin, Texas 78705-3224
(312) 503-0135 Telephone	(512) 232-9391 Telephone
(312) 503-8977 Facsimile	(512) 232-9171 Facsimile
robert.owen@law.northwestern.edu	rschonemann@law.utexas.edu

APPLICATION TO FILE SECOND OR SUCCESSIVE HABEAS CORPUS PETITION

Example Application #1—Robert James Campbell (cont.)

Case: 14-20293   Document: 00512624851   Page: 2   Date Filed: 05/09/2014

No. _____

IN THE
UNITED STATES COURT OF APPEALS
FOR THE FIFTH CIRCUIT

_____

In re ROBERT JAMES CAMPBELL,

Movant.

_____

**MOTION FOR ORDER AUTHORIZING
CONSIDERATION OF SECOND PETITION FOR
WRIT OF HABEAS CORPUS UNDER 28 U.S.C. § 2254**

Movant, Robert James Campbell, is a state prisoner on death row in Texas. He respectfully moves, pursuant to 28 U.S.C. § 2244(b)(3)(C), for an order authorizing the filing and consideration of a second petition for writ of habeas corpus, a copy of which is attached as Exhibit 1 to this motion. Mr. Campbell's application is based on *Atkins v. Virginia*, 536 U.S. 304 (2002). Mr. Campbell is ineligible for execution under *Atkins*, because he is intellectually disabled.

Example Application #1—Robert James Campbell (cont.)

Case: 14-20293   Document: 00512624851   Page: 3   Date Filed: 05/09/2014

INTRODUCTION

Robert James Campbell seeks authorization to file a claim that he is intellectually disabled and is constitutionally ineligible for a death sentence under *Atkins v. Virginia*. As confirmed by a comprehensive mental ability assessment conducted last month – the first and only such assessment ever performed on him – Mr. Campbell is a person with intellectual disability (the condition formerly called "mental retardation").

In June 2002, the Supreme Court categorically banned executing defendants with mental retardation (intellectual disability). *Atkins v. Virginia*, 536 U.S. 304 (2002). In 2003, without benefit of resources to develop the facts that might conclusively establish Mr. Campbell's intellectual disability, Justin Waggoner, then Mr. Campbell's appointed federal habeas counsel, filed a habeas application in the state convicting court "based upon a good faith belief that Campbell m[ight] be mentally retarded." In that application, Mr. Waggoner alleged that all four categories of risk factors described in the 2002 American Association on Mental Retardation ("AAMR") Manual – behavioral, social, educational, and biomedical – that may interact to cause mental retardation were present in Mr. Campbell's case. *Id.* at 5-7. In support of the application, Mr. Waggoner attached two pages of school records from 1985 to 1989 demonstrating that Mr. Campbell made failing grades in junior and senior high school. The application requested a remand to the

APPLICATION TO FILE SECOND OR SUCCESSIVE HABEAS CORPUS PETITION

Example Application #1—Robert James Campbell (cont.)

Case: 14-20293   Document: 00512624851   Page: 4   Date Filed: 05/09/2014

trial court for discovery and an evidentiary hearing for full development of the facts. *Id.* at 10.

In response, the State moved to dismiss Mr. Campbell's application, arguing that Mr. Campbell's allegations did not establish a *prima facie* case of mental retardation. The State argued that while Mr. Campbell's "sparse school records ... show that [he] made failing grades in middle school," they failed to establish that he met the criteria to establish mental retardation. Respondent's Motion to Dismiss Applicant's Subsequent Application for Writ of Habeas Corpus at 20. In conclusion, the State asserted that "there is no credible evidence of mental retardation and no credible basis for believing that the applicant is a mentally retarded person in terms of the prevailing diagnostic standards." *Id.* at 21.

Endorsing the position asserted by the State, the Texas Court of Criminal Appeals dismissed that application, viewing the preliminary factual support submitted by Mr. Waggoner as insufficient "to raise a *bona fide* claim of mental retardation." *Ex parte Campbell*, No. WR–44,551–02 (Tex. Crim. App. July 2, 2003) (not designated for publication).

Mr. Campbell then moved this Court for authorization to file a successive federal habeas petition raising the *Atkins* claim. In support of that motion, Mr. Campbell again attached witness affidavits and the two pages of junior and senior high school records. The State opposed the motion, again arguing that the

APPLICATION TO FILE SECOND OR SUCCESSIVE HABEAS CORPUS PETITION

Example Application #1—Robert James Campbell (cont.)

Case: 14-20293   Document: 00512624851   Page: 5   Date Filed: 05/09/2014

proffered "evidence d[id] not meet the established criteria for mental retardation." *In re Robert James Campbell*, No. 03-20700, Response in Opposition at 13-14. As the State argued:

> Although school records reveal that Campbell received failing grades from 1985 to 1989, alone, this does not support a finding of significantly sub-average general intellectual functioning (Criterion A) as set out in *Atkins*.... Thus, it is quite clear that Campbell is *not* mentally retarded and is therefore *not* within the ambit of *Atkins*.

Id. at 13-14.

This Court concluded that no evidence showed that Mr. Campbell "[wa]s mentally retarded within the understanding of *Atkins*" – "only that, according to one set of factors, he [wa]s *at risk* for mental retardation." *In re Campbell*, 82 Fed. Appx. 349, 351 (5th Cir. 2003) (unpublished). Accordingly, it refused to authorize a new habeas proceeding in district court.

The present motion seeks to alert the Court to a gravely troubling fact: when it denied Mr. Campbell's 2003 motion for authorization, the Court was laboring under a mistaken impression about the available evidence. Undersigned counsel have discovered records of prior IQ scores – records that existed in 2003, but were not reasonably available to Mr. Campbell's counsel. And those scores are strongly indicative of significantly sub-average intellectual functioning. Had they been presented in 2003, it is highly likely that this Court would have given Mr. Campbell a full opportunity to develop the relevant facts and, potentially, show

---

39

that he may not legally be put to death.[1] In these highly unusual circumstances, all the equities weigh in favor of giving Mr. Campbell one fair chance to prove his *Atkins* claim before permitting Texas to execute him.

> **1. Previously unavailable school records indicating significantly sub-average intellectual functioning in the developmental period, including an IQ score of 68 when Mr. Campbell was 9 years old.**

Mr. Waggoner made diligent efforts to obtain copies of Mr. Campbell's school records; he contacted each of the schools Mr. Campbell had attended, provided them with signed releases from Mr. Campbell, and asked for any records whatsoever concerning Mr. Campbell. The only school that had any records was Jones High School, which Mr. Campbell attended for parts of two different school years (both in the ninth grade) before abandoning school at age 17. Jones High provided Mr. Waggoner with just two pages of records. One reflected a (partial) record of Mr. Campbell's middle-school years; the other Mr. Campbell's two failed attempts to make it through the ninth grade at Jones. Neither page reflected any IQ testing or any other type of standardized intelligence or academic achievement testing that showed Mr. Campbell's performance compared to that of a national peer group. *See* Exhibit 3 (School records). Thus, despite Mr. Waggoner's having made a systematic and diligent search, those two pages were

---

[1] Indeed, if these records had been available in 2003, it is almost certain that the state courts would have authorized further proceedings on Mr. Campbell's *Atkins* claim, and the case might well have been resolved without any need to return to federal court.

APPLICATION TO FILE SECOND OR SUCCESSIVE HABEAS CORPUS PETITION

Example Application #1—Robert James Campbell (cont.)

Case: 14-20293   Document: 00512624851   Page: 7   Date Filed: 05/09/2014

the only school records that Mr. Waggoner was able to submit in support of Mr. Campbell's 2003 motion for authorization attempting to present a claim under *Atkins*.

In the first week of March 2014, undersigned counsel Robert C. Owen discovered while reviewing Mr. Waggoner's files that in January 1991, prior to Mr. Campbell's trial, the District Attorney's office had subpoenaed a complete set of all available high school records concerning Mr. Campbell. *See* Exhibit 9 (subpoena). Accordingly, Mr. Owen requested that the District Attorney's office provide Mr. Campbell a copy of whatever school records had been produced in response to the State's January 1991 subpoena. The District Attorney's office disclosed the additional two pages of records from Mr. Campbell's elementary school years. *See* Exhibit 3 (School records).

Those additional records would have satisfied the requirement for evidence of "*significantly* sub-average general intellectual functioning," because they show the results of two standardized mental ability tests (the Otis-Lennon Mental Ability Test and the Metropolitan Readiness Test) on which Mr. Campbell's performance fell more than two standard deviations below the mean, *see* Exhibit 2 (Dr. Rosenstein report), as well as a deviation IQ score of 68 on the Otis-Lennon.

These records existed in 2003 and were in the State's possession, although not in Mr. Waggoner's, and their existence was simply unknown to the Court.

APPLICATION TO FILE SECOND OR SUCCESSIVE HABEAS CORPUS PETITION

Example Application #1—Robert James Campbell (cont.)

Case: 14-20293   Document: 00512624851   Page: 8   Date Filed: 05/09/2014

While Mr. Campbell has no reason to believe that the State acted knowingly in failing to disclose these records in 2003 when either the state courts or this Court was considering his initial *Atkins* application, the records make clear that this Court's 2003 decision warrants reconsideration. In concluding that Mr. Campbell "d[id] not state a *prima facie* case of mental retardation within the understanding of *Atkins*," 82 Fed. Appx. at 350, the Court reasonably assumed that the only available evidence of Mr. Campbell's intellectual disability was (1) his very poor performance in middle and high school – which admittedly could have sprung from many causes – and (2) the inference one might draw from the fact that Mr. Campbell's background revealed a range of "risk factors" for mental retardation. *See Campbell*, 82 Fed. Appx. at 351 ("Campbell does not allege that he *is* mentally retarded within the understanding of Atkins, only that, according to one set of factors, he is *at risk* for mental retardation."). We now know that assumption was mistaken. The question before this Court is whether Mr. Campbell should die without having an opportunity to present the full and true facts, which were unknown to his counsel in 2003 and would likely have resulted in a different outcome to the authorization request. That is the only fair outcome, and this Court can ensure it by granting this motion for authorization to permit full and fair litigation of Mr. Campbell's *Atkins* claim.

APPLICATION TO FILE SECOND OR SUCCESSIVE HABEAS CORPUS PETITION

Example Application #1—Robert James Campbell (cont.)

Case: 14-20293   Document: 00512624851   Page: 9   Date Filed: 05/09/2014

2. Previously undisclosed TDCJ IQ score.

Equity also calls for intervention by this Court to ensure that Mr. Campbell receives merits review of his *Atkins* claim because Texas prison authorities affirmatively misled Mr. Waggoner about the existence of other IQ testing records concerning Mr. Campbell that provide yet more evidence of significantly sub-average intellectual functioning. Despite Mr. Waggoner's diligent efforts to obtain all TDCJ records reflecting IQ testing of Mr. Campbell, the Texas Department of Criminal Justice not only failed to provide them to him but made affirmative misrepresentations to Mr. Waggoner, which misled him about IQ testing that TDCJ had performed on Mr. Campbell.

Mr. Waggoner originally contacted TDCJ in March 2003, requesting "any and all intellectual functioning tests" concerning Mr. Campbell. *See* Exhibit 6 (TDCJ letter and social history summary) at 1. Ten days later, he received a response from TDCJ's Office of the General Counsel:

> I am writing in response to your request dated March 21, 2003 asking for any and all intellectual functioning tests completed by inmate Campbell while incarcerated on a previous conviction under TDCJ # 546059. *As you know, inmates sentenced to death receive no intellectual testing upon incarceration.*
>
> Our records indicate that inmate Campbell was previously sentenced to a five-year term for robbery on April 23, 1990 and received by TDCJ in May 1990. The admission summary for that conviction indicates an IQ test score of 84. Because the actual IQ test instruments are kept for only a few months, any

such test instrument for inmate Campbell would have been destroyed long ago.

Id. (emphasis added).

Relying on that sweeping representation – that "inmates sentenced to death receive no intellectual testing upon incarceration" – Mr. Waggoner understandably took no further steps to press for additional relevant TDCJ records concerning Mr. Campbell that might have, in connection with other information, persuaded this Court to authorize further proceedings on his *Atkins* claim in 2003. Nor did he look critically at the claimed 84 IQ score from 1990.

As it turns out, those representations are demonstrably false: Mr. Campbell – and every other new arrival on Death Row, at least in the early 1990's – *did* "receive ... intellectual testing upon incarceration." According to TDCJ-CID clinic notes recently obtained by undersigned counsel within the past week, in July 1992 Mr. Campbell was administered a "WAIS-R IQ Short Form," and he scored 71. *See* Exhibit 5 (short form 71 page). Because such tests "have been shown to overestimate Full Scale IQs when compared to contemporary Wechsler Adult Intelligence Scales," *see* Exhibit 2 (Dr. Rosenstein report) at 2, that short form test score of 71, particularly alongside the derivative IQ score of 68 reflected in Mr. Campbell's elementary school records, would have served as strong evidence that Mr. Campbell's *Atkins* claim was and is substantial. In fairness, the Court must assume that had TDCJ informed Mr. Waggoner of the existence of this record, Mr.

APPLICATION TO FILE SECOND OR SUCCESSIVE HABEAS CORPUS PETITION

Example Application #1—Robert James Campbell (cont.)

Case: 14-20293   Document: 00512624851   Page: 11   Date Filed: 05/09/2014

Waggoner would have brought it to this Court's attention, providing the "individualized, fact specific [showing] ... that a movant must make in order to have a motion for leave to file a successive habeas petition granted by this Court."[2] *Campbell*, 82 Fed. App. at 351. Instead, by falsely informing Mr. Waggoner that no such intelligence testing was conducted on incoming death row inmates (and thus that he need not pursue the issue further), TDCJ officials contributed to this Court's decision to deny Mr. Campbell's motion for authorization to *Atkins* claim on the basis of an incomplete and misleading factual record. This unfairness deserves correction, and the most direct path to that correction is for the Court to grant Mr. Campbell's motion for authorization.

Thus, through no fault of his own, Mr. Campbell faces execution without ever having received in state or federal court any meaningful inquiry into whether his intellectual disability entitles him to protection from execution under *Atkins*. While any claimed malfunction of the system of post-trial review is troubling in a death penalty case, Mr. Campbell's situation is uniquely disturbing. *Atkins* is not a technicality or a procedural nicety – it imposes "a substantive restriction" on the state's power to punish by killing. *Atkins*, 536 U.S. at 321 (quoting *Ford v.*

---

[2] It would also have assisted Mr. Waggoner in showing why the purported 84 score from 1990, as a clear outlier, deserves little weight. Of course, given that *absolutely nothing* is known about that test – what test it was, who administered it, what training that person had, what conditions prevailed at the time of the test, whether the test was scored correctly, etc. – it should receive little weight in any event. *See infra*.

APPLICATION TO FILE SECOND OR SUCCESSIVE HABEAS CORPUS PETITION

Example Application #1—Robert James Campbell (cont.)

Case: 14-20293   Document: 00512624851   Page: 12   Date Filed: 05/09/2014

Wainwright, 477 U.S. 399, 405 (1986)). Executing Mr. Campbell under these circumstances would be profoundly arbitrary and unfair.

This Court should ensure that Mr. Campbell is not executed until it is reliably determined whether putting him to death would violate *Atkins*. The most straightforward route to ensuring a reliable outcome – and avoiding any chance of an *Atkins* violation – would be for the Court to grant the present motion for authorization and permit Mr. Campbell to file a second federal habeas petition presenting his *Atkins* claim, as it plainly satisfies the standards for consideration of a successive claim. If for any reason the Court concludes that anything in the law limits its authority to grant a second motion for authorization on the same underlying constitutional claim, then the Court should exercise its discretion to recall the mandate from the 2003 proceeding, because the integrity of its result was fatally compromised when the Court based its ruling on a record that, through no fault of Mr. Campbell or his counsel, lacked the essential facts.

As set forth fully *infra*, this Court can – and should – act to ensure both that Mr. Campbell receives the meaningful review of his eligibility for execution under *Atkins* that he would have received if adequate resources had been available and the State had not suppressed the other available evidence pointing to a diagnosis of intellectual disability.

Case: 14-20293   Document: 00512624851   Page: 13   Date Filed: 05/09/2014

I. JURISDICTION.

This Court has subject matter jurisdiction of this case pursuant to 28 U.S.C. § 2244(b). Mr. Campbell is under a judgment and sentence of death entered in the 232nd District Court of Harris County, Texas. Mr. Campbell seeks leave to challenge his sentence in the underlying successive petition for writ of habeas corpus.

II. PROCEDURAL HISTORY.

Mr. Campbell was convicted of capital murder in May 1992 in the 232nd District Court of Harris County.

The judgment was affirmed on direct appeal in June 1995. *Campbell v. State*, 910 S.W.2d 475 (Tex. Crim. App. 1995) (partial publication), *cert. denied*, 517 U.S. 1140 (1996).

Mr. Campbell's first state habeas application was filed on April 23, 1997. On November 11, 1999, the convicting court recommended that all relief be denied; on March 8, 2000, the Texas Court of Criminal Appeals adopted the trial court's recommendation and denied relief. *Ex parte Campbell*, No. WR–44,551–01 (Tex. Crim. App. Mar. 8, 2000) (not designated for publication).

On November 2, 2000, represented by new counsel appointed by the federal court, Mr. Campbell filed a petition for writ of habeas corpus in the United States

APPLICATION TO FILE SECOND OR SUCCESSIVE HABEAS CORPUS PETITION

Example Application #1—Robert James Campbell (cont.)

Case: 14-20293 Document: 00512624851 Page: 14 Date Filed: 05/09/2014

District Court for the Southern District of Texas. On March 20, 2003, the district court entered an order denying relief. On March 28, 2003, Mr. Campbell filed a timely motion to vacate or amend the judgment pursuant to Fed. R. Civ. P. 59(e).

While the motion to vacate or amend judgment remained pending before the federal district court, on May 28, 2003, Mr. Campbell filed a second state habeas application alleging, "based upon a good faith belief that Campbell may be mentally retarded," that his execution "would violate the constitutional prohibition on execution of mentally retarded individuals recently recognized by the U.S. Supreme Court in *Atkins v. Virginia*, 536 U.S. 304 (2002)." *Ex parte Campbell*, No. 586190-B, Application for Postconviction Writ of Habeas Application, at 3.

On July 2, 2003, the Texas Court of Criminal Appeals dismissed Mr. Campbell's second state habeas application,

> After a careful review of all the materials submitted by applicant, we conclude that he has failed to meet the threshold factual burden. The evidence he has submitted to this Court consists of school records from 1985 to 1989 and affidavits from six individuals, all friends or relatives. No results of IQ tests, or assertions that applicant was never tested, are presented. Although the records submitted to this Court indicate that applicant received failing grades in every subject except physical education, music, and basic mathematics, the "sufficient specific facts" that would support a finding of *significantly* sub-average general intellectual functioning required under Atkins are not set out in this record. The affidavits assert that applicant suffered terrible abuse suffered during his childhood, but do not allege any inability to learn, or any maladaptive behavior. The application urges that, because applicant experienced risk factors in all four areas, he "may suffer from mental retardation." Such an assertion, unsupported

APPLICATION TO FILE SECOND OR SUCCESSIVE HABEAS CORPUS PETITION

Example Application #1—Robert James Campbell (cont.)

Case: 14-20293   Document: 00512624851   Page: 15   Date Filed: 05/09/2014

by specific factual allegations, is insufficient.

Ex parte Campbell, No. WR–44,551–02 (Tex. Crim. App. July 2, 2003), at 4 (emphasis in original).

Mr. Campbell then filed with this Court a motion for authorization to file a successive habeas petition raising the *Atkins* claim. The State filed an opposition to the motion. On November 13, 2003, this Court denied the motion for authorization on the ground that Mr. Campbell's allegations did not establish a *prima facie* showing of mental retardation. *In re Campbell*, 82 Fed.Appx. 349 (5th Cir. 2003).

In August 2006, Mr. Campbell filed a state habeas application seeking review of three claims related to post-trial revelations of improprieties in forensic testing by the Harris County Crime Lab at the time of Mr. Campbell's trial. The state court dismissed that petition in April 2007. *Ex parte Campbell*, 226 S.W.3d 418 (Tex. Crim. App.), *cert. denied*, 552 U.S. 1044 (2007). This Court denied in an unpublished order Mr. Campbell's motion for authorization to file a successive federal habeas petition raising those claims. *In re Campbell*, No. 07-20305 (5th Cir., October 3, 2007).

Another successive state habeas application on Mr. Campbell's behalf was filed in September 2012 raising a *Penry* claim in light of Texas state court decisions applying the Supreme Court's decisions in *Abdul-Kabir v. Quarterman*,

550 U.S. 233 (2007); *Brewer v. Quarterman*, 550 U.S. 286 (2007); and *Smith v. Texas*, 550 U.S. 297 (2007). The Texas Court of Criminal Appeals denied that claim on the merits in November 2012. *Ex parte Campbell*, No. 76,907 (Tex. Crim. App. Nov. 7, 2012) (not designated for publication), *cert. denied*, 134 S. Ct. 53 (2013).

On May 5, 2014, Mr. Campbell filed a subsequent application for writ of habeas corpus in state court alleging that Mr. Campbell's death sentence was unconstitutional because he had mental retardation and providing *prima facie* evidence in support thereof. Mr. Campbell alleged a second claim that he was denied effective assistance of counsel at the penalty phase of his trial. That application remains pending before the Texas state courts at this time.

III. THIS COURT SHOULD AUTHORIZE REVIEW OF MR. CAMPBELL'S *ATKINS* CLAIM PURSUANT TO 28 U.S.C. § 2244.

"The relevant provisions of the AEDPA-amended habeas statutes, 28 U.S.C. §§ 2244(b)(1)–(3), impose three requirements on second or successive habeas petitions: First, any claim that has already been *adjudicated* in a previous petition must be dismissed. § 2244(b)(1)." *Gonzalez v. Crosby*, 545 U.S. 524, 529–30 (2005) (emphasis added). Mr. Campbell's *Atkins* claim has not been adjudicated in a prior petition. No federal court previously acquired jurisdiction over Mr. Campbell's *Atkins* claim because authorization to adjudicate the claim was denied

APPLICATION TO FILE SECOND OR SUCCESSIVE HABEAS CORPUS PETITION

Example Application #1—Robert James Campbell (cont.)

Case: 14-20293 Document: 00512624851 Page: 17 Date Filed: 05/09/2014

by this Court. This understanding of § 2244(b)(1) is consistent with this Court's decisions in the case of Texas death row inmate Jose Rivera. Mr. Rivera moved for authorization to file a successive petition raising an *Atkins* claim. *Rivera v. Quarterman*, 505 F.3d 349, 352 (5th Cir. 2007). The Court denied the motion because Mr. Rivera had failed to make a *prima facie* showing of mental retardation. *Id.* In the first authorization proceeding, this Court was precluded from considering all of the existing evidence because some of it was unexhausted. *Id.* After Mr. Rivera returned to the state courts and exhausted his evidence, Mr. Rivera:

> *filed a second motion for authorization to file a successive petition* with this court. Now able to consider all of Rivera's evidence, this court concluded that Rivera had made a *prima facie* showing of mental retardation, authorized the successive petition on that issue only, and stayed his execution.

Id. (emphasis added).

Mr. Campbell's case is, for all practical purposes, essentially identical to Mr. Rivera's. In both cases, this Court was initially precluded from considering existing compelling evidence that the petitioner was a person with intellectual disability. In *Rivera*, the bar to consideration stemmed from the petitioner's failure to exhaust state court remedies. Here, the evidence was not before the Court because, despite Mr. Campbell's diligent efforts to secure the documentary evidence, described *supra*, the evidence in 2003 remained within the exclusive

APPLICATION TO FILE SECOND OR SUCCESSIVE HABEAS CORPUS PETITION

Example Application #1—Robert James Campbell (cont.)

Case: 14-20293   Document: 00512624851   Page: 18   Date Filed: 05/09/2014

possession of the State of Texas – indeed, it remained there until the last eight weeks.

Second, in this context, the movant must show that the claim he seeks to raise in the successive petition "relies on a new rule of constitutional law, made retroactive to cases on collateral review by the Supreme Court, that was previously unavailable." 28 U.S.C. § 2244(b)(2)(A). Mr. Campbell's first federal habeas application was filed on November 2, 2000, almost two years before the Supreme Court's decision in *Atkins*.

Third, this Court, acting in a "gatekeeping" role, must determine whether a petitioner has made a "prima facie" showing that his application satisfies the requirements of section 2244(b). 28 U.S.C. § 2244(b)(3)(C). A "prima facie" showing is "simply a sufficient showing of possible merit to warrant a fuller exploration by the district court." *In re Morris*, 328 F.3d 739, 740 (5th Cir. 2003) (quoting *Bennett v. United States*, 119 F.3d 468, 469 (7th Cir. 1997)); see also *In re Johnson*, 334 F.3d 403 (5th Cir. 2003). But see *Ochoa v. Sirmons*, 485 F.3d 538, 542 (10th Cir. 2007) ("the plain language of the statute directs us to focus solely on the conditions Congress has designated as controlling with respect to the authorization of second or successive habeas petitions. And those conditions specified in § 2244(b)(2)(A) for the pursuit of claims resting on new rules of constitutional law do not involve the appellate court in any preliminary assessment of the merit of the claims for which second or successive authorization is sought.").

As demonstrated in Section V, *infra*, Mr. Campbell easily satisfies this threshold showing.

IV. IN THE ALTERNATIVE, THIS COURT SHOULD EXERCISE ITS POWER TO RECALL THE MANDATE.

Federal appeals courts "have an inherent power to recall their mandates,"[3] though it is to be exercised only in "extraordinary circumstances."[4] Fifth Circuit Rule 41.2 provides that a mandate may be recalled "to prevent injustice." This Court exercises that power sparingly but has ordered the mandate recalled where that was the only vehicle available to prevent injustice.[5] In each instance critically important facts were made known to the Court only after the mandate had been issued. Precisely the same is true here.

---

[3] *Calderon v. Thompson*, 523 U.S. 538, 549 (1998); *see also United States v. Tolliver*, 116 F.3d 120, 123 (5th Cir. 1997) ("Our authority to recall our own mandate is clear.").

[4] *Calderon*, 523 U.S. at 550.

[5] *See, e.g., Spence v. Holder*, 414 Fed. App'x 637 (5th Cir. Feb. 8, 2011) (unpublished) (recalling mandate where defendant had not received notice of the appellate decision and a subsequent Supreme Court decision provided a ground for reversing that decision); *United States v. Fraga-Araigo*, 281 F.3d 1278 (5th Cir. 2001) (unpublished) (recalling mandate and reopening appeal because of new decision by the Circuit); *Tolliver*, 116 F.3d at 123–24 (recalling mandate as to one of several co-defendants who did not petition for certiorari so that he could have his conviction reviewed in light of new Supreme Court decision that made clear the previous Fifth Circuit decision was wrong, and other co-defendants who had petitioned had their judgments vacated by the Supreme Court and remanded for reconsideration); *Ordonez v. United States*, 588 F.2d 448, 449 (5th Cir. 1979) (recalling and reissuing mandate to allow defendant an opportunity to bring a timely certiorari petition, where defendant's counsel had promised to file a petition but failed to do so).

Case: 14-20293   Document: 00512624851   Page: 20   Date Filed: 05/09/2014

Circumstances that "call[] into question the very legitimacy of the judgment" — such as fraud on the appellate court — are the type of situation where recall of a mandate is appropriate, and the restrictions against successive habeas petitions do not operate.[6] As a member of this panel has explained, it is not always necessary to show bad faith:

> "[A] federal court may provide equitable intervention in a state criminal proceeding even in the absence of the usual prerequisites of bad faith and harassment when extraordinary circumstances in which the necessary irreparable injury can be shown are present." *Gilliam v. Foster*, 75 F.3d 881, 904 (4th Cir. 1996) (quoting *Kugler v. Helfant*, 421 U.S. 117, 123 . . . 1975)) (internal quotation marks omitted). The Supreme Court explained that federal injunctive relief against pending state prosecutions are appropriate only where there is proven harassment or prosecutions taken in bad faith, or where there are "other extraordinary circumstances where irreparable injury can be shown." *Kugler*, 421 U.S. at 123 . . . . The extraordinary circumstances must "creat[e] a threat of irreparable injury both great and immediate" in order to enable federal court intervention. *Id.* at 123 . . . .

Chester v. Thaler, 522 Fed. Appx. 208, 209 (5th Cir. June 11, 2013) (Dennis, J., concurring).

A motion to recall the mandate may not be used to circumvent the strict rules against successive habeas petitions set forth in 28 U.S.C. § 2244(b).[7] The current motion is not a disguised successive habeas petition. Mr. Campbell's argument for recalling the mandate is not a challenge to his conviction or his

---

[6] *Calderon*, 523 U.S. at 557.

[7] *See Gonzalez v. Crosby*, 545 U.S. 524, 531–32 (2005) (discussing restriction on the use of motions in the district court under Civil Rule 60(b)); *Calderon*, 523 U.S. at 553–59 (same).

APPLICATION TO FILE SECOND OR SUCCESSIVE HABEAS CORPUS PETITION

Example Application #1—Robert James Campbell (cont.)

Case: 14-20293   Document: 00512624851   Page: 21   Date Filed: 05/09/2014

sentence. This motion challenges only the integrity of the appellate process. It falls within the exception recognized in *Gonzalez v. Crosby* for motions that challenge the integrity of the federal proceedings and do not attack the substance of the federal courts' resolution of the underlying substantive claim on the merits.[8]

As described *supra*, the extraordinary circumstances of this case call into question the integrity of the prior proceedings. In the wake of *Atkins*, Mr. Waggoner diligently submitted requests for records from the schools that Mr. Campbell attended, as well as for the Houston Independent School District records. He was given just a few pages; more important, he was *not* supplied with the record that showed that Mr. Campbell had a 68 IQ at age eight. This document, evidence of Mr. Campbell's sub-average intellectual functioning prior to the age of 18, was apparently within the exclusive possession of the Harris County District Attorney's Office at the time Mr. Campbell attempted to litigate his *Atkins* claim in both state and federal court.

Likewise, Mr. Waggoner diligently pursued any intellectual functioning testing in the possession of the Respondent in these proceedings, the Texas Department of Criminal Justice. The Respondent affirmatively misled Mr. Waggoner by telling him that death-sentenced prisoners receive no intellectual

---

[8] *See Gonzalez*, 545 U.S. at 532.

APPLICATION TO FILE SECOND OR SUCCESSIVE HABEAS CORPUS PETITION

Example Application #1—Robert James Campbell (cont.)

Case: 14-20293   Document: 00512624851   Page: 22   Date Filed: 05/09/2014

testing.[9] But for the Respondent's misdirection, this Court would have had before it a pre-*Atkins* IQ score of 71 — obtained by a state-employed psychologist — on a short-form test that tends to over-estimate Full Scale IQs.

Mr. Campbell's attempts to litigate an *Atkins* claim in both state and federal court were met with stiff opposition from the State of Texas, which was at the time — knowingly or not — sitting on evidence that would have undoubtedly resulted in a different outcome in both authorization-stage proceedings. Moreover, had the claim been authorized in federal court, Mr. Waggoner could have secured the resources necessary for a forensic evaluation which would resulted in a report like Dr. Rosenstein's, confirming the diagnosis of mental retardation that bars Texas from putting Mr. Campbell to death.

The record is silent as to why the State of Texas failed to come forward with the compelling evidence in its files of Mr. Campbell's intellectual disability. But it is clear that the absence of this evidence fatally compromised the integrity of the prior proceeding and resulted in a decision not to authorize review of Mr. Campbell's *Atkins* claim. It is truly extraordinary that Mr. Waggoner's diligent record-gathering effort came up empty, particularly because Mr. Waggoner's request to the Respondent was made in the aftermath of *Atkins*, a time when the

---

[9] For purposes of this proceeding, it makes no difference whether this misdirection was intentional. What matters is that, as a result, Mr. Waggoner *and this Court* were deprived of available and powerfully probative evidence of a pre-*Atkins* IQ score of 71.

APPLICATION TO FILE SECOND OR SUCCESSIVE HABEAS CORPUS PETITION

Example Application #1—Robert James Campbell (cont.)

Case: 14-20293   Document: 00512624851   Page: 23   Date Filed: 05/09/2014

legal community and prison officials alike were highly attuned to the issue of intelligence testing of death row inmates.

To prioritize finality interests now, ahead of Mr. Campbell's interest in securing one fair opportunity to present his *Atkins* claim, would be an injustice. Indeed, the very retroactivity of *Atkins* itself demonstrates that finality interests are secondary to preventing the execution of a class of offenders whose diminished moral culpability renders execution, as a matter of law, *categorically* cruel and unusual punishment. "This court unquestionably has the power to recall its mandate and render a new judgment in this matter." *See, e.g., Chester v. Thaler*, 522 Fed. Appx. at 209 (Dennis, J., concurring). If this Court concludes that it cannot authorize review of Mr. Campbell's *Atkins* claim pursuant to 28 U.S.C. § 2244, it can and should recall the mandate from the prior authorization to prevent the injustice that would otherwise result from allowing the Respondent to execute an intellectually disabled offender after — inadvertently or otherwise — failing to disclose until the last minute requested evidence of his intellectual disability.

V. MR. CAMPBELL'S *ATKINS* CLAIM SATISFIES THE *PRIMA FACIE* SHOWING OF INTELLECTUAL DISABILITY NECESSARY FOR AUTHORIZATION UNDER § 2244(b)(3)(C).

A. The Intellectual Disability Standard.

The execution of an intellectually disabled person violates the Eighth Amendment's proscription against cruel and unusual punishment. *Atkins*, 536 U.S., at 321.

The Texas Legislature has not provided a statutory definition of mental retardation. In the absence of such a statutory definition, it is appropriate for this Court in assessing whether a *prima facie* case has been made to rely on the definitions set out by the American Association of Mental Retardation ("AAMR") and the American Psychiatric Association ("APA").[10] *Atkins*, 536 U.S. at 309 n.3. Each organization recognizes that mental retardation is a disability characterized by (1) "significantly sub-average" (APA) or "significant limitations" in (AAMR) intellectual functioning, (2) accompanied by "significant limitations" in adaptive behavior, (3) the onset of which occurs prior to the age of 18. *See* AAMR, *Mental Retardation: Definition, Classification, and Systems of Supports* 1 (10th ed. 2002) [hereinafter 2002 AAMR Manual]; APA, *Diagnostic and Statistical Manual of*

---

[10] The AAMR is now called the American Association on Intellectual and Developmental Disabilities ("AAIDD"). Mr. Campbell will use AAMR to refer to the manual published under that name, but will use AAIDD to refer to the organization itself and publications published under the new name.

Mental Disorders 41 (Text Revision, 4th ed. 2000) [hereinafter DSM-IV]; *Atkins*, 536 U.S. at 309 n.3.

Significantly sub-average intellectual functioning is defined as an IQ of about 70 or below, or approximately two standard deviations below the mean. *Briseno*, 135 S.W.3d, at 7 n.24 (citing DSM-IV at 39). However, both the AAMR Manual and the DSM-IV take into account the standard error of measurement in assessing IQ (approximately 5 points), which, in effect, "expands the operational definition of mental retardation to 75." 2002 AAMR Manual at 58-59; DSM-IV-TR at 41-42. *See also Atkins*, 536 U.S., at 309 n.5 (score of 75 is typically considered the cutoff IQ score for the intellectual functioning prong of the mental retardation definition); *Ex parte Modden*, 147 S.W.3d 293, 298 (Tex. Crim. App. 2004) (70-75 IQ score "generally indicates sub-average general intellectual functioning"). Additionally, the AAIIDD User's Guide to the 2002 AAMR Manual recommends that clinicians take the Flynn Effect, discussed *infra*, into account when interpreting IQ scores and assessing intellectual functioning. *See* AAIDD, USER'S GUIDE: MENTAL RETARDATION, DEFINITION, CLASSIFICATION, AND SYSTEMS OF SUPPORTS—10TH EDITION 20-21 (2007) [hereinafter AAIDD USER'S GUIDE].

The AAMR Manual requires that there be "significant limitations . . . in adaptive behavior as expressed in conceptual, social, and practical skills." 2002

AAMR Manual at 1. "Significance" can be established by the limitations in one of the three domains. AAMR 2002, at 74, 77-78. The AAMR Manual provides examples of "representative skills" in each of the three domains. Representative **conceptual skills** are "language, reading and writing, money concepts, and self-direction." *Id.* at 82. Representative **social skills** are "interpersonal, responsibility, self-esteem, gullibility, naiveté, follows rules, obeys laws, avoids victimization." *Id.* Representative **practical skills** are "activities of daily living, instrumental activities of daily living, occupational skills, and maintains safe environments." *Id.* The APA definition requires that there be "significant limitations" in at least two of the following eleven domains:

- communication
- self-care
- home living
- social/interpersonal skills
- use of community resources
- self-direction
- health
- safety
- functional academics
- leisure
- work

DSM-IV-TR, at 41.[11]

---

[11] The AAIDD and APA adaptive behavior domains are consistent with each other. Prior to the present edition of the 2002 AAMR Manual, the 1992 AAMR Manual (9th ed.1992) utilized a description of adaptive behavior domains similar to the description of the eleven domains still utilized by the APA in the DSM-IV. The only differences were the APA domain "social/interpersonal skills" was called "social skills" in the 1992 AAMR Manual; the APA

APPLICATION TO FILE SECOND OR SUCCESSIVE HABEAS CORPUS PETITION

Example Application #1—Robert James Campbell (cont.)

Case: 14-20293   Document: 00512624851   Page: 27   Date Filed: 05/09/2014

The 2002 AAMR Manual describes four categories of risk factors that may interact to cause mental retardation. The four categories of risk factors are: (1) biomedical: factors that relate to biologic processes, such as genetic disorders or nutrition; (2) social: factors that relate to social and family interaction, such as stimulation and adult responsiveness; (3) behavioral: factors that relate to

---

domain "use of community resources" was called "community use" in the 1992 AAMR Manual; and the two APA domains, "health" and "safety" were combined into a single "health and safety" domain in the 1992 AAMR Manual. *See* AAMR, *Mental Retardation: Definition, Classification, and Systems of Supports* 1 (9th ed. 1992) [hereinafter 1992 AAMR Manual]. Although the 2002 AAMR Manual shifted from a focus upon ten domains to three broader domains of adaptive behavior, each of the ten 1992 skill areas fits neatly within at least one 2002 AAMR Manual domain:

Relationships of 1992 and 2002 Adaptive Behavior Skills

Adaptive Behavior Skill Areas in 2002 Definition	Representative Skills in 2002 Definition	Skill Areas Listed in 1992 Definition
Conceptual	Language Reading and Writing Money concepts Self-direction	Communication Functional academics Self-direction Academics
Social	Interpersonal Responsibility Self-esteem Gullibility Naiveté Follows rules Obeys laws Avoid victimization	Social skills Leisure
Practical	Activities of daily living Instrumental activities of daily living Occupational skills Maintains safe environments	Self-care Home living Community use Health and safety Work

2002 AAMR Manual, Table 5.2. Thus, the current AAMR and APA domains are likewise compatible.

APPLICATION TO FILE SECOND OR SUCCESSIVE HABEAS CORPUS PETITION

Example Application #1—Robert James Campbell (cont.)

Case: 14-20293   Document: 00512624851   Page: 28   Date Filed: 05/09/2014

potentially causal behaviors, such as dangerous (injurious) activities or maternal substance abuse; and (4) educational: factors that relate to the availability of educational supports that promote mental development and the development of adaptive skills. 2002 AAMR Manual at 126. The 2002 AAMR Manual emphasizes that "the impairment of functioning that is present when an individual meets the criteria for a diagnosis of mental retardation usually reflects the presence of several risk factors that interact over time." *Id.*

B.   Robert Campbell Has Intellectual Disability.

Mr. Campbell has intellectual disability. The evidence shows that: (1) his IQ, as reflected in the results of IQ tests administered to him is significantly sub-average; (2) he has significant limitations in his adaptive functioning; and (3) he exhibited these diagnostic features before the age of eighteen.

1.   Mr. Campbell manifests significantly sub-average intellectual functioning.

Mr. Campbell has been administered what is recognized as the "gold standard" testing instrument for intellectual testing – the Wechsler Adult Intelligence Scale IV (WAIS-IV). It showed him to have significantly sub-average intellectual functioning.

The comprehensive evaluation of Mr. Campbell was performed by Dr.

APPLICATION TO FILE SECOND OR SUCCESSIVE HABEAS CORPUS PETITION

Example Application #1—Robert James Campbell (cont.)

Case: 14-20293   Document: 00512624851   Page: 29   Date Filed: 05/09/2014

Leslie D. Rosenstein on April 4, 2014, at the Polunsky Unit of TDCJ.[12] *See* Exhibit 2 (Dr. Rosenstein report) at 1.

Mr. Campbell's full scale composite IQ score – derived from 10 subtest scores – was 69. Exhibit 2 (Dr. Rosenstein report) at 2. Dr. Rosenstein reported the results as follows:

Test Scores

Wechsler Adult Intelligence Scale-IV (WAIS-IV):

Scale Scores*		Subtest Scores**		Subtest Scores**	
Full Scale IQ	69	Similarities	3	Block Design	6
Verbal Comprehension	70	Vocabulary	6	Matrix Reasoning	5
Perceptual Reasoning	75	Information	5	Visual Puzzles	6
Working Memory Index	77	Digit Span#	7	Symbol Search	5
Processing Speed Index	74	Forward	(6)	Coding	5
		Backward	(9)		
		Sequencing	(7)		
		Arithmetic	5		

*Mean = 100; Standard Deviation = 15
**Mean = 10; Standard Deviation = 3
#Max Forward Digits = 5 (4 for two consecutive trials); Max Backward Digits = 4 (both trials)

Her narrative summary of the results of the testing was as follows:

On April 4, 2014, comprehensive assessment of intellectual

---

[12] Dr. Rosenstein is a clinical neuropsychologist in private practice, board-certified by the American Board of Professional Psychology and licensed to practice in Texas. In 2009, she was appointed by Governor Perry to serve a six-year term as one of nine members of the Texas State Board of Examiners of Psychologists. Her curriculum vitae is included in Exhibit 2.

APPLICATION TO FILE SECOND OR SUCCESSIVE HABEAS CORPUS PETITION

Example Application #1—Robert James Campbell (cont.)

> Case: 14-20293   Document: 00512624851   Page: 30   Date Filed: 05/09/2014
>
> functioning was completed with the Wechsler Adult Intelligence Scale-4th Edition. The test environment was noted to be quiet and comfortable, and, as outlined above, Mr. Campbell cooperated with the procedures and demonstrated good effort. The Full Scale IQ obtained during this assessment was very close to the Deviation IQ of 68 from 1981; the current Full Scale IQ was 69. With regard to verbal intellectual skills, which were borderline to mildly deficient, overall, Mr. Campbell demonstrated low average to borderline receptive vocabulary as noted above, moderately deficient verbal abstract reasoning and knowledge of super ordinate semantic categories, and mildly deficient general fund of factual knowledge. In terms of the perceptual reasoning subtests, Mr. Campbell demonstrated low average to borderline speeded visual constructional assembling skill, mildly deficient nonverbal reasoning and pattern analysis, and low average to borderline visual spatial reasoning. With regard to span of attention and working memory, he performed within the low average to borderline range on a measure of span of attention for simple auditory verbal stimuli (*i.e.*, forward digit repetition), within the average range on one measure of working memory for auditory verbal stimuli (reverse digit repetition), within the low average range on a second measure of working memory (digit sequencing), and within the mildly deficient range on a measure requiring both working memory and applied arithmetic problem solving. With regard to psychomotor/processing speed, Mr. Campbell performed within the mildly deficient range on both a measure of graphomotor/ copying speed and incidental learning and on a measure of visual scanning and processing speed.
>
> Exhibit 2 (Dr. Rosenstein report) at 2-3. She diagnosed Mr. Campbell as having "mild mental retardation," *id.* at 3, and noted that this performance was consistent with, and corroborated by, his performance on other standardized measures of intelligence when he was a child:
>
> > As early as age 9, he performed more than two standard deviations below the population mean on a measure of mental ability, and as early as age 8 he scored within the deficient range (5th percentile) on a composite measure of basic skills, also demonstrating lack of

progress from the previous year (Grade Equivalent in 2nd grade = 1.4; Grade Equivalent in 1st grade = 1.7). On April 4, 2014, he performed more than two standard deviations below the population mean on a comprehensive measure of intelligence in spite of demonstrating good effort for the evaluation.

Id. at 3.

Mr. Campbell's performance on a separate measure of effort was consistent with his performance on a measure of effort embedded in the WAIS-IV itself, and supported Dr. Rosenstein's conclusion that no malingering was present, and that the WAIS-IV result is valid, *i.e.*, it accurately reflects Mr. Campbell's actual level of intellectual ability:

> Test Validity/Effort: In addition to not appearing overly anxious or depressed, Mr. Campbell was cooperative with the test procedures, and he performed normally on a measure of effort as well as on an embedded measure of effort. His pattern of errors was also consistent with good effort, with increased failures on more difficult items, and more successes on easier items. He also persisted when completing test items.

Id. at 1.

Mr. Campbell's performance on the WAIS-IV is mutually corroborated by other early childhood evidence concerning his intellectual ability. For example, as Dr. Rosenstein notes:

> At the age of 9, Mr. Campbell obtained a Deviation IQ of 68 on the Otis-Lennon Mental Ability Test, Form R. He also performed in the "Low" (lowest) range on all subtests of the Metropolitan Readiness Test at the age of 7; his Pre-Reading composite Stanine was reported as a 2, but with a percentile rank of 4th %ile (which would indicate a Stanine of 1), and his Total Quantitative score was reported as a

APPLICATION TO FILE SECOND OR SUCCESSIVE HABEAS CORPUS PETITION

Example Application #1—Robert James Campbell (cont.)

Case: 14-20293   Document: 00512624851   Page: 32   Date Filed: 05/09/2014

Stanine of 1 with a 1st %ile rank.

Id. at 2; *see also* Exhibit 3 (elementary school standardized test scores). As Dr. Rosenstein points out later in her report, it is significant that Mr. Campbell's scores on both the Otis-Lennon and the Metropolitan Readiness Test, both of which measure mental ability, are more than two standard deviations below the population mean.[13] *See* Exhibit 2 (Dr. Rosenstein report) at 3.

In addition, Mr. Campbell was annually administered standardized academic achievement tests during his abbreviated school career. His performance on these tests likewise is consistent with significantly sub-average intellectual functioning:

> At ages 7 through 12 years, Mr. Campbell was assessed through school with the Iowa Tests of Basic Skills on an annual basis. Keeping in mind that he repeated grades and he was older than his peers for much of these school years, his grade-based percentile ranks for the Composite Score on the Iowa Tests each year were: 46th%ile (first grade, age 7), 5th%ile (second grade, age 8), 2nd%ile (third grade, age 9), 11th%ile (3rd grade, age 10), 4th%ile (4th grade, age 11), and 8th%ile (5th grade, age 12).

Exhibit 2 (Dr. Rosenstein report) at 2.

Mr. Campbell's grades in school are also consistent with his performance on the WAIS-IV, as is his failure to progress beyond the ninth grade. As this

---

[13] The Stanine (STAndard NINE) scale is a nine-point scale with a mean of 5 and a standard deviation of two; thus, a Stanine score of 3 is one standard deviation below the mean, and a Stanine score of 1 is two standard deviations below the mean. *See* http://en.wikipedia.org/wiki/Stanine.

Court acknowledged in 2003, Mr. Campbell's records "indicate that [he] received failing grades in every subject except physical education, music, and basic mathematics." *Ex parte Campbell*, No. 44,551-02 (Tex. Crim. App. July 2, 2003) at 4. In addition, it is now plain from the available school records that Mr. Campbell failed at least two grades in school.[14]

In addition, Mr. Campbell's trial counsel arranged to have him interviewed prior to trial by psychologist Dr. Walter Quijano. *See* Exhibit 4 (Declaration of Dr. Walter Quijano). Dr. Quijano did not administer any intelligence testing to Mr. Campbell, and trial counsel did not provide Dr. Quijano with any of Mr. Campbell's school records. Nevertheless, "based on [his] extensive prior professional experience," Dr. Quijano "formed the impression that Mr. Campbell's IQ might be sub-average from the manner in which Mr. Campbell

---

[14] The records show that Mr. Campbell took the third-grade administration of the Iowa Tests of Basic Skills in *both* March 1982 and March 1983 (the computer-printed score summaries for both those administrations say "GR 03"), indicating that he failed the third grade in 1981-82 and repeated it in 1982-83. *See* Exhibit 3 (School records). In addition, the records show that Mr. Campbell was enrolled in the seventh grade at Attucks Middle School in September 1986 and withdrew in November 1986, and that he was next enrolled at Attucks from September 1988 to April 1989 as an eighth-grader. *Id.* The records do not reflect where Mr. Campbell was in school from November 1986 through Spring 1988, a period of about a year and a half (he is reported to have been enrolled in at least one other middle school), but the only explanation for his having been enrolled in the seventh and eighth grades 18 months apart is that he failed one or the other (*i.e.*, he could have failed the seventh grade in the 1986-87 school year and then repeated it at another school in the 1987-88 school year, or he could have been promoted to the eighth grade at the end of the 1986-87 school year but then failed the eighth grade in the 1987-88 year – meaning that when he was enrolled in the eighth grade at Attucks in 1988-89, he was repeating the grade which he had failed elsewhere). In any event, the only inference that can be drawn from the records is that Mr. Campbell failed two grades between first and eighth, which is consistent with his performance on the WAIS-IV.

APPLICATION TO FILE SECOND OR SUCCESSIVE HABEAS CORPUS PETITION

Example Application #1—Robert James Campbell (cont.)

Case: 14-20293 Document: 00512624851 Page: 34 Date Filed: 05/09/2014

answered [Dr. Quijano's] questions during the evaluation." *Id.* Dr. Quijano has now reviewed Mr. Campbell's available school records, and notes that they "show multiple test scores falling two or more standard deviations below the population mean as well as a history of failing academic performances," which is "consistent with the impression [Dr. Quijano] formed in April 1992 that [Mr. Campbell] might have a sub-average IQ." *Id.*

Dr. Rosenstein also notes that "[a]t least two individuals who knew [Mr. Campbell] as a child stated that they believed he was in Special Education classes." Exhibit 2 (Dr. Rosenstein First Addendum).

Two other IQ test scores deserve mention here, one because it essentially corroborates Dr. Rosenstein's diagnosis, and one because it deserves no weight whatsoever. The first: in 1992, when Mr. Campbell had just arrived on Death Row, he was administered what is described in TDCJ-ID clinic notes as a "WAIS-R IQ short form." *See* Exhibit 5 (Clinic Note dated July 13, 1992 from TDC medical records of Robert James Campbell). According to the clinic notes, Mr. Campbell scored a 71. Given that such "short form" screening tests "ha[ve] been shown to overestimate Full Scale IQs when compared to contemporary Wechsler Adult Intelligence Scales," *see* Exhibit 2 (Dr. Rosenstein report) at 2, and that Dr. Rosenstein's score both rests on the "gold standard" WAIS-IV and was obtained as part of the only comprehensive assessment ever performed of Mr. Campbell's cognitive ability, there is every reason to conclude that Dr. Rosenstein's 69 is the more accurate score.[15] In any event, taking the standard measure of error into account, the 71 score on the WAIS-R short form is statistically indistinguishable from the 68 score measured on the Otis-Lennon in 1982 and the 69 score recently measure on the WAIS-IV. All three scores are clearly in the same statistical range indicating significant sub-average intellectual functioning.

The remaining score is contained in the "Social and Criminal History" form completed in May 1990 by TDCJ (then TDC) officials when Mr. Campbell first entered TDCJ custody. On the first page of the document is a line marked "I.Q.," and on that line the number 84. When TDCJ officials disclosed this score to Mr. Campbell's then counsel in 2003, they described it as follows:

> The admission summary for [Mr. Campbell's initial] conviction indicates an IQ test score of 84. Because the actual IQ test instruments are kept for only a few months, any such test instrument for inmate Campbell would have been destroyed long ago. Additionally, our records indicate that there was no referral for any

---

[15] The 71 may well overstate Mr. Campbell's cognitive ability for another reason. The WAIS-R – from which subtests were drawn to improvise the "short form" IQ test that Mr. Campbell completed in 1992 – was normed in 1979. To correct for IQ gains over time in the general population (the "Flynn Effect"), Mr. Campbell's scores must be adjusted down by .30 points per year from the time the test was normed until the test was administered. Thus, when Mr. Campbell took the "short form" WAIS-R in 1992, it had been 13 years since the test was normed. Application of the Flynn Effect (13 years x .30 = 3.9, rounded down conservatively to 3) to the IQ score reported for Mr. Campbell from 1992 (71 – 3) would result in an IQ score of 68. Although this Court has not formally decided whether to require courts to address the "Flynn Effect," the presence of this question is just another reason to dismiss the "short form" score as insignificant, and to credit the Full Scale IQ score of 69 obtained through Dr. Rosenstein's comprehensive evaluation.

APPLICATION TO FILE SECOND OR SUCCESSIVE HABEAS CORPUS PETITION

Example Application #1—Robert James Campbell (cont.)

> Case: 14-20293   Document: 00512624851   Page: 36   Date Filed: 05/09/2014
>
> other intellectual testing so that TDCJ has nothing further on inmate Campbell in that regard.
>
> Exhibit 6 (TDC letter to Waggoner accompanying Social and Criminal History of Robert James Campbell) at 1. By TDCJ's own admission, "nothing further" is known about this score. It is not known what test was administered, the qualifications of the person who administered it, whether it was administered individually, what subtests (if any) might have comprised it, what Mr. Campbell's scores on the subtests were, or what the respective verbal and performance scores were. It is not known whether the person who scored the test made mathematical or other interpretive errors in doing so, and it is not possible to double-check that person's work against the raw data. In such circumstances, the fog of uncertainty that envelops this score, in contrast to what is known and readily available about Dr. Rosenstein's evaluation, counsels giving this 84 no weight whatsoever. *See Rivera v. Quarterman*, 505 F.3d 349, 362 (5th Cir. 2007) (where a "paucity of details surround[ed the] administration and scoring" of certain screening IQ tests used in the Texas prisons, including the fact that "the circumstances surrounding the [ ] administration [of the four tests were] either totally unknown or less than ideal," district court was entitled to give those scores less weight).
>
> These facts and circumstances, taken together, establish by any standard of proof that Mr. Campbell suffers from significantly sub-average general intellectual functioning.

2. Mr. Campbell manifests significant deficits in adaptive functioning.

The second prong requires an examination of deficits in adaptive behavior. The AAIDD (AAMR) has determined that three areas are applicable in determining intellectual disability: conceptual skills, social skills and practical skills. *Id.* The Texas Court of Criminal Appeals has cited the former AAMR's definitions of these areas:

Conceptual skills include skills related to language, reading and writing, money concepts, and self-direction. Social skills include skills related to interpersonal relationships, responsibility, self-esteem, gullibility, naivete, following rules, obeying laws, and avoiding victimization. Practical skills are skills related to activities of daily living and include occupational skills and maintaining a safe environment. *Hearn*, 310 S.W.3d at 428 at n. 9 (citing AAMR at 82).

Briseno notes that "[i]mpairments in adaptive behavior are defined as significant limitations in an individual's effectiveness in meeting the standards of maturation, learning, personal independence, and/or social responsibility that are expected for his or her age level and cultural group, as determined by clinical assessment and, usually, standardized scales." 135 S.W.3d at 7 n. 25 (citation omitted).¹⁶ Texas Health and Safety Code § 591.003(1) similarly explains that adaptive behavior means "the effectiveness with or degree to which a person meets the standards of personal independence and social responsibility expected of the person's age and cultural group."¹⁷

Although it has not yet been possible to complete standardized questionnaires regarding Mr. Campbell's adaptive functioning, *see* Exhibit 2 (Dr. Rosenstein report) at 1, Dr. Rosenstein has obtained sufficient historical information to conclude that Mr. Campbell's impairments in adaptive functioning warrant diagnosing him as a person with mental retardation.

First, as part of her comprehensive evaluation, Dr. Rosenstein assessed Mr. Campbell's functional academic skills by administering the Woodcock-Johnson-

---

[16] The Texas Court of Criminal Appeals requires that the defendant's deficits in adaptive functioning be linked to his sub-average intellectual functioning, to establish that they reflect that "deficit ... and not a personality disorder." *Hearn*, 310 S.W.3d at 428 To that end, the Court of Criminal Appeals has established a list of evidentiary factors to be considered by the fact-finder. See *Briseno*, 135 S.W.3d at 8-9. We address the applicability of the *Briseno* factors *infra*.

[17] It is important in this context to not confuse "adaptive behavior" with the term "maladaptive behavior." As one reviewer noted:

> "Maladaptive behavior" is a separate and independent construct of adaptive behavior. The presence or absence of "maladaptive behaviors" has little relationship to an individual's adaptive functioning. These behaviors can occur in individuals with poor adaptive behavior (*e.g.*, someone bangs their head because they are unable to communicate that they have a headache), and they can occur in individuals with good adaptive behavior, but for whom they are associated to a co-occurring mental health problem (*e.g.*, depression and aggressive behavior). "Maladaptive behaviors" are not part of the diagnostic criteria of mental retardation.

Marc J. Tassé, "Adaptive Behavior Assessment and the Diagnosis of Mental Retardation in Capital Cases," *Applied Neuropsychology*, 16:114-123 (2009).

APPLICATION TO FILE SECOND OR SUCCESSIVE HABEAS CORPUS PETITION

Example Application #1—Robert James Campbell (cont.)

Case: 14-20293   Document: 00512624851   Page: 39   Date Filed: 05/09/2014

II-NU Tests of Achievement: Passage Comprehension, Applied Problems, Writing Samples. *See* Exhibit 2 (Dr. Rosenstein report) at 1. In combination with Mr. Campbell's academic history as revealed by his available school records, his performance on the academic achievement test revealed significant deficits, *i.e.*, "applied academic skills consistent with an individual midway through the fifth grade." *Id.* at 2.

Mr. Campbell also demonstrated significantly impaired conceptual and practical skills in that he had difficulty performing ordinary monetary calculations ("he was able to count and add change," but "was not consistently accurate in calculating change from a purchase," and "could not answer simple questions about ... money savings"). *Id.* Mr. Campbell also had to ask a friend to read the time on his [Mr. Campbell's] non-digital watch. Exhibit 8 (declaration of Otha Lee Norton) at 1.

Mr. Campbell also manifested difficulties in reading and in written communication: he "failed to consistently write complete sentences," and although "[h]e was able to read and comprehend short sentences and short passages," he "sometimes missed the gist of the sentence completely," as indicated by his "filling in blanks with a word or phrase [that was] opposite [to] the correct response." *Id.* "Some of his responses involved simply offering words or phrases from the reading passage or completing the sentence with a common

APPLICATION TO FILE SECOND OR SUCCESSIVE HABEAS CORPUS PETITION

Example Application #1—Robert James Campbell (cont.)

Case: 14-20293 Document: 00512624851 Page: 40 Date Filed: 05/09/2014

phrase that did not match the context or meaning of the sentence." *Id.* Queried about the meaning of some of the words he used, he "often ... could not explain the meaning of the word or phrase correctly." *Id.*

Other adaptive functioning deficits were noted with respect to the fact that Mr. Campbell never obtained a driver's license, and that although he was known to drive, he experienced a number of minor driving incidents that suggested a degree of difficulty with his driving skill. *See*, *e.g.* 65 RR 1722 (testimony that while driving a stolen car, Mr. Campbell "hit a mailbox" and "ran [the car] into the ditch;" *see also* 64 RR 1503 (testimony that when driving a different car, Mr. Campbell "seemed to be having trouble driving [a] stick shift"). Another informant states that Mr. Campbell could not read the gas gauge on a car, and always had to ask others whether there was enough fuel to get to the destination. Exhibit 8 (declaration of Otha Lee Norton dec) at 1.

In addition, Mr. Campbell never obtained any gainful employment beyond physical labor (*i.e.*, mowing lawns) or which resulted in, *e.g.*, IRS W-2 filings. *See also*, *e.g.*, 65 RR 1791 (trial testimony of Mr. Campbell's cousin Marcus Arvey that he and Mr. Campbell had "cut yards" from the time that Arvey was "about five years old" until Mr. Campbell was eighteen or so); 65 RR 1797 (Mr. Campbell went around "cutting people's yards"); 65 RR 1792-93 (trial testimony that Mr. Campbell had tried to find a job "[d]owntown" in Houston, applying at

APPLICATION TO FILE SECOND OR SUCCESSIVE HABEAS CORPUS PETITION

Example Application #1—Robert James Campbell (cont.)

Case: 14-20293   Document: 00512624851   Page: 41   Date Filed: 05/09/2014

"Kroger's ... Rice and ... Family Dollar," but no one would hire him).

Dr. Rosenstein found other adaptive functioning deficits with respect to social skills. Dr. Rosenstein observes that "individuals who knew Mr. Campbell in childhood and adolescence" described him as "small and mentally slow / impaired," and noted that he was teased by others about his size and behavior, and (perhaps as a consequence) that he spent time with children much younger than he. Exhibit 2 (Dr. Rosenstein First Addendum). These informants also "noted that [Mr. Campbell] was a follower, and not a leader." *Id.*

To help "fact-finders in the criminal trial context" distinguish between effects of intellectual disability and those of personality disorders, the Texas Court of Criminal Appeals has identified the following evidentiary factors as relevant:

> Did those who knew the offender during the developmental stage - his family, friends, teachers, employers, authorities - think he was mentally retarded at that time, and if so, act in accordance with that determination?
>
> Has the person formulated plans and carried them through or is his conduct impulsive?
>
> Does his conduct show leadership or does it show that he is led around by others? Is his conduct in response to external stimuli rational and appropriate, regardless of whether it is socially acceptable?
>
> Does he respond coherently, rationally, and on point to oral and written questions, or do his responses wander from subject to subject?
>
> Can the person hide facts or lie effectively in his own or others"

APPLICATION TO FILE SECOND OR SUCCESSIVE HABEAS CORPUS PETITION

Example Application #1—Robert James Campbell (cont.)

Case: 14-20293   Document: 00512624851   Page: 42   Date Filed: 05/09/2014

interests?

Putting aside any heinousness or gruesomeness surrounding the capital offense, did the commission of that offense require forethought, planning and complex execution of purpose?

Briseno, 135 S.W.3d at 8-9.

Although we acknowledge that this Court has upheld the *Briseno* factors against constitutional challenge, we respectfully maintain that *Briseno*'s aim – to identify whether a claimant suffers such a "level and degree of mental retardation" that "a consensus of Texas citizens" would agree that he should be exempt from execution, 135 S.W.3d at 6 – is fundamentally at odds with *Atkins*. *Briseno* "departs from the scientific definition of mental retardation and supplants clinical criteria with non-scientific factors, resulting in a grossly underinclusive definition of mental retardation." *Amicus Curiae* Brief of American Association on Intellectual and Developmental Disabilities in Support of Petitioner, *Wilson v. Thaler*, No. 12-5349 (U.S. Sup. Ct.) (available at http://tinyurl.com/q7jclhs) at 3-4. *Atkins* does not permit states to displace clinically accepted standards for assessing adaptive functioning in favor of judicially created ones. In considering strengths to the exclusion of limitations and focusing on the particulars of the crime itself, "the *Briseno* factors ... have no basis in research and capitalize on entrenched prejudices." *Id*. at 4. Thus, reliance on the *Briseno* factors creates a substantial risk that people who are mentally retarded will be excluded from

APPLICATION TO FILE SECOND OR SUCCESSIVE HABEAS CORPUS PETITION

Example Application #1—Robert James Campbell (cont.)

Case: 14-20293   Document: 00512624851   Page: 43   Date Filed: 05/09/2014

Atkins' protection, in violation of due process and the Eighth Amendment. We object to any reliance on the *Briseno* factors to deny Mr. Campbell relief under *Atkins*.

However, to the extent they apply at all to the circumstances of Mr. Campbell's case, these factors all point toward intellectual disability as the underlying cause of Mr. Campbell's adaptive deficits. For example, Dr. Rosenstein notes that "individuals who knew Mr. Campbell in childhood and adolescence" – *i.e.*, "during the developmental stage" – described him as mentally slow / impaired." Exhibit 8 (Dr. Rosenstein First Addendum 1) at 2. Moreover, "[a]t least two individuals who knew [Mr. Campbell] as a child ... believe[] he was in Special Education classes," which would indicate that responsible officials in the school system "act[ed] in accordance with th[e] determination" that Mr. Campbell was cognitively impaired. *Id.*; *Briseno*, 135 S.W.3d at 8.

Evidence also indicates Mr. Campbell's criminal behavior has been marked by impulsivity rather than the formulation and carrying through of plans. To take just one example, the abduction of Susan Casey and her son from the Toys 'R' Us store appears to have been an utterly spur-of-the-moment event. It began when the vehicle stolen from Ms. Rendon, being driven by Mr. Campbell, ran out of gas – likely because Mr. Campbell could not read the gas gauge. *See* Exhibit 8 (declaration of Otha Lee Norton) at 1; *see also* 64 RR 1640-41. Mr. Campbell

APPLICATION TO FILE SECOND OR SUCCESSIVE HABEAS CORPUS PETITION

Example Application #1—Robert James Campbell (cont.)

Case: 14-20293   Document: 00512624851   Page: 44   Date Filed: 05/09/2014

and two companions, Otha Norton and Rochelle Pearson, pushed the car into a gas station. *Id.* Remarkably, it was the *same* gas station from which Mr. Campbell and Lawrence Thomas had abducted Ms. Rendon just days earlier, and Mr. Campbell told his companions that that was the location where he'd originally gotten the car. *Id.* at 1642. Mr. Campbell and his companions then began walking to a nearby mall because it wasn't "that far" from where they were, and they wanted "to go into Toys R Us because it was right after Christmas." *Id.* at 1643. Mr. Norton and Ms. Pearson got in line to buy some snacks, and without any warning, Mr. Campbell came into the store and began to talk to them about "robbing the lady [Ms. Casey] and taking her vehicle." *Id.* at 1646. As Mr. Norton and Ms. Pearson came out the door of Toys 'R' Us, Mr. Campbell rushed up to Ms. Casey's car with his handgun drawn "and pushed her in." *Id.* at 1647.

In short, everything about the Casey carjacking-abduction was spontaneous and impulsive. There is no evidence of any plan,[18] and the presence of Mr. Campbell and his co-participants at the store in the first place was entirely fortuitous, since it followed from their having run out of gas in Ms. Rendon's car a short distance away.

---

[18] Mr. Campbell's behavior in the course of the Casey abduction also bespeaks impulsivity and lack of any settled plan; co-participant Otha Norton testified that Mr. Campbell initially said he wanted to "kill [Ms. Casey] and drown [her son]," *see* 64 RR 1651, but abandoned that idea after "maybe three or four minutes" when Mr. Norton protested. *Id.* at 1654.

APPLICATION TO FILE SECOND OR SUCCESSIVE HABEAS CORPUS PETITION

Example Application #1—Robert James Campbell (cont.)

Case: 14-20293   Document: 00512624851   Page: 45   Date Filed: 05/09/2014

As to being a "leader," Dr. Rosenstein reports that "individuals who knew Mr. Campbell in childhood and adolescence" say "he was a follower, and not a leader." Exhibit 2 (Dr. Rosenstein First Addendum) at 2. While there is evidence that Mr. Campbell took part in crimes with other people, there is no evidence that he "led" the other participants in any meaningful way. *Briseno* plainly uses "leader" to mean someone who directs the actions of others who in turn are voluntarily following his lead. That description does not fit Mr. Campbell's relationship to, *e.g.*, Mr. Norton and Ms. Pearson in the Casey carjacking-abduction. In that case, Mr. Campbell's actions in drawing a gun and rushing Ms. Casey's car may have "forced their hand" in choosing whether to come along or stay behind, but there is no indication that he was telling either of them what to do. Indeed, in the only aspect of the Casey crime with respect to which Mr. Campbell purportedly asserted an intention was that he wanted to kill the victims; rather than "leading" or "directing" Mr. Norton and/or Ms. Pearson to make that happen, he was talked out of that idea by Mr. Norton. Thus, there is no evidence supporting a characterization of Mr. Campbell as "show[ing] leadership."

While Mr. Campbell appears somewhat capable of "respond[ing] coherently, rationally, and on point to oral and written questions," his ability to respond to anything in writing is impaired by the reading comprehension problems identified by Dr. Rosenstein, *supra*. Perhaps more to the point, his

APPLICATION TO FILE SECOND OR SUCCESSIVE HABEAS CORPUS PETITION

Example Application #1—Robert James Campbell (cont.)

Case: 14-20293   Document: 00512624851   Page: 46   Date Filed: 05/09/2014

responses are limited in their sophistication and depth, due to his intellectual impairment.

The last two *Briseno* factors (whether the person can "hide facts" or "lie effectively," and whether committing the capital offense "require[d] forethought, planning, and complex execution of purpose") can and should be considered together, since they effectively ask the fact-finder to evaluate the defendant's criminal sophistication. Mr. Campbell demonstrates no criminal sophistication. He does not appear ever to have committed a crime by himself (he was one of four defendants in the robbery that sent him to prison at 17; one of two persons involved in the Du Vong carjacking-abduction; one of two persons involved in the Alexandra Rendon carjacking, abduction, and murder; and one of three persons involved in the Susan Casey carjacking-abduction). More important, far from taking steps to hide his involvement in the offenses and evade detection, Mr. Campbell did things that effectively broadcast his role. He made inculpatory statements. He drove the victims' cars around his own neighborhood in broad daylight. Finally, rather than convert Ms. Rendon's personal property (*e.g.*, by selling it at a pawnshop) and then giving the money to his friends or buying them gifts, Mr. Campbell simply gave some of Ms. Rendon's personal property directly to his mother and his girlfriend. All of this behavior showed an utter lack of criminal sophistication, contrary to the focus of *Briseno*.

APPLICATION TO FILE SECOND OR SUCCESSIVE HABEAS CORPUS PETITION

Example Application #1—Robert James Campbell (cont.)

Case: 14-20293   Document: 00512624851   Page: 47   Date Filed: 05/09/2014

Since none of the *Briseno* factors weighs significantly against Mr. Campbell, they should not bar relief here.

> **3. Mr. Campbell's significantly sub-average intellectual functioning and his significant deficits in adaptive functioning manifested themselves during the developmental period.**

Dr. Rosenstein notes that Mr. Campbell performed more than two standard deviations below the population mean on a measure of mental ability "as early as age 9," *see* Exhibit 2 (Dr. Rosenstein report) at 3, and that he had "a long history *throughout childhood* of academic failures, poor test performances, inability to live independently, inability to obtain gainful employment, and inability to stay out of trouble." *Id.* (emphasis added). These facts establish that Mr. Campbell's intellectual disability manifested itself during the developmental period (*i.e.*, prior to age 18).

PRAYER FOR RELIEF

ACCORDINGLY, Mr. Campbell asks this Court to:

1. Authorize the district court to consider the merits of his *Atkins* claim;

2. Grant such other relief as law and justice require.

Respectfully submitted,

/s/ Robert C. Owen

ROBERT C. OWEN
Texas Bar No. 15371950
Bluhm Legal Clinic
Northwestern University
 School of Law
375 East Chicago Ave.
Chicago, Illinois 60611
(312) 503-0135 voice
(312) 503-8977 facsimile
robert.owen@law.northwestern.edu

RAOUL D. SCHONEMANN
Texas Bar No. 00786233
Capital Punishment Clinic
School of Law
The University of Texas at Austin
727 East Dean Keeton Street
Austin, Texas 78705-3224
(512) 232-9391 voice
(512) 232-9171 facsimile

Attorneys for Robert James Campbell

APPLICATION TO FILE SECOND OR SUCCESSIVE HABEAS CORPUS PETITION

Example Application #1—Robert James Campbell (cont.)

Case: 14-20293   Document: 00512624851   Page: 49   Date Filed: 05/09/2014

CERTIFICATE OF SERVICE

On May 7, 2014, I electronically submitted the foregoing document to the Clerk of Court for the United States Court of Appeals for the Fifth Circuit, using the electronic case filing system of the court. I hereby certify that I have served all counsel and/or *pro se* parties of record electronically or by another manner authorized by Federal Rule of Civil Procedure 5 (b)(2).

/s/ *Robert C. Owen*
Robert C. Owen

No. 06-4120

IN THE
**United States Court of Appeals
for the Sixth Circuit**

IN RE: DEWITT MCDONALD JR.,

Movant.

**On Motion For An Order Authorizing
A Second Or Successive Petition For A Writ Of Habeas Corpus
Pursuant To 28 U.S.C. § 2244(b)(3)(A)**

MOTION OF DEWITT MCDONALD JR.

MEIR FEDER
ROBERT T. SMITH
(Counsel of Record)
JONES DAY
222 East 41st Street
New York, NY 10017
(212) 326-3939

*Counsel for Movant
(Appointed Pursuant to the
Criminal Justice Act)*

APPLICATION TO FILE SECOND OR SUCCESSIVE HABEAS CORPUS PETITION

Example Application #2—Dewitt McDonald, Jr. (cont.)

TABLE OF CONTENTS

Page

TABLE OF AUTHORITIES iii
INTRODUCTION 1
STATEMENT OF JURISDICTION 2
STATEMENT OF THE ISSUE PRESENTED 2
STATEMENT OF THE CASE 4
STATEMENT OF THE FACTS 7
    A. The Shooting 9
    B. The Investigation 11
    C. Harris's Initial Grand Jury Testimony 12
    D. Harris's Subsequent Grand Jury Testimony 13
    E. McDonald's Trial 14
    F. McDonald's First § 2254 Petition 20
    G. Harris's Recantation 22
    H. Caston's § 2254 Petition 22
    I. McDonald's First Petition for State Post-Conviction Relief 24
    J. Caffey's Confession 24
    K. McDonald's Second Petition for State Post-Conviction Relief 25
    L. McDonald's Second § 2254 Petition 25
SUMMARY OF ARGUMENT 26
ARGUMENT 28
I.   MCDONALD IS ENTITLED TO FILE A SECOND § 2254
    PETITION UNDER AEDPA 28
    A.   This Court Evaluates A Second-Or-Successive Motion Under A
        Lenient Prima Facie Standard And Grants Such A Motion If It
        Presents Allegations Of Fact Sufficient To Warrant A Fuller
        Exploration In The District Court. 28
    B.   McDonald Has Made A "Prima Facie Showing" Under The
        Statute. 31

-i-

TABLE OF CONTENTS
(continued)

Page

- 1. McDonald Has Easily Made A Prima Facie Showing That, But For Constitutional Error, No Reasonable Factfinder Would Have Found Him Guilty Of The Underlying Offense..31
    - a. The Application Makes A Prima Facie Showing Of Constitutional Error...32
        - i. The Knowing Use Of Perjured Testimony..........32
        - ii. The Failure To Disclose Information That Could Have Been Used To Impeach Important Inculpatory Testimony 35
        - iii. The Denial Of The Right To Present A Witness In One's Own Defense 36
    - b. The Application Makes The Required Showing That, But For The Constitutional Error, No Reasonable Factfinder Would Have Convicted McDonald Of The Underlying Offense.........................38
- 2. The Factual Predicate For McDonald's Claims Could Not Have Been Previously Discovered Through The Exercise Of Due Diligence. 41
- 3. None Of McDonald's Claims Has Been Presented In A Prior Application...42

C. A Movant Is Not Required To Make A Prima Facie Showing Beyond The Requirements Of § 2244(b) 42

CONCLUSION 45

-ii-

Example Application #2—Dewitt McDonald, Jr. (cont.)

TABLE OF AUTHORITIES

                                                                     Page

Bell v. United States,
    296 F.3d 127 (2d Cir. 2002) 29

Bennett v. United States,
    119 F.3d 468 (7th Cir. 1997) 26, 29, 30, 32, 39

Brady v. Maryland,
    373 U.S. 83 (1963)..32, 35, 40

Byrd v. Collins,
    209 F.3d 486 (6th Cir. 2000) 33

Caston v. Mitchell,
    12 Fed. Appx. 208 (6th Cir. 2001) 23, 24

Chambers v. Mississippi,
    410 U.S. 284 (1973)..32, 36

Christie v. Hollins,
    409 F.3d 120 (2d Cir. 2005) 38

Cooper v. Woodford,
    358 F.3d 1117 (9th Cir. 2004) 29, 32, 38, 43

Davis v. Straub,
    430 F.3d 281 (6th Cir. 2005), *cert. denied*, 127 S. Ct. 929 (2007) 38

In re Fowlkers,
    326 F.3d 542 (4th Cir. 2003) 42

Giglio v. United States,
    405 U.S. 150 (1972)...32

House v. Bell,
    126 S. Ct. 2064 (2006)..30, 31, 39

-iii-

TABLE OF AUTHORITIES
(continued)

                                                                                                  Page

Jackson v. Virginia,
    443 U.S. 307 (1979)..30

Jamison v. Collins,
    291 F.3d 380 (6th Cir. 2002) 34

In re Johnson,
    322 F.3d 881 (5th Cir. 2003) 29, 32, 39, 43

Jordan v. Secretary, Department of Corrections,
    485 F.3d 1351 (11th Cir. 2007) 32, 38, 43

Kyles v. Whitley,
    514 U.S. 419 (1995)...33, 35

In re Lott,
    366 F.3d 431 (6th Cir. 2004) .... *passim*

Napue v. Illinois,
    360 U.S. 264 (1959)...32, 36

In re Provenzano,
    215 F.3d 1233 (11th Cir. 2000) 41

Sawyer v. Whitley,
    505 U.S. 333 (1992)..30

Schlup v. Delo,
    513 U.S. 298 (1995)...30, 31

In re Siggers,
    132 F.3d 333 (6th Cir. 1997) 28

Souter v. Jones,
    395 F.3d 577 (6th Cir. 2005) 44

Spirko v. Mitchell,
    368 F.3d 603 (6th Cir. 2004) 36

TABLE OF AUTHORITIES
(continued)

                                                                                                                 Page

Strickler v. Greene,
    527 U.S. 263 (1999)..35

Sustache-Rivera v. United States,
    221 F.3d 8 (1st Cir. 2000)..29

United States v. Agurs,
    427 U.S. 97 (1976)..33

United States v. Bagley,
    473 U.S. 667 (1985)..33

United States v. Emuegbunam,
    268 F.3d 377 (6th Cir. 2001) 37

United States v. Lochmondy,
    890 F.2d 817 (6th Cir. 1989) 33

United States v. Thomas,
    488 F.2d 334 (6th Cir. 1973) 37, 38

Washington v. Texas,
    388 U.S. 14 (1967)..36

Webb v. Texas,
    409 U.S. 95 (1972)..32, 36, 37, 38

STATE CASES

State v. McDonald,
    679 N.E.2d 309 (Ohio 1997) 4

State v. Johnson,
    754 N.E.2d 796 (Ohio 2001) 34, 40

State v. McDonald,
    830 N.E.2d 1169 (Ohio 2005) 6

TABLE OF AUTHORITIES
(continued)

Page

State v. McDonald,
No. E-95-046, 1997 WL 51221 (Ohio Ct. App. Feb. 7, 1997) 4

State v. McDonald,
2005 Ohio 798 (Ohio Ct. App. 2005) 6

State v. McDonald,
2007 Ohio 2148 (Ohio Ct. App. 2007) ....passim

DOCKETED CASES

Caston v. Mitchell,
No. 3:98-cv-7099 (N.D. Ohio Oct. 13, 1999) 23

State v. McDonald,
No. 94-CR-357 (Erie County Ct. of Common Pleas) 5, 6

State v. McDonald,
No. E-95-046 (Ohio Ct. App. June 10, 1997) 5

FEDERAL STATUTES

28 U.S.C. § 2241 2

28 U.S.C. § 2241(d) 2

28 U.S.C. § 2244(b)(1) 3, 26, 29, 31

28 U.S.C. § 2244(b)(2) ....*passim*

28 U.S.C. § 2244(b)(3) ....*passim*

28 U.S.C. § 2244(b)(4) 43

28 U.S.C. § 2244(d)(1) 44

28 U.S.C. § 2244(d)(2) 44

TABLE OF AUTHORITIES
(continued)

Page

28 U.S.C. § 2254 .... *passim*

Pub. L. No. 104-132, 110 Stat. 1214 28

STATE STATUTES

Ohio Rev. Code Ann. § 2901.13(A)(1)(a) 5

Ohio Rev. Code Ann. § 2903.01 4

Ohio Rev. Code Ann. § 2903.02 4

Ohio Rev. Code Ann. § 2903.11 4

Ohio Rev. Code Ann. § 2921.11 5

Ohio Rev. Code Ann. § 2923.01 4

Ohio Rev. Code Ann. § 2923.02 4

Ohio Rev. Code Ann. § 2923.03 ....4, 40

Ohio Rev. Code Ann. § 2923.161 4

Ohio Rev. Code Ann. § 2953.21 6

Ohio Rev. Code Ann. § 2953.23 6

MISCELLANEOUS

2 RANDY HERTZ & JAMES S. LIEBMAN, FEDERAL HABEAS CORPUS PRACTICE
AND PROCEDURE (5th ed. 2005) 43

FED. R. GOVERNING § 2254 CASES 44

INTRODUCTION

Movant Dewitt McDonald Jr. is currently serving a sentence of 20 years to life on a conviction secured largely on the strength of one woman's testimony, Krista Harris.

Nearly two years after Mr. McDonald's first § 2254 petition had been denied, Ms. Harris came forward and admitted that she had provided false testimony at Mr. McDonald's trial. She filed a sworn affidavit in state court, in which she accused Mr. McDonald's prosecutor, Kevin Baxter, of having knowingly procured her perjured testimony through threats and a coerced sexual relationship. These accusations have been corroborated, under oath, by Mr. Baxter's brother, Edward Baxter.

Mr. McDonald now moves this Court, pursuant to 28 U.S.C. § 2244(b)(3), for an order authorizing the United States District Court for the Southern District of Ohio to consider a second § 2254 petition. His application easily satisfies the "lenient prima facie standard" that governs such motions. *In re Lott*, 366 F.3d 431, 433 (6th Cir. 2004). As is most relevant here, he has made the required showing that it is *possible* that the District Court may ultimately conclude, on a more fully developed record, that no reasonable factfinder would have convicted him based on the overall, newly supplemented record. *See* 28 U.S.C. § 2244(b)(2)(B), (b)(3)(C). Accordingly, this Court should grant his motion.

Example Application #2—Dewitt McDonald, Jr. (cont.)

STATEMENT OF JURISDICTION

This is an original motion filed in the United States Court of Appeals for the Sixth Circuit pursuant to 28 U.S.C. § 2244(b)(3)(A). A three-judge panel is authorized to consider this motion pursuant to 28 U.S.C. § 2244(b)(3)(B). If this Court should grant the motion, then the United States District Court for the Southern District of Ohio would have jurisdiction to consider Movant's underlying petition for a writ of habeas corpus pursuant to 28 U.S.C. §§ 2241, 2254. Because Movant is currently in custody in the Southern District of Ohio but was convicted and sentenced in a state court in the Northern District of Ohio, venue would lie in either judicial district pursuant to 28 U.S.C. § 2241(d).

STATEMENT OF THE ISSUE PRESENTED

Dewitt McDonald is incarcerated for aiding and abetting two other men in the commission of a 1994 drive-by shooting that resulted in the death of one woman and the injury of another. From the beginning, the State proceeded on the theory that Mr. McDonald was present at the time of the shooting. As a consequence, the State's case against him faltered when Krista Harris told both investigators and a grand jury that Mr. McDonald had been with her at that time. It was resurrected, however, when Ms. Harris changed her story and testified, among other things, that Mr. McDonald had not been with her. She provided this and

APPLICATION TO FILE SECOND OR SUCCESSIVE HABEAS CORPUS PETITION

Example Application #2—Dewitt McDonald, Jr. (cont.)

other evidence necessary to secure both Mr. McDonald's indictment and conviction.

Years later, after Mr. McDonald's first § 2254 petition had been denied, Ms. Harris filed a sworn affidavit in state court, in which she asserted that Mr. McDonald's prosecutor coerced her into providing false testimony at Mr. McDonald's trial. Other evidence corroborates the accusations in her affidavit and supports Mr. McDonald's claims that his conviction was secured through constitutional error. These claims include: (1) the knowing use of perjured testimony, (2) the failure to disclose information that could have been used to impeach important inculpatory evidence, and (3) the denial of the right to present witnesses in his own defense.

This motion presents the following issue:

1. Whether Mr. McDonald has made a "prima facie showing" (i) that the facts underlying his claims "could not have been previously discovered through the exercise of due diligence," (ii) that those facts, "if proven and viewed in the light of the evidence as a whole, would be sufficient to establish by clear and convincing evidence that, but for constitutional error, no reasonable factfinder would have found the applicant guilty of the underlying offense," and (iii) that his claims have not been "presented in a prior application." 28 U.S.C. § 2244(b)(1), (b)(2)(B), (b)(3)(C).

APPLICATION TO FILE SECOND OR SUCCESSIVE HABEAS CORPUS PETITION

Example Application #2—Dewitt McDonald, Jr. (cont.)

STATEMENT OF THE CASE

In June 1995, Dewitt McDonald Jr. was convicted of complicity to commit the following offenses: (1) aggravated murder with a firearm specification, OHIO REV. CODE ANN. §§ 2903.01, 2923.03; (2) the lesser included offense of murder with a firearm specification, *id.* §§ 2903.02, 2923.03; (3) improperly discharging a firearm into a habitation with specifications for harm and a firearm, *id.* §§ 2923.161, 2923.03; (4) felonious assault with a firearm specification, *id.* §§ 2903.11(A)(2), 2923.03; (5) attempted aggravated murder with a firearm specification, *id.* §§ 2903.01(A), 2923.02, 2923.03; and (6) felonious assault with a firearm specification, *id.* §§ 2903.11(A)(2), 2923.03. (A0063.) The trial judge merged Mr. McDonald's conviction for aggravated murder with his conviction for murder and sentenced him principally to a term of life in prison with no eligibility for parole for 20 years. (A0064-A0066.) A final judgment was entered in the Erie County Court of Common Pleas on June 27, 1995. (A0063.)

Mr. McDonald pursued direct appeals through the Ohio court system. On February 7, 1997, the Ohio Court of Appeals for the Sixth Appellate District affirmed the judgment of the trial court. *State v. McDonald*, No. E-95-046, 1997 WL 51221 (Ohio Ct. App. Feb. 7, 1997) (unpublished). On May 7, 1997, the Supreme Court of Ohio denied him leave to appeal. *State v. McDonald*, 679 N.E.2d 309 (Ohio 1997). Finally, on June 10, 1997, the Ohio Court of Appeals denied an application by Mr. McDonald to reopen his appeal. *State v. McDonald*, No. E-95-046 (Ohio Ct. App. June 10, 1997) (unpublished).

On May 28, 1998, Mr. McDonald filed a timely petition for a writ of habeas corpus in the United States District Court for the Northern District of Ohio. (A0002.) On May 18, 1999, the District Court issued an opinion and order denying the petition. (A0031.) A certificate of appealability was likewise denied. (A0040-A0041.)

On June 16, 1999, Mr. McDonald filed a notice of appeal with the District Court. (A0042.) This Court construed the notice of appeal as an application for a certificate of appealability and denied that application in an order dated February 1, 2000. (A0044.)

Nearly two years later, Ms. Harris filed an affidavit in state court, in which she asserted that Erie County Prosecutor Kevin Baxter coerced her into providing false testimony at Mr. McDonald's trial. (A0045.) The affidavit was filed slightly more than six years after Mr. McDonald's trial. The statute of limitations for perjury is six years in Ohio. *See* OHIO REV. CODE ANN. §§ 2901.13(A)(1)(a), 2921.11(F).

On May 1, 2003, Mr. McDonald commenced the first of two state post-conviction proceedings in the Erie County Court of Common Pleas. Petition for McDonald, *State v. McDonald*, No. 94-CR-357 (Erie County Ct. of Common

Example Application #2—Dewitt McDonald, Jr. (cont.)

Pleas). In the first proceeding, Mr. McDonald moved for post-conviction relief, a new trial, and an order declaring the Ohio statute governing post-conviction relief unconstitutional, *see* OHIO REV. CODE ANN. §§ 2953.21, 2953.23. Petition for McDonald, *State v. McDonald*, No. 94-CR-357 (Erie County Ct. of Common Pleas).

On January 21, 2004, the Court of Common Pleas denied Mr. McDonald's motions and entered judgment for the State. *State v. McDonald*, No. 94-CR-357 (Erie County Ct. of Common Pleas Jan. 21, 2004) (unpublished). The Ohio Court of Appeals for the Sixth Appellate District affirmed, *State v. McDonald*, 2005 Ohio 798 (Ohio Ct. App. 2005), and on July 13, 2005, the Supreme Court of Ohio denied leave to appeal, *State v. McDonald*, 830 N.E.2d 1169 (Ohio 2005).

On October 29, 2005, Mr. McDonald filed a second petition for State post-conviction relief. Petition for McDonald, *State v. McDonald*, No. 94-CR-357 (Erie County Ct. of Common Pleas). This petition was based on evidence not presented in the previous state post-conviction proceeding. *Id*.

On February 3, 2006, the Court of Common Pleas denied Mr. McDonald's motion and entered judgment for the State. *State v. McDonald*, No. 94-CR-357 (Erie County Ct. of Common Pleas Feb. 3, 2006) (unpublished). The Ohio Court of Appeals has since affirmed. *State v. McDonald*, 2007 Ohio 2148 (Ohio Ct. App. 2007).

APPLICATION TO FILE SECOND OR SUCCESSIVE HABEAS CORPUS PETITION

Example Application #2—Dewitt McDonald, Jr. (cont.)

On June 30, 2006, while his second petition for post-conviction relief was still pending in state court, Mr. McDonald sent to this Court a *pro se* motion for an order authorizing the United States District Court to consider a second or successive petition for a writ of habeas corpus. *See* Addendum C. The motion was filed on August 17, 2006. *Id.*

On March 19, 2007, this Court issued an order directing the Clerk of the Court to appoint counsel to represent Mr. McDonald. (A0001.) The Clerk appointed the undersigned counsel to prepare a revised motion and present oral argument on Mr. McDonald's behalf.

STATEMENT OF THE FACTS

Dewitt McDonald's incarceration stems from charges that he aided and abetted two other men in the commission of a drive-by shooting. Despite the flexibility inherent in those charges, the State proceeded on the theory that Mr. McDonald was present at the time of the shooting. (A0222-A0228, A0375-A0376, A0381, A0388-A0389.)

When the State first brought its case to a grand jury, it was unable to secure an indictment. (A0103, A0300-A0301.) At those proceedings, Krista Harris testified that she had made arrangements to meet Mr. McDonald at a motel room, that she had rented a room on the evening of the shooting, and that Mr. McDonald had arrived well before the shooting occurred. (A0122-A0124.)

Example Application #2—Dewitt McDonald, Jr. (cont.)

Several months later, however, Ms. Harris suddenly reversed course. (A0125.) At a second grand jury proceeding, she testified, *inter alia*, that Mr. McDonald was not with her at the time of the shooting, that when he did arrive he appeared nervous and shaken, that he went to retrieve the gun used in the shooting later that morning, that he threatened to harm her if she cooperated with the police, and that he intended to use her as an alibi witness. (A00140-A0146, A0149-A0150, A0156, A0159.) The grand jury returned an indictment. (*See* A0103, A0300-A0301.)

At trial, the State did not present any evidence that Mr. McDonald had assisted the other men in the commission of the shooting. There was no evidence, for example, that he provided the other men with the car or the weapon used during the shooting. Similarly, there was no evidence placing him at the scene of the shooting. Instead, the State relied principally on Ms. Harris's testimony to obtain Mr. McDonald's conviction. (A0389-A0390.)

Ms. Harris has since admitted that she provided false testimony against Mr. McDonald. (A0045.) She contends that the prosecuting attorney knowingly procured her perjured testimony through threats and a non-consensual sexual relationship. (*Id.*)

APPLICATION TO FILE SECOND OR SUCCESSIVE HABEAS CORPUS PETITION

Example Application #2—Dewitt McDonald, Jr. (cont.)

A. The Shooting

In the early morning hours of June 6, 1994, Shawn Caston, Daryl Turner, and Dewitt McDonald were seen drinking at Whitlee's Bar in Sandusky, Ohio. (A0078-A0081.) At some point during the night, Shawn Caston got into an argument with another man, Jerome Caffey. (*Id*.; A0280-A0282.)

After the argument ended, Caston fumed about Caffey. (A0079-A0080.) He was overheard saying that Caffey did not know "who he [was] messing with." (A0080.) Caston also said, "[H]e better be glad I'm riding with someone else and they aren't ready to go." (*Id*.) "[I]f I had my little Chevy," Caston apparently continued, "Jerome would see who he was fuckin [sic] with." (*Id*.) And Caston would later remark, "[F]uck this, I am gonna to show that nigger." (*Id*.)

As Caston fumed, Daryl Turner said that "Caston should just take care of business." (A0079.) Apparently, Caston was also told that he should "just cap one of those little niggers." (A0080.)

At around 2:15 - 2:30 am, the three men left the bar in Mr. McDonald's car, a white Mercury Sable. (A0079, A0081, A0094, A0249-A0251, A0257, A0282, A0307.) They were seen later that evening at a Shell gas station. (A0079, A0249-A0251, A0257, A0282.) At the gas station, Shawn Caston was apparently asking other people for a ride so that he could go get a gun at Turner's house. (A0094, A0185-A0186.)

Example Application #2—*Dewitt McDonald, Jr. (cont.)*

At around 3:00 am, a small, dark Chevrolet sat in the middle of East Parish Street, directly in front of Caffey's residence. (A0071, A0297, A0367.) As a woman stepped out from the house, someone from within the car began to open fire. (A0229, A0244, A0367.) The woman thought she saw two men sitting in the car. (A0371, A0171.)

As one of the last shots echoed in the night, people from within the house heard what sounded like glass popping. (A0172-A0173, A0368.) The car sped away, heading west on East Parish Street. (A0261.)

At almost the same time, Jerome Caffey exited the house, gun already in hand. (A0258, A0262.) He ran across the street to a neighbor's house—Russell Huff's residence. (A0258, A0263.)

A call was placed to the police at 3:00 am, moments after the shooting ended. (A0071, A0297.) Just five minutes after the police and paramedics arrived, however, a gun shot went off across the street at Russell Huff's house. (A0247, A0253.) The police ordered the house's occupants out onto the front lawn and arrested them. (A0072, A0264.) During a subsequent search of the house, the police found Jerome Caffey's gun hidden in a dryer. (A0265.) Apparently, Mr. Caffey had discharged the weapon while trying to remove a round from the chamber. (A0264.) He was eventually charged with unlawful possession of firearm by a felon under disability. (A0102, A0167-A0168.)

APPLICATION TO FILE SECOND OR SUCCESSIVE HABEAS CORPUS PETITION

Example Application #2—Dewitt McDonald, Jr. (cont.)

The paramedics treated Sharon McGill for a gunshot wound to the thigh. (A0071, A0253.) She had been in Caffey's house at the time of the shooting. The bullet remains lodged somewhere in her abdomen. (A0253-A0254.)

The paramedics also attended to Vivian Johnson, who was bleeding from both sides of her neck. (A0071-A0072, A0309, A0369, A0370.) Ms. Johnson had been sitting in a car that was parked in front of Caffey's house at the time of the shooting. (A0071-A0072, A0367-A0368.) The car's passenger and driver's side windows had been shot out. (A0190, A0242, A0368.)

Ms. Johnson was rushed to a hospital and eventually airlifted to a medical center in Cleveland. (A0072, A0369.) She died on the following day. (A0069-A0070, A0370.) On her emergency room report, the attending physician indicated that a bullet had entered the right side of her neck and exited out the left. (A0067.) The emergency room doctor's conclusion was consistent with the bullet having been fired from Caffey's residence, where Mr. Caffey had been seen exiting with a gun, not from the car that had fired upon the house from East Parish Street.

B. The Investigation

Almost immediately after the shooting, the police began to focus their attention on Caston, Turner, and McDonald. (A0081, A0300-A0303.)

The State quickly secured indictments against the former two. (A0088, A0095, A0294, A0296.) In addition to what is recounted above, the State had learned that Caston's girlfriend owned a small, dark Chevrolet Celebrity. (A0083-A0084.) Although an initial search of the vehicle produced nothing of interest, on a subsequent inspection the police discovered a shell casing cradled between the windshield and the front hood. (A0083-A0084, A0087, A0292-A0294.) This casing matched casings that had been found at the crime scene. (A0294, A0330-A0333.) The State also had learned that Daryl Turner owned a gun that was capable of firing the bullets that had been found at the crime scene, and that Turner had given his gun to Caston on the night of the shooting. (A0085, A0090, A0291.)

In contrast, the State's investigation of Mr. McDonald revealed exculpatory evidence. (A0103, A0300-A0301.) The police had learned that Mr. McDonald had been with Krista Harris in a motel room at the time of the shooting. (A0305-A0306.) They also learned that Ms. Harris had, in fact, rented a room at the Budget Inn in Sandusky. (A0306.)

C. Harris's Initial Grand Jury Testimony

At the grand jury proceedings, Ms. Harris testified—consistent with her prior statements to the police—that Mr. McDonald had been with her at the time of the shooting. (A0122.) Specifically, she testified, under oath, that Mr. McDonald had arrived at the motel around 2:30 am. (A0124.) During this line of questioning, Kevin Baxter showed signs of anger; he threatened to charge Ms. Harris with being an accessory to murder. (A0111-A0112, A0355.)

APPLICATION TO FILE SECOND OR SUCCESSIVE HABEAS CORPUS PETITION

Example Application #2—Dewitt McDonald, Jr. (cont.)

At the conclusion of these proceedings, the State lacked probable cause to secure an indictment against Mr. McDonald. (A0103, A0300-A0301.)

D. Harris's Subsequent Grand Jury Testimony

Later that summer, however, Ms. Harris suddenly reversed course. At a subsequent grand jury proceeding, she testified that Mr. McDonald was not with her at the time of the shooting. (A0126, A0140.) She also testified that Mr. McDonald had called Daryl Turner on the morning of the shooting, that he had learned that the three men were rumored to have been involved in the shooting, and that upon learning this he told Turner that "things were all fucked up" and they needed to get the gun. (A00140-A0142, A0183-A0184, A0356-A0360.) She then testified that Mr. McDonald left the motel to pick up Turner, and when the two men returned, Turner was carrying a duffle bag. (A0143-A0146, A0184, A0356-A0360.) Finally, she testified that Mr. McDonald told her that he intended to use her as an alibi witness, and that he had made veiled threats to keep her from cooperating with the police. (A0149-A0150, A0156, A0159.) The grand jury returned an indictment. (*See* A0103, A0300-A0301.)

Example Application #2—Dewitt McDonald, Jr. (cont.)

E. McDonald's Trial

Mr. Baxter tried the three men in separate jury trials before the same judge. Dewitt McDonald was the last to be tried.[1]

During opening statements, Mr. Baxter stated that the evidence would show that Shawn Caston had gotten into a fight with Jerome Caffey at a bar; that the three men were seen later that morning in a car at a gas station; that a different car was used during the shooting; that a neighbor saw three men sitting in the car; and that Mr. McDonald did not arrive at the motel until 3:15 am. (A0222-A0226.) He also stated that the evidence would show, *inter alia*, that Mr. McDonald went with Daryl Turner to retrieve the firearm, that he planned to use Ms. Harris as an alibi witness, and that he had threatened her. (A0226-A0228.)

Aside from Krista Harris's testimony, the State only presented three pieces of evidence that suggested that Mr. McDonald was involved directly in the shooting.

---

[1] A jury found Daryl Turner guilty of complicity to commit the following offenses: (1) murder, (2) the lesser included offense of involuntary manslaughter, (3) improperly discharging a firearm into a habitation, (4) the felonious assault of Sharon McGill, and (5) the felonious assault of Jerome Caffey. (A0187-A0189.) He was found not guilty of complicity to commit aggravated murder and complicity to commit attempted murder. (*Id.*)

Shawn Caston was found guilty of complicity to commit the following offenses: (1) murder, (2) the felonious assault of Sharon McGill, (3) improperly discharging a firearm into a habitation, and (4) the felonious assault of Jerome Caffey. (A0217-A0219.) He was found not guilty of complicity to commit aggravated murder and complicity to commit attempted aggravated murder. (*Id.*)

Example Application #2—Dewitt McDonald, Jr. (cont.)

First, Danielle Fenderson testified that, at Whitlee's Bar, she overheard Mr. McDonald tell Shawn Caston that "he wouldn't waste his time on one of them[; h]e would cap one of them." (A0282.) On cross-examination, Ms. Fenderson admitted that she did not initially tell the police that she had heard that statement, and she admitted that she had not previously attributed that statement to Mr. McDonald. (A0284-A0286.) She also admitted that, in the interim, the police had threatened her with charges of perjury. (A0287-A0288.)

Sharon McGill contradicted Ms. Fenderson's testimony. She testified that Mr. McDonald "didn't say anything." (A0256.) She also testified that Mr. McDonald did not appear to be upset.[2] (A0255.)

Second, the State presented evidence that Mr. McDonald was with the other men at a gas station at around 2:30 am. (A0249-A0251, A0257, A0283.) The men were seen in Mr. McDonald's white Mercury Sable—not the car that was used in the shooting. (*Id.*)

Finally, the State elicited from Terry McDonald—a distant relative of Dewitt McDonald but a close friend of Shawn Caston—testimony that he had observed Jerome Caffey get into an argument with Dewitt McDonald the day

---

[2] Similarly, another woman told the police that Mr. McDonald did not make any incriminating or suggestive remarks to Caston at the bar. (A0081.) Neither the State nor the defense called her to testify. (A0220-A0221.)

Example Application #2—Dewitt McDonald, Jr. (cont.)

before the shooting. (A0313-A0315.) Even the State had reason to doubt the veracity of this testimony. (A0201-A0202, A0203-A0208.)

At Shawn Caston's trial, the defense had called Terry McDonald as its principal alibi witness. (A0192, A0216, A0318.) Terry testified that Mr. Caston was severely intoxicated on the night in question—that he was too drunk to have carried out the shooting. (A0196-A0200, A0323.) He also testified that he had observed Jerome Caffey and Dewitt McDonald get into an argument the day before the shooting. (A0193-A0195.)

Mr. Baxter responded with disbelief. (A0201-A0202.) When Terry McDonald appeared before the grand jury, he had testified that he did not have any information of relevance to the investigation of Dewitt McDonald. (*Id.*) During a vigorous cross-examination at Shawn Caston's trial, Mr. Baxter suggested that Terry McDonald was telling a different story to help his friend, Shawn Caston. (*Id.*; A0203-A0208.) And during his closing argument, Mr. Baxter stated that Terry McDonald had "lied." (A0216.)

None of that stopped Mr. Baxter from calling Terry McDonald as a witness at Mr. McDonald's trial. (A0311.) Even though Terry's prior testimony had been inconsistent with the State's case against Shawn Caston, Mr. Baxter proceeded to elicit the same testimony from him at Mr. McDonald's trial. (A0313-A0315, A0317, A0321-A0322; *cf.* A0203-A0208.) The witness who Baxter had accused

APPLICATION TO FILE SECOND OR SUCCESSIVE HABEAS CORPUS PETITION

Example Application #2—Dewitt McDonald, Jr. (cont.)

of lying to protect his friend now testified that Mr. McDonald had been in an argument with Mr. Caffey the day before the shooting. (*Compare* A0203-A0208, *with* A0316, A0323-0324, A0377-A0378.)

In addition to the three pieces of evidence that suggested that Mr. McDonald had some direct involvement in the shooting, the State presented evidence that there had been three men in the small car that had been used to carry out the shooting. (A0260.) Russell Huff testified that he had seen the shooting from his window across the street, and that there were three men in the car. (*Id.*)

Russell Huff's testimony, however, differed from his testimony before the grand jury, and it differed from the statement he had given to the police. (A0077-A0078, A0270.) At the grand jury, he testified—consistent with his prior statement to the police—that he did not see the shooting. (A0272.) He explained that he had been asleep in his living room at that time. (A0270; *cf.* A0078.) He awoke to the sound of gun fire but thought that the noise was coming from a television set that he had left on. (A0271.) It was only after he turned off the television set that he realized that actual shots were being fired. (*Id.*) Having grown up in a rough neighborhood in Cleveland, Mr. Huff said he knew what to do next: He fell to the ground and took cover. (A0272.)

Since testifying at the grand jury, however, Mr. Huff had pled guilty to passing bad checks and was serving the first of two 30-day sentences. (A0174,

A0267, A0275.) He also had an unrelated felony charge looming over his head. (A0274, A0279.) He told the police that he had lied to the grand jury. (A0267.) He was now willing to testify that he saw a small, four-door car fire upon Jerome Caffey's house. (A0191, A0259.) More importantly, he claimed to have seen three men sitting in the car. (A0260.) Based on these statements, Mr. Baxter was able to assist Mr. Huff in obtaining an early release from his second 30-day sentence.[3] (A0269, A0276, A0278.) At the time of Mr. McDonald's trial, Mr. Huff still had not gone to trial on his own felony charge. (A0175, A0274.)

In any event, Mr. Huff's new account contradicted another witness's testimony. (A0171, A0371.) The victim's own sister, Tammy Johnson, testified that she had seen only two men in the car at the time of the shooting. (*Id.*)

Mr. Baxter called Krista Harris as his second-to-last witness. (A0221.) She testified that Mr. McDonald did not arrive at the motel room until 3:15 am, and that when he did arrive he appeared shaken and nervous. (A0335-A0336.) She also testified that, later that morning, upon hearing of their rumored involvement, Mr. McDonald told Mr. Turner that "things were all fucked up and . . . that they had to get the gun." (A0337.) According to Ms. Harris, Mr. McDonald then went to pick up Turner, and when the two men returned, Turner was carrying a duffle

---

[3] During his closing statement, Mr. Baxter argued that by releasing Russell Huff from jail early, the judge had vouched for his veracity: "Does it make sense that Judge Ridge is going to let someone out who lied?" (A0376.)

Example Application #2—Dewitt McDonald, Jr. (cont.)

bag. (A0337-A0338.) Ms. Harris then testified that, on another occasion, Mr. Turner admitted to her that he had given Shawn Caston his gun to take out Jerome Caffey, and that he (Turner) had been in the car at the time of the shooting. (A0340-A0341.) Finally, Ms. Harris testified that Mr. McDonald intended to use her as an alibi witness, and that he had made repeated and specific threats to her throughout the summer.[4] (A0339, A0341-A0345, A0364.)

The defense did not call any witnesses, and Mr. McDonald elected not to testify in his own defense. (A0372-A0373.)

During closing statements, Mr. Baxter argued that all of the evidence established that Mr. McDonald was "involved in the murder," but he neglected to explain how Mr. McDonald was involved. (A0374.) Instead, he emphasized that Mr. McDonald was present at the time of the shooting, and that he had helped Mr. Turner hide the weapon afterwards. (A0390.) He would go so far as to suggest that Mr. McDonald could be convicted solely on this basis: "All these things are so very evident of guilt, so very clear. The gun missing. Where's it at? They had to get the gun. Complicity." (*Id.*)

Mr. Baxter also argued that Ms. Harris had "stripped" Mr. McDonald of "any defense in this case." (A0389.) He continued, "Krista Harris is a hero in this case." (*Id.*) She "burie[d]" the defense. (A0390.)

---

[4] During cross-examination, counsel pointed out several discrepancies in Ms. Harris's testimony. (A0350-A0354, A0361-A0364.)

Example Application #2—Dewitt McDonald, Jr. (cont.)

The jury deliberated for 16 hours before convicting Mr. McDonald on all counts. (A0392.) The trial judge sentenced him principally to a term of life in prison with no eligibility for parole for 20 years. (A0063-A0066.) At his sentencing hearing, Mr. McDonald stated:

> There [were] two tragedies done this past year, the first one being Miss Vivian Johnson's death, and the second one is me going to jail. I was innocent. I didn't have anything to do with it, and I think that's very tragic for a person to be a citizen of the United States and go to jail for something he did not do.

(A0391.)

F. McDonald's First § 2254 Petition

After pursuing direct appeals in the Ohio Court of Appeals for the Sixth Appellate District and the Supreme Court of Ohio, the specifics of which are recounted in the application attached to this motion, *see* Addendum B, Mr. McDonald filed a timely petition for a writ of habeas corpus in the United States District Court for the Northern District of Ohio. His petition raised six claims:

(1) "Due process and a fair trial were denied Petitioner when a principal witness for the State testified that the police had given the accused a polygraph test."

(2) "A due process violation occurred when the court failed to give a proper instruction of complicity. This follows because the given instructions did not advise the jury that an aider and abetter [sic] must act with the specific intent required for the commission of the charged offense or offenses."

(3) "The accused did not receive a fair trial consistent with the Sixth and Fourteenth Amendments to the Constitution when he was

victimized by a willful pattern of prosecutorial misconduct that permeated the trial."[5]

(4) "The accused did not have the benefit of the effective assistance of trial counsel under the Sixth and Fourteenth Amendments to the Constitution, when counsel failed to object to a considerable quantity of inadmissible, egregiously prejudicial evidence."

(5) "When a prosecution witness is permitted to testify regarding the contents of statements attributed (by the witness) to any alleged accomplice who, not only, confessed therein to supplying the gun used in the crimes alleged, but who also implicated Petitioner as a participant, the resultant effect was a denial of Petitioner's right of confrontation and to a fair trial."

(6) "It was a constitutional violation for the prosecutor, who called a witness a 'liar' in a separate trial of a co-defendant of Petitioner, to then vouch for his credibility when he called this same witness to testify in favor of the prosecution in the later trial of the Petitioner."

(A0009.)

On May 18, 1999, the District Court issued an opinion and order denying the petition. (A0030, A0031, A0040.) The Court held that Mr. McDonald had failed to exhaust claims one through four, and that those claims were now procedurally defaulted. (A0036, A0039.). The Court denied claims five and six on the merits. (A0039-A0040.) A certificate of appealability was likewise denied. (A0030, A0040-A0041.)

---

[5] Mr. McDonald's prosecutorial misconduct claim was based on certain statements that the prosecutor made during voir dire, testimony that he elicited at trial, and arguments that he made in closing. (A0020-A0022.)

Example Application #2—Dewitt McDonald, Jr. (cont.)

On February 1, 2000, this Court also denied Mr. McDonald a certificate of appealability. (A0044.) This marked the end of Mr. McDonald's first application for federal collateral relief.

G. Harris's Recantation

Almost two years after Mr. McDonald's first petition had been denied, Ms. Harris filed an affidavit in State court, in which she asserted that Erie County Prosecutor Kevin Baxter coerced her into providing false testimony at Mr. McDonald's trial. (A0045.) Specifically, she stated that she had provided "false testimony in the trials of State v. Daryl Turner and State v. Dewitt McDonald." (*Id.*) She also stated that Erie County Prosecutor Kevin Baxter knowingly procured her perjured testimony through "threat of false criminal charges" and a "non-consensual sexual relationship." (*Id.*)

These accusations have been corroborated by Mr. Baxter's brother, Edward Baxter, who has likewise signed a sworn affidavit. (A0048.) In that affidavit, Edward Baxter states that he "has first[]hand knowledge that Erie County Prosecutor, Kevin Baxter, coerced Krista Harris to lie in a drive-by shooting [case] then forced her into a non[-]consensual sexual relationship." (A0051.)

H. Caston's § 2254 Petition

In the mean time, Shawn Caston had challenged his conviction in the United States District Court for the Northern District of Ohio. *See* Petition of Caston,

Example Application #2—Dewitt McDonald, Jr. (cont.)

Caston v. Mitchell, No. 3:98-cv-7099 (N.D. Ohio). He alleged that he had received the ineffective assistance of trial and appellate counsel in failing to object and raise on appeal the introduction of statements that the police had obtained from Caston in violation of his constitutional rights. *Id.* Judge John Potter concluded that the police had violated Mr. Caston's constitutional rights, that the statements that the police had obtained were highly prejudicial, and that counsel's failure to move to suppress the statements at trial and to raise this argument on appeal were objectively unreasonable. *Caston v. Mitchell*, No. 3:98-cv-7099 (N.D. Ohio Oct. 13, 1999) (unpublished). He granted conditionally Caston's petition for a writ of habeas corpus and ordered that the writ would issue if the State failed to grant Caston a new trial within 90 days from date on which the order became final. *Id.* This Court affirmed in an unpublished opinion. *Caston v. Mitchell*, 12 Fed. Appx. 208 (6th Cir. 2001) (per curiam).

After this Court issued its decision, Shawn Caston negotiated a plea deal with Mr. Baxter. According to the terms of the deal, Mr. Caston agreed to plead guilty to a reduced charge of voluntary manslaughter and received credit for time served. (A0394.)

Before accepting his plea, however, the Erie County Court of Common Pleas ordered Shawn Caston to submit to a polygraph examination. During that examination, Mr. Caston stated that "he (Caston) drove by" Jerome Caffey's house,

Example Application #2—Dewitt McDonald, Jr. (cont.)

pointed "a Tech 9 handgun" out the driver's side window, "and fired several times at the house." (A0058.) He also stated that "[a]fter driving by he turned off and while leaving the area threw the Tech 9 into the bushes on McKinley Street." (*Id.*) Mr. Caston did not state that Mr. McDonald was with him at the time of the shooting. (*Id.*) The examiner concluded that Caston had "told the substantial truth during the examination." (*Id.*)

I. McDonald's First Petition for State Post-Conviction Relief

Shortly after Ms. Harris filed her affidavit and Mr. Caston had taken his polygraph examination, Mr. McDonald filed in the Erie County Court of Common Pleas a petition for state post-conviction relief. The court denied the petition; the Ohio Court of Appeals affirmed; and on July 13, 2005, the Supreme Court of Ohio denied leave to appeal. *See* Addendum B.

J. Caffey's Confession

On September 19, 2005, Vivian Johnson's son, Jermaine Johnson, signed a sworn affidavit, in which he stated that Jerome Caffey had confessed to him, "I killed [your] momma." (A0061.) Mr. Johnson's wife, Jihan Johnson, signed a similar affidavit. (A0062.) These statements corroborated the emergency room doctor's conclusion that the bullet that killed Ms. Johnson had entered from the right side of her neck. (A0067.)

K. McDonald's Second Petition for State Post-Conviction Relief

On October 29, 2005, Mr. McDonald filed a second petition for state post-conviction relief based on the Johnson affidavits. Once again, the Erie County Court of Common Pleas denied the petition, and the Ohio Court of Appeals affirmed. *See* Addendum B.

L. McDonald's Second § 2254 Petition

On June 30, 2006, Mr. McDonald sent to this Court a *pro se* motion for an order authorizing the United States District Court to consider a second or successive petition for a writ of habeas corpus. *See* Addendum C. The Southern Christian Leadership Conference subsequently filed an *amicus curiae* brief in support of Mr. McDonald's motion and his claim of actual innocence.

On March 19, 2007, this Court issued an order directing the Clerk of the Court to appoint counsel to represent Mr. McDonald. (A0001.) The Clerk appointed the undersigned counsel to prepare a revised motion and present oral argument on Mr. McDonald's behalf.

Recognizing that Mr. McDonald's "motion presents a significant question that warrants further development and oral argument," this Court specifically directed counsel to "prepare a revised motion that addresses McDonald's claim involving the allegedly perjured testimony of Krista Harris as well as any other claims that counsel deems appropriate." (*Id.*)

Example Application #2—Dewitt McDonald, Jr. (cont.)

SUMMARY OF ARGUMENT

Mr. McDonald is entitled to file a second petition for a writ of habeas corpus. In order to obtain the necessary authorization from this Court, he is simply required to make a "prima facie showing" (i) that the facts underlying his claims "could not have been discovered previously through the exercise of due diligence," (ii) that those facts, "if proven and viewed in the light of the evidence as a whole, would be sufficient to establish by clear and convincing evidence that, but for constitutional error, no reasonable factfinder would have found the applicant guilty of the underlying offense," and (iii) that his claims have not been "presented in a prior application." 28 U.S.C. § 2244(b)(1), (b)(2)(B), (b)(3)(C).

A prima facie showing "is not a difficult standard to meet." *In re Lott*, 366 F.3d 431, 432 (6th Cir. 2004). A movant is simply required to show that it is "'possible'" that the district court might ultimately conclude, on a more fully developed record, that the applicant has made the required showing under § 2244(b). *See id.* at 432-33 (quoting *Bennett v. United States*, 119 F.3d 468, 469 (7th Cir. 1997)); *see also* 28 U.S.C. § 2244(b)(3)(C).

Mr. McDonald's motion easily satisfies this standard. *First*, he has made "a prima facie showing of constitutional . . . error that, if proved in the district court, may be sufficient to cause the fact finder to reach" the conclusion that the petitioner was not guilty of the underlying offense. *Lott*, 366 F.3d at 434.

Example Application #2—Dewitt McDonald, Jr. (cont.)

Specifically, he has made a prima facie showing that Prosecutor Kevin Baxter prevented Krista Harris from providing critical, exculpatory evidence for the defense; that Mr. Baxter used threats and a non-consensual sexual relationship to coerce Ms. Harris into providing false, inculpatory testimony against Mr. McDonald; and that Mr. Baxter failed to disclose to the defense his relationship with Ms. Harris. Moreover, Mr. McDonald has made a prima facie showing that his conviction was secured through these constitutional violations—namely, (i) the knowing use of perjured testimony, (ii) the failure to disclose information that could be used to impeach inculpatory testimony, and (iii) the denial of right to present witnesses in one's own defense.

Second, Mr. McDonald has made a prima facie showing that the factual predicate for his claim "could not have been discovered previously through the exercise of due diligence." 28 U.S.C. § 2244(b)(2)(B)(i). He has demonstrated that Ms. Harris did not come forward until after his first § 2254 petition had been denied, that Ms. Harris could not come forward until after the statute of limitations for perjury expired, and that Mr. Baxter actively sought to hide the nature of his relationship with Ms. Harris.

Finally, none of Mr. McDonald's claims were presented in his previous § 2254 petition. These claims relate to evidence that was not previously available and therefore could not have been asserted in his prior petition.

Example Application #2—Dewitt McDonald, Jr. (cont.)

ARGUMENT

I. **MCDONALD IS ENTITLED TO FILE A SECOND § 2254 PETITION UNDER AEDPA.**

   A. **This Court Evaluates A Second-Or-Successive Motion Under A Lenient Prima Facie Standard And Grants Such A Motion If It Presents Allegations Of Fact Sufficient To Warrant A Fuller Exploration In The District Court.**

Section 106 of the Antiterrorism and Effective Death Penalty Act of 1996 (AEDPA) established the court of appeals as a gatekeeper for petitions deemed "second or successive." Pub. L. No. 104-132, § 106, 110 Stat. 1214, 1220-21 (amending 28 U.S.C. § 2244). Under the Act, a prospective second-or-successive petitioner must file a motion in "the appropriate court of appeals for an order authorizing the district court to consider the [underlying] application." 28 U.S.C. § 2244(b)(3)(A). A three-judge panel should grant the motion "if it determines that the application makes a prima facie showing that the application satisfies the requirements of [§ 2244(b)]." *Id.* § 2244(b)(3)(B), (C).[6]

As relevant here, the Court must determine that the movant has made a "prima facie showing" (i) that the facts underlying his claims "could not have been discovered previously through the exercise of due diligence," (ii) that those facts,

---

[6] The statute also provides that the "court of appeals shall grant or deny the authorization to file a second or successive application not later than 30 days after the filing of the motion." 28 U.S.C. § 2244(b)(3)(D). However, this Court has held that the statutory deadline is "advisory or hortatory rather than mandatory." *In re Siggers*, 132 F.3d 333, 335 (6th Cir. 1997).

Example Application #2—Dewitt McDonald, Jr. (cont.)

"if proven and viewed in the light of the evidence as a whole, would be sufficient to establish by clear and convincing evidence that, but for constitutional error, no reasonable factfinder would have found the applicant guilty of the underlying offense," and (iii) that his claims have not been "presented in a prior application." 28 U.S.C. § 2244(b)(1), (b)(2)(B), (b)(3)(C).

In *Lott*, this Court explained that a prima facie showing "is not a difficult standard to meet." *Lott*, 366 F.3d at 432. "'Prima facie' in this context means simply sufficient allegations of fact together with some documentation that would 'warrant a fuller exploration in the district court.'" *Id.* at 433 (quoting *Bennett*, 119 F.3d at 469). As a result, this Court simply must determine whether it is "'possible'" that the district court might conclude, on a more fully developed record, that applicant has made the required showing under § 2244(b). *Id.* at 432.[7] *See also* 28 U.S.C. § 2244(b)(3)(C).

---

[7] *Accord Cooper v. Woodford*, 358 F.3d 1117, 1119 (9th Cir. 2004) (en banc) ("By 'prima facie showing' we understand simply a sufficient showing of *possible* merit to warrant a fuller exploration." (internal quotation marks omitted)); *In re Johnson*, 322 F.3d 881, 882 (5th Cir. 2003) (per curiam) (stating that a prima facie showing is "simply a sufficient showing of possible merit to warrant a fuller exploration by the district court" (emphasis omitted)); *cf. Sustache-Rivera v. United States*, 221 F.3d 8, 15 (1st Cir. 2000) ("In judging whether to permit the filing of a second petition, the court of appeals, as gatekeeper, does not definitely decide these issues. Rather, . . . the precise question is whether 'jurists of reason' would find each of these points 'debatable.'"); *Bell v. United States*, 296 F.3d 127, 128 (2d Cir. 2002) (per curiam) ("A prima facie showing is not a particularly high standard. An application need only show sufficient likelihood of satisfying the

Example Application #2—Dewitt McDonald, Jr. (cont.)

In this case, the Court must determine whether it is possible that the no reasonable fact finder "*would* have found the applicant guilty of the underlying offense" based on the "evidence as a whole," including the new "facts underlying the claim." 28 U.S.C. § 2244(b)(2)(B)(ii) (emphasis added). The Court does *not* engage in a sufficiency of the evidence inquiry to resolve that question—*i.e.*, whether "no rational trier of fact *could* have found proof of guilt beyond a reasonable doubt," *Jackson v. Virginia*, 443 U.S. 307, 324 (1979) (emphasis added). *See Schlup v. Delo*, 513 U.S. 298, 323 & n.28 (1995) (explaining that the nearly identical use of the word "would" in *Sawyer v. Whitley*, 505 U.S. 333, 336 (1992), resulted in a standard that "falls short of the *Jackson* standard governing habeas review of claims of insufficiency of the evidence"). Instead, the use of the word "would" has been interpreted to require a "federal court to assess how reasonable jurors *would* react to the overall, newly supplemented record." *House v. Bell*, 126 S. Ct. 2064, 2078 (2006) (applying *Schlup*). Accordingly, this Court simply must determine whether it is possible that the district court might ultimately conclude that no reasonable fact finder would have convicted the applicant based on the overall, newly supplemented record. *See* 28 U.S.C. § 2244(b)(2)(B)(ii); *see*

(continued...)

strict standards of § 2255 to 'warrant a fuller exploration by the district court.'" (quoting *Bennett*, 119 F.3d at 469)).

also House, 126 S. Ct. at 2078; *Schlup*, 513 U.S. at 323 & n.28; *Lott*, 366 F.3d at 432-33.

B. McDonald Has Made A "Prima Facie Showing" Under The Statute.

As explained below, Mr. McDonald's application easily satisfies the "lenient prima facie standard." *Lott*, 366 F.3d at 433. *First*, "[t]aking the evidence as a whole," his motion "makes a prima facie showing of constitutional . . . error that, if proved in the district court, may be sufficient" to establish, by clear and convincing evidence, that no reasonable factfinder would have convicted Mr. McDonald of the underlying offense. *Id.* at 434; *see also* 28 U.S.C. § 2244(b)(2)(B)(ii). *Second*, the facts underlying his claims could not have been discovered through due diligence prior to the filing of his first § 2254 petition. *See* 28 U.S.C. § 2244(b)(2)(B)(i). *Finally*, none of Mr. McDonald's claims has been presented in a prior application. *See id.* § 2244(b)(1).

1. McDonald Has Easily Made A Prima Facie Showing That, But For Constitutional Error, No Reasonable Factfinder Would Have Found Him Guilty Of The Underlying Offense.

Under the governing standard, Mr. McDonald is simply required to make "a prima facie showing of constitutional . . . error that, if proved in the district court, *may* be sufficient to cause the factfinder to reach" the conclusion that the petitioner was not guilty of the underlying crime. *Lott*, 366 F.3d at 434 (emphasis added). As this and other circuits have made plain, the showing is one of "possible"—not

Example Application #2—Dewitt McDonald, Jr. (cont.)

certain—merit. *Id*. at 432-33 (quoting *Bennett*, 119 F.3d at 469); *accord Jordan v. Sec'y, Dep't of Corrs*., 485 F.3d 1351, 1358 (11th Cir. 2007); *Cooper*, 358 F.3d at 1119; *Johnson*, 322 F.3d at 882. Mr. McDonald easily satisfies this requirement.

        a.   The Application Makes A Prima Facie Showing Of Constitutional Error.

The factual allegations in Mr. McDonald's application, together with the supporting documentation, make a prima facie showing of flagrant violations of Mr. McDonald's constitutional rights. Specifically, Mr. McDonald has proffered evidence (i) that Mr. Baxter knowingly used perjured testimony, *Napue v. Illinois*, 360 U.S. 264 (1959); (ii) that he failed to disclose information that could have been used to impeach important inculpatory testimony, *Giglio v. United States*, 405 U.S. 150 (1972); *see also Brady v. Maryland*, 373 U.S. 83 (1963); and (iii) that Mr. Baxter's conduct effectively rendered unavailable a witness that would have provided evidence critical to Mr. McDonald's defense, *see Webb v. Texas*, 409 U.S. 95 (1972) (per curiam); *see also Chambers v. Mississippi*, 410 U.S. 284 (1973). These are egregious examples of prosecutorial misconduct that cannot be countenanced.

        i.   The Knowing Use Of Perjured Testimony.

"'[A] conviction obtained by the knowing use of perjured testimony is fundamentally unfair, and must be set aside if there is any reasonable likelihood that the false testimony could have affected the judgment of the jury.'" *Kyles v.*

APPLICATION TO FILE SECOND OR SUCCESSIVE HABEAS CORPUS PETITION

Example Application #2—Dewitt McDonald, Jr. (cont.)

Whitley, 514 U.S. 419, 433 n.7 (1995) (quoting *United States v. Agurs*, 427 U.S. 97, 103 (1976)); *see also United States v. Lochmondy*, 890 F.2d 817, 822 (6th Cir. 1989). In order to establish such a denial of due process, a habeas petitioner "must show that the statement in question was false, that the prosecution knew it was false, and that it was material." *Byrd v. Collins*, 209 F.3d 486, 517 (6th Cir. 2000). A statement is material "'if there is a reasonable probability that, had the evidence been disclosed to the defense, the result of the proceeding would have been different.'" *Kyles*, 514 U.S. at 434 (quoting *United States v. Bagley*, 473 U.S. 667, 682 (1985) (plurality)). "[A] 'reasonable probability' is a probability sufficient to undermine confidence in the outcome." *Bagley*, 473 U.S. at 682 (internal quotation marks omitted).[8]

Mr. McDonald has proffered evidence that the attorney who prosecuted him, Kevin Baxter, knowingly procured false testimony through threats and a non-consensual sexual relationship. *See* A0045, A0051. This testimony was undoubtedly material.

---

[8] The Supreme Court has made clear that materiality is "not a sufficiency of the evidence test." *Kyles*, 514 U.S. at 434. In other words, "[a] defendant need not demonstrate that after discounting the inculpatory evidence in light of the undisclosed evidence, there would not have been enough left to convict." *Id.* at 434-35. Rather, materiality is demonstrated "by showing that the favorable evidence could reasonably be taken to put the whole case in such a different light as to undermine confidence in the verdict." *Id.* at 435.

APPLICATION TO FILE SECOND OR SUCCESSIVE HABEAS CORPUS PETITION

Example Application #2—Dewitt McDonald, Jr. (cont.)

Although the State charged Mr. McDonald with complicity, it proceeded on the theory that he was present at the time of the shooting, A0222-A0228, A0375-A0376, A0381, A0388-A0389, and it did so for good reason: The jury was permitted to rely on Mr. McDonald's alleged presence in the car as evidence that he was complicit in the shooting—even though that evidence, standing alone, would have been insufficient to convict Mr. McDonald of complicity. *See State v. Johnson*, 754 N.E.2d 796, 799, 801-02 (Ohio 2001). No other witness—indeed, no other evidence—placed Mr. McDonald in the car at the time of the shooting.

The State's remaining evidence was contradictory and certainly does not instill confidence that the jury's verdict was unaffected by Ms. Harris's testimony: Mr. Huff testified that there were three people in the car, whereas Tammy Johnson only saw two; Ms Fenderson claimed to have heard Mr. McDonald say that "he wouldn't waste his time on" Caffey, "he would cap" him, whereas Ms. McGill heard nothing of the sort. A0255-A0256, A0260, A0281-A0282, A0371, *see also* A0171. And there were reasons to doubt the veracity of the State's witnesses on these points. A0266-A0268, A0284-A0288. Under these circumstances, Ms. Harris's testimony was not simply material; it was determinative. *See Jamison v. Collins*, 291 F.3d 380, 389-91 (6th Cir. 2002) (affirming a grant of the writ on a lesser showing that, even though the undisclosed evidence did not eliminate the petitioner as a perpetrator of the crime, the evidence nevertheless undermined the prosecutor's theory of the case and contradicted the testimony of the prosecution's chief witness).

    ii. **The Failure To Disclose Information That Could Have Been Used To Impeach Important Inculpatory Testimony.**

The well-established rule of *Brady v. Maryland* provides that the suppression by the State of evidence favorable to the accused violates the Due Process Clause where the evidence is material either to guilt or punishment, irrespective of the good or bad faith of the prosecutor. *Strickler v. Greene*, 527 U.S. 263, 280 (1999). To establish a *Brady* violation, a habeas petitioner must show (1) that the prosecution failed to disclose evidence, (2) that such evidence was favorable to the petitioner, either because it is exculpatory or it may impeach important inculpatory evidence, and (3) that such evidence is material. *See id.* at 280-81. As noted above, materiality is demonstrated "by showing that the favorable evidence could reasonably be taken to put the whole case in such a different light as to undermine confidence in the verdict." *Kyles*, 514 U.S. at 435.

Here, Mr. McDonald has proffered evidence that the attorney who prosecuted him, Kevin Baxter, failed to disclose his inappropriate sexual relationship with the State's key witness—evidence that could have been used to impeach her trial testimony. *See* A0045, A0051. This information was undoubtedly material. Although Mr. McDonald's trial counsel attempted to

Example Application #2—Dewitt McDonald, Jr. (cont.)

impeach Ms. Harris based on her original grand jury testimony, he could not develop a favorable explanation as to why she had changed her testimony. A0382-A0386. In the absence of such an explanation, the prosecution was able to argue that Ms. Harris had decided to come clean after initially succumbing to Mr. McDonald's repeated—but undocumented—threats. A0379-A0380. Moreover, Ms. Harris admitted in her affidavit that the sexual relationship had an undue influence on her testimony. *See* A0045; *cf. Spirko v. Mitchell*, 368 F.3d 603, 613 (6th Cir. 2004) (explaining that, there, the petitioner had failed to explain "how [a witness's] testimony was affected by [her] alleged relationship with the [State's chief] investigator"). Given the otherwise thin evidence of guilt, there is a reasonable probability that, had the prosecutor's inappropriate sexual relationship been disclosed, the result of the proceeding would have been different. *See Napue*, 360 U.S. at 269 ("The jury's estimate of the truthfulness and reliability of a given witness may well be determinative of guilt or innocence, and it is upon such subtle factors as the possible interest of the witness in testifying falsely that a defendant's life or liberty may depend.").

    iii. **The Denial Of The Right To Present A Witness In One's Own Defense.**

A defendant's right to present witnesses in his own defense is a fundamental element of due process and is protected by the Sixth Amendment. *See Chambers*, 410 U.S. at 302; *Webb*, 409 U.S. at 98; *Washington v. Texas*, 388 U.S. 14, 19

Example Application #2—Dewitt McDonald, Jr. (cont.)

(1967). "Various prosecutorial and judicial actions aimed at discouraging defense witnesses from testifying deprive a defendant of this right." *United States v. Emuegbunam*, 268 F.3d 377, 400 (6th Cir. 2001). Thus, in *Webb*, the Supreme Court held that a trial judge's repeated admonishments about the dangers of perjury, "directed only at the single witness for the defense, effectively drove that witness off the stand, and thus deprived the petitioner of due process of law under the Fourteenth Amendment." 409 U.S. at 98. Similarly, in *United States v. Thomas*, this Court applied *Webb* to a case where a prosecutor had sent a Secret Service agent to communicate *ex parte* with a potential witness and threatened that witness with prosecution if he testified. 488 F.2d 334, 335-36 (6th Cir. 1973). In holding that the defendant's constitutional rights were violated after the witness took the stand but failed to testify on the defendant's behalf, the Court explained: "[T]he Government's action here substantially interfered with any free and unhampered determination the witness might have made as to whether to testify and if so as to the content of such testimony." *Id.* at 336.

Similarly, here, the prosecutor engaged in conduct that interfered with any free and unhampered determination by Ms. Harris as to the content of her testimony. A0045, A0051. Mr. Baxter achieved this interference through repeated threats of criminal prosecution and a coerced sexual relationship. *Id.* He not only prevented a key witness for the defense from testifying on Mr. McDonald's behalf, but also he managed to coerce the witness into providing false testimony for the State. *Compare* A0122-A0124, *with* A0335-A0338. This conduct undoubtedly rises to the level of intimidation present in *Webb* and *Thomas*. *Cf. Davis v. Straub*, 430 F.3d 281, 287 (6th Cir. 2005) (affirming the denial of the writ after concluding, in that case, that the prosecutor's conduct—requesting a sidebar with the judge at which point he informed the court that the witness was a suspect and should be informed of his constitutional rights—"d[id] not rise to the level of intimidation present in *Webb* and *Thomas*"), *cert. denied*, 127 S. Ct. 929 (2007). Indeed, the contrasting outcomes between the first grand jury proceeding, where Mr. Baxter failed to establish probable cause to indict, and Mr. McDonald's trial "present the equivalent of a controlled experiment that demonstrates the critical nature of [Ms. Harris's] testimony to [Mr. McDonald's] defense." *Christie v. Hollins*, 409 F.3d 120, 126 (2d Cir. 2005) (Newman, J.).

> b. **The Application Makes The Required Showing That, But For The Constitutional Error, No Reasonable Factfinder Would Have Convicted McDonald Of The Underlying Offense.**

Mr. McDonald also has made a prima facie showing that, but for the constitutional error, no reasonable fact finder would have convicted him of the underlying offense. As explained above, at the prima-facie-showing stage, Mr. McDonald merely has to show that it is "possible" that he will ultimately prevail. *Lott*, 366 F.3d at 432; *accord Jordan*, 485 F.3d at 1358; *Cooper*, 358 F.3d at 1119;

Example Application #2—Dewitt McDonald, Jr. (cont.)

Johnson, 322 F.3d at 882; *Bennett*, 119 F.3d at 469. Applying that standard to the present motion, it is plain that Mr. McDonald has made the required showing.

Mr. McDonald was not only convicted based largely on Ms. Harris's false inculpatory testimony, but also he was denied the opportunity to present critical exculpatory evidence in the form of Ms. Harris's original grand jury testimony. As mentioned above, the fact that the State charged him with complicity does not alter this conclusion. The State sought to prove his involvement by arguing that he was present at the time of the shooting. A0222-A0228, A0375-A0376, A0381, A0388-A0389. Without this evidence, the State failed even to convince a grand jury that there was probable cause to indict Mr. McDonald. A0103, A0300-A0301.

The remaining evidence presented at trial does not even come close to overcoming the obvious effect of the prosecutor's misconduct. No other witness—indeed, no other evidence—placed Mr. McDonald in the car at the time of the shooting, and Ms. Harris's initial grand jury testimony would have put that issue to rest. A0122-A0124. Moreover, this Court is permitted to consider the likely effect that this new evidence would have had on "the credibility of the witnesses presented at trial." *See House*, 126 S. Ct. at 2078 (citation and internal quotation marks omitted). The already questionable testimony of Mr. Huff, Ms. Fenderson, and Terry McDonald is rendered even more questionable after a fact finder is presented with evidence that Mr. McDonald was not present at the time of the shooting. Finally, just as the jury was permitted to rely on Mr. McDonald's alleged presence in the car as evidence that he was complicit in the shooting, *see Johnson*, 754 N.E.2d at 801-02, it was similarly entitled to infer, based on his absence, that he did not form the intent necessary to be convicted of complicity, *see id.* at 800 (explaining that, there, the defendant "could have abandoned the plan to kill" the intended victim at several points, but instead "he chose to continue on" in the car ultimately responsible for a drive-by shooting); *see also* OHIO REV. CODE ANN. § 2923.03(A) (requiring the State to prove that the defendant was "acting with the kind of culpability required for the commission" of the underlying offense).

In this way, Mr. McDonald's motion makes at least as strong a showing as the motion approved by this Court in *Lott*. There, the movant made a prima facie showing of *Brady* error based largely on the withholding evidence that related to the murder victim's dying description of his assailant. *Lott*, 366 F.3d at 433. As Chief Judge Boggs explained in his dissenting opinion, the difference between the victim's description and the movant's appearance was not all that dramatic, and other evidence tended to confirm the movant's guilt. *See id.* at 436-37 (Boggs, C.J., dissenting). Nevertheless, the Court determined that the movant had made a sufficient showing of possible merit to warrant adjudication in the district court. *Id.* at 434.

At a minimum, then, Mr. McDonald has presented "sufficient allegations of fact together with [the] documentation" necessary to "warrant a fuller exploration in the district court." *Id.* at 433 (internal quotation marks omitted).[9]

> **2. The Factual Predicate For McDonald's Claims Could Not Have Been Previously Discovered Through The Exercise Of Due Diligence.**

Similarly, Mr. McDonald has made a prima facie showing that the factual predicate for his claim "could not have been previously discovered through the exercise of due diligence." 28 U.S.C. § 2244(b)(2)(B)(i). "Previously" in this context means prior to the filing of the first § 2254 petition. *E.g., In re Provenzano*, 215 F.3d 1233, 1236 (11th Cir. 2000).

Here, no exercise of diligence could have revealed, prior to the filing of Mr. McDonald's first § 2254 petition, the inappropriate conduct of Mr. Baxter. Ms.

---

[9] Mr. McDonald has presented other, credible evidence that likewise casts doubt on his guilt and supports his claim of actual innocence. *First*, Mr. Caston's statements during his polygraph examination suggest that Mr. McDonald was not present at the time of the shooting. *See* A0058. This suggestion draws support from other evidence in the record, including statements that Mr. Caston allegedly made on the night of the shooting. For example, at least one witness overheard Caston say that Caffey was lucky that he did not have his "little Chevy" because Turner and McDonald "aren't ready to go." A0080.

Second, the victim's own son and daughter-in-law have signed sworn affidavits, in which they state that Jerome Caffey had confessed to them that he killed Vivian Johnson. A0061, A0062. These statements corroborate the emergency room doctor's conclusion that the bullet that killed Ms. Johnson entered from the right side of her neck—the side of her neck closest to the house where Caffey was seen holding a gun. A0067.

Harris only came forward after the statute of limitations for perjury expired, which was still more than a year after this Court denied Mr. McDonald's application for a certificate of appealability over the denial of his first § 2254 petition. Moreover, according to Ms. Harris, Mr. Baxter took significant steps to hide his conduct, including relocating Ms. Harris to Cleveland, Ohio. A0045, A0051. Under these circumstances, and in light of the fact that the vast majority of prosecutors act in good faith, it would be manifestly unfair to hold that a habeas petitioner must anticipate the sort of prosecutorial misconduct engaged in by Mr. Baxter and raise it in a first petition.

3. None Of McDonald's Claims Has Been Presented In A Prior Application.

Finally, none of Mr. McDonald's claims has been presented in a prior application. *Compare* Addendum B, *with* A0002-A0029. His new claims relate to evidence that was not previously available and therefore could not have been asserted in a previous petition. Thus, unlike *In re Fowlkers*, 326 F.3d 542, 545 (4th Cir. 2003), where the movant had previously presented the same claims and relied on the same evidence, here the movant relies on neither.

C. A Movant Is Not Required To Make A Prima Facie Showing Beyond The Requirements Of § 2244(b).

In its opposition to Mr. McDonald's *pro se* motion, the State argued that he must demonstrate that his underlying application satisfies requirements beyond those specified in § 2244(b). *See* Opp'n to *Pro Se* Mot. at 7-10. This argument is contrary to AEDPA's plain text, which limits the scope of this Court's review to the requirements of "th[at] subsection." 28 U.S.C. § 2244(b)(3)(C).

The Act's hierarchy also makes plain the error in the State's argument. Whereas the court of appeals simply must ensure that any one claim satisfies *subsection (b)*, the district court must ultimately ensure that each claim satisfies the requirements of the *entire section*. *Compare id*. § 2244(b)(3)(C) (using the phrase "this subsection"), *with id*. § 2244(b)(4) (using the phrase "this section"). *See also Cooper*, 358 F.3d at 1123.[10] If Congress had wanted the court of appeals to analyze the requirements of the entire section, it very easily could have said so. Because it did not, the court of appeals should not concern itself with such requirements as the applicable limitations period, which resides in § 2244*(d)*, not § 2244*(b)*. *See* 28 U.S.C. § 2244(b)(3)(C); *see also* 2 HERTZ & LIEBMAN, *supra*, at 1447-48 & n.120 ("The statute limits the scope of review at [the motion] stage to the specific question whether the motion makes a *prima facie* showing that any of

---

[10] If the court of appeals grants a second or successive motion, then the district court must engage in a plenary review of the entire application that underlines that motion. *See* 28 U.S.C. § 2244(b)(4); *see also Jordan*, 485 F.3d at 1358; *Johnson*, 322 F.3d at 883; 2 RANDY HERTZ & JAMES S. LIEBMAN, FEDERAL HABEAS CORPUS PRACTICE AND PROCEDURE 1454 (5th ed. 2005). AEDPA requires the district court to "dismiss any claim presented in a second or successive application that the court of appeals has authorized to be filed" if the applicant cannot "show[] that the claim satisfies the requirements of [the *entire*] section." 28 U.S.C. § 2244(b)(4) (emphasis added).

Example Application #2—Dewitt McDonald, Jr. (cont.)

the claims in the petition satisfy AEDPA's substantive successive standards, thereby evidently rendering irrelevant other possible grounds for dismissal such as ultimate lack of merit, nonexhaustion, procedural default, and the like." (citing authorities)).[11]

---

[11] There are a number of good reasons why Congress did not require the court of appeals to concern itself with the applicable statute of limitations at the motion stage. *First*, the statute of limitations is an affirmative defense that normally must be raised by the State in its answer. *See* FED. R. GOVERNING § 2254 CASES 5(b). *Second*, the limitations period must be evaluated on a claim-by-claim basis. *Third*, the applicable limitations period that will most often govern claims in a second-or-successive petition, § 2244(d)(1)(D), often requires factual development to determine when the factual predicate "could have been discovered." 28 U.S.C. § 2244(d)(1)(D). *Fourth*, the applicant may be entitled to statutory tolling, which again requires a detailed factual analysis, including an analysis of whether an application was "properly filed" in state court. *Id.* § 2244(d)(2). *Finally*, equitable tolling may be available, including tolling based on a showing of actual innocence. *See Souter v. Jones*, 395 F.3d 577 (6th Cir. 2005).

CONCLUSION

For the foregoing reasons, the Court should grant Mr. McDonald's motion for an order authorizing the United States District Court for the Southern District of Ohio to consider his second petition for a writ of habeas corpus.

Respectfully submitted,

_____
MEIR FEDER
ROBERT T. SMITH
Counsel of Record
JONES DAY
222 East 41st Street
New York, NY 10017
(212) 326-3939

*Counsel for Movant
Dewitt McDonald Jr.*

Dated: July 26, 2007

CERTIFICATE OF COMPLIANCE

I hereby certify that, in accordance with the general requirements set forth in Federal Rule of Appellate Procedure 32(a) and (c)(2), this motion is proportionately spaced, has a typeface of 14-point, and contains **9,604** words, exclusive of the material not counted under Federal Rule of Appellate Procedure 32(a)(7)(B)(iii). The Clerk's Office has informed counsel that no page or word limitation governs this motion.

_____
Robert T. Smith
Counsel for Movant

CERTIFICATE OF SERVICE

I hereby certify that on this 26th day of July, 2007, I sent an original and four copies of the foregoing motion to the Clerk of the United States Court of Appeals for the Sixth Circuit by Federal Express. In addition, on this same day, I served the foregoing motion by causing two copies to be sent to the following counsel by Federal Express:

Jerri L. Fosnaught, Esq.
Office of the Attorney General
Corrections Litigation Section
150 E. Gay Street
16th Floor
Columbus, Ohio 43215-6001

Bishop Richard E. Cox
SCLC Redress Committee
Dayton Chapter SCLC
2132 W. Third Street
Dayton, Ohio 45417

                                              Robert T. Smith
                                              Counsel for Movant

APPLICATION TO FILE SECOND OR SUCCESSIVE HABEAS CORPUS PETITION

Example Application #3—Leslie A. Parker

Case: 16-13814   Date Filed: 06/21/2016   Page: 1 of 20

UNITED STATES COURT OF APPEALS
ELEVENTH CIRCUIT

[Stamp: U.S. COURT OF APPEALS, JUN 21 2016, ATLANTA, GA]

APPLICATION FOR LEAVE TO FILE A SECOND OR
SUCCESSIVE MOTION TO VACATE, SET ASIDE
OR CORRECT SENTENCE
28 U.S.C. § 2255
BY A PRISONER IN FEDERAL CUSTODY

Name Leslie A. Parker   Prisoner Number 19109-018

Institution Orlando RRM

Street Address 6303 County Road 500

City Wildwood   State FL   Zip Code 34785

INSTRUCTIONS—READ CAREFULLY

(1) This application must be legibly handwritten or typewritten and signed by the applicant under penalty of perjury. Any false statement of a material fact may serve as the basis for prosecution and conviction for perjury.

(2) All questions must be answered concisely in the proper space on the form.

(3) The Judicial Conference of the United States has adopted the 8½ x 11 inch paper size for use throughout the federal judiciary and directed the elimination of the use of legal size paper. All pleadings must be on 8½ x 11 inch paper, otherwise we cannot accept them.

(4) All applicants seeking leave to file a second or successive petition are required to use this form, except in capital cases. In capital cases only, the use of this form is optional.

(5) Additional pages are not permitted except with respect to additional grounds for relief and facts which you rely upon to support those grounds. DO NOT SUBMIT SEPARATE PETITIONS, MOTIONS, BRIEFS, ARGUMENTS, ETC., EXCEPT IN CAPITAL CASES.

28 U.S.C. § 2255 Application   Page 1   *Revised 1/02/01*

APPLICATION TO FILE SECOND OR SUCCESSIVE HABEAS CORPUS PETITION

Example Application #3—Leslie A. Parker (cont.)

(6) In accordance with the "Antiterrorism and Effective Death Penalty Act of 1996," as codified at 28 U.S.C. § 2255, effective April 24, 1996, before leave to file a second or successive motion can be granted by the United States Court of Appeals, <u>it is the applicant's burden</u> to make a <u>prima facie</u> showing that he satisfies either of the two conditions stated below.

> A second or successive motion must be certified as provided in [28 U.S.C.] section 2255 by a panel of the appropriate court of appeals to contain—
>
>> (1) newly discovered evidence that, if proven and viewed in light of the evidence as a whole, would be sufficient to establish by clear and convincing evidence that no reasonable factfinder would have found the movant guilty of the offense; or
>>
>> (2) a new rule of constitutional law, made retroactive to cases on collateral review by the Supreme Court, that was previously unavailable.

(7) When this application is fully completed, the original and three copies must be mailed to:

**Clerk of Court
United States Court of Appeals for the Eleventh Circuit
56 Forsyth Street, N.W.
Atlanta, Georgia 30303**

28 U.S.C. § 2255 Application   Page 2   *Revised 1/02/01*

APPLICATION TO FILE SECOND OR SUCCESSIVE HABEAS CORPUS PETITION

Example Application #3—Leslie A. Parker (cont.)

Case: 16-13814   Date Filed: 06/21/2016   Page: 3 of 20

APPLICATION

1. (a) State and division of the United States District Court which entered the judgment of conviction under attack U.S. District Court, Middle District of Florida, Tampa Division

   (b) Case number 8:95-cr-00227-SDM-1

2. Date of judgment of conviction 5/10/1996

3. Length of sentence 293 Months   Sentencing Judge William J. Castagna

4. Nature of offense or offenses for which you were convicted: Felon in Possession of a Firearm (count 1).

5. Related to this conviction and sentence, have you ever filed a motion to vacate in any federal court?
   Yes (x) No ( ) If "yes", how many times? 1 (if more than one, complete 6 and 7 below as necessary)
   (a) Name of court U.S. District Court, Middle District of Florida, Tampa Division
   (b) Case number 8:98-cv-627-SDM
   (c) Nature of proceeding Motion to vacate, set aside, or correct a sentence under 28 U.S.C. § 2255

   (d) Grounds raised (list all grounds; use extra pages if necessary)
   Counsel was ineffective by failing to inquire with the State Attorney's Office as to whether the State was also going to prosecute him for being a felon in possession of a firearm, despite Mr. Parker's request that he do so.

   (e) Did you receive an evidentiary hearing on your motion? Yes ( ) No (x)
   (f) Result Denied
   (g) Date of result April 19, 2000

6. As to any second federal motion, give the same information:
   (a) Name of court
   (b) Case number
   (c) Nature of proceeding

28 U.S.C. § 2255 Application   Page 3   *Revised 1/02/01*

APPLICATION TO FILE SECOND OR SUCCESSIVE HABEAS CORPUS PETITION

Example Application #3—Leslie A. Parker (cont.)

Case: 16-13814 Date Filed: 06/21/2016 Page: 4 of 20

(d) Grounds raised (list <u>all</u> grounds; use extra pages if necessary) _____

_____
_____
_____
_____

(e) Did you receive an evidentiary hearing on your motion? Yes ( ) No ( )
(f) Result _____
_____
(g) Date of result _____

7. As to any third federal motion, give the same information:
   (a) Name of court _____
   (b) Case number _____
   (c) Nature of proceeding _____
   _____
   _____

   (d) Grounds raised (list <u>all</u> grounds; use extra pages if necessary) _____
   _____
   _____
   _____
   _____

   (e) Did you receive an evidentiary hearing on your motion? Yes ( ) No ( )
   (f) Result _____
   _____
   (g) Date of result _____

8. Did you appeal the result of any action taken on your federal motion? (Use extra pages to reflect additional petitions if necessary)
   (1) First motion   No (x) Yes ( ) Appeal No. _____
   (2) Second motion   No ( ) Yes ( ) Appeal No. _____
   (3) Third motion   No ( ) Yes ( ) Appeal No. _____

9. If you did <u>not</u> appeal from the adverse action on any motion, explain briefly why you did not: Mr. Parker was without the assistance of counsel. _____
_____
_____
_____
_____

28 U.S.C. § 2255 Application   Page 4   Revised 1/02/01

APPLICATION TO FILE SECOND OR SUCCESSIVE HABEAS CORPUS PETITION

Example Application #3—Leslie A. Parker (cont.)

Case: 16-13814 Date Filed: 06/21/2016 Page: 5 of 20

10. State <u>concisely</u> every ground on which you <u>now</u> claim that you are being held unlawfully. Summarize <u>briefly</u> the <u>facts</u> supporting each ground.

   A. Ground one: Increasing Leslie A. Parker's sentence under the Armed Career Criminal Act's residual clause violated due process.

   Supporting FACTS (tell your story briefly without citing cases or law):
   The U.S. Supreme Court has declared the Armed Career Criminal Act's residual clause unconstitutionally vague, and it held that increasing a defendant's sentence under that clause violated due process. The district court enhanced Mr. Parker's sentence under the Act's residual clause and subjected him to a mandatory minimum 15-year sentence. Accordingly, he was denied due process. The Supreme Court has ruled that the decision in Johnson is retroactive in cases on collateral review. PLEASE CONTINUE ON ATTACHED PAGES

   Was this claim raised in a prior motion? Yes ( ) No (X)

   Does this claim rely on a "new rule of law?" Yes (X) No ( )
   If "yes," state the new rule of law (give case name and citation):
   Johnson v. United States, 135 S. Ct. 2551 (2015).
   Welch v. United States, 136 S. Ct. 1257, 1268 (2016).

   Does this claim rely on "newly discovered evidence?" Yes ( ) No (X)
   If "yes," briefly state the newly discovered evidence, and why it was not previously available to you n/a

   B. Ground two: n/a

   Supporting FACTS (tell your story briefly without citing cases or law):
   n/a

   Was this claim raised in a prior motion? Yes ( ) No ( )

   28 U.S.C. § 2255 Application   Page 5   Revised 1/02/01

APPLICATION TO FILE SECOND OR SUCCESSIVE HABEAS CORPUS PETITION

Example Application #3—Leslie A. Parker (cont.)

Continuation of Question 10A

In denying Leslie Parker's prior application for leave to file a second or successive motion to vacate, correct, or set aside a federal sentence pursuant to 28 U.S.C. § 2255 ("SOS Application") based on *Samuel Johnson v. United States*, 135 S. Ct. 2551 (2015) (*Samuel Johnson*), the Court relied on *Turner v. Warden Coleman FCI (Medium)*, 709 F.3d 1328, 1338 (11th Cir. 2013), to summarily conclude his two 1980 aggravated assault convictions qualify under the ACCA's elements clause, and relied on the facts in the pre-sentence report to conclude his 1983 conviction for burglary of a dwelling qualified under the enumerated offenses clause. *See In re Parker*, No. 16-12635, Order at 4 (11th Cir. June 16, 2016). The Court also relied on *In re Hires*, ___ F.3d ___, 2016 WL 3342668 (11th Cir. June 15, 2015) (No. 16-12744), in observing that *Samuel Johnson* "also does not serve as a portal for Parker to raise a *Descamps*[1] claim and challenge whether his burglary conviction would count today under the enumerated crimes clause, given *Descamps*'s holding on divisibility." *See In re Parker*, Order at 5 (footnote added).

In light of the Court's recent published order in *In re Rogers*, ___ F.3d ___ (11th Cir. June 17, 2016) (No. 16-12626), and the unsettled law related to Florida burglary and aggravated assault, Mr. Parker respectfully submits this second SOS

---

[1] *Descamps v. United States*, 133 S. Ct. 2276 (2013).

Page 5(a)

Application.² As demonstrated below, he has made the requisite prima facie showing and so should be allowed to present his claim to the district court to resolve the merits in the first instance.

In *In re Rogers*, the Court clarified that *Samuel Johnson* is "'implicated' as a new rule of constitutional law, and the application should be granted, in situations where neither the record nor current binding precedent makes undeniably clear that, absent the residual clause, an enhanced sentence validly was entered." *In re Rogers*, Slip Op. at 5. The Court explained:

> Read together, *Adams*,³ *Hires*,⁴ and *Thomas*⁵ establish a "clear or unclear" test that turns on the sentencing court's findings and on-point binding precedent regarding whether a particular crime categorically qualifies under a still-valid ACCA clause offense (precedent that includes *Descamps*). When neither the sentencing court's finding on which ACCA clause or clauses applied nor binding on-point

---

² Because there are no avenues available for seeking further review, Mr. Parker has filed this application requesting that the Court reconsider its denial of leave to file a second or successive § 2255 motion, as other Panels have done. *See, e.g., In re Troy Robinson*, No. 16-12616 (11th Cir. June 8, 2016) (granting re-filed application upon concluding that its earlier denial in a published opinion "was not correct"); *In re Michael Turner*, No. 16-13012 (11th Cir June 14, 2016) (granting re-filed application after having denied an earlier application).

³ *In re Adams*, ___ F.3d ___, 2016 WL 3269704 (11th Cir. June 15, 2015) (No. 16-12519).

⁴ *In re Hires*, ___ F.3d ___, 2016 WL 3342668 (11th Cir. June 15, 2015) (No. 16-12744).

⁵ *In re Thomas*, ___ F.3d ___, 2016 WL 3000325 (11th Cir. May 25, 2015) (No. 16-12065).

precedent forecloses an applicant's assertion that his sentence arose under the ACCA's residual clause, we look to *Descamps* "to ensure we apply the correct meaning of the ACCA's words." *Adams*, slip op. at 8. And at this point, unless post-*Descamps* binding precedent clearly resolves the residual clause ambiguity the applicant has demonstrated, his application "contain[s]" a *Johnson* claim such that his application is due to be granted. *See* 28 U.S.C. § 2255(h).

In re Rogers, Slip Op. at 6-7 (footnotes added).

Concerning the statement in *Hires* that was relied upon to deny Mr. Parker's prior SOS Application, the Court in *Rogers* stated:

> Although *Hires* suggested that "*Descamps* cannot serve as a basis, independent or otherwise, for authorizing a successive § 2255 motion," we do not read this statement as applying even when the application "contain[s]" a *Johnson* claim as described above. *Hires*, No. 16-12744, slip op. at 10 (emphasis added). We acknowledge that *Hires*'s statement is in tension with our holding in *Adams*, but because *Adams* was decided before *Hires*, its holding established prior panel precedent that *Hires* could not overrule. *See Morrison v. Amway Corp.*, 323 F.3d 920, 929 (11th Cir. 2003).

Id. at 5 n.6.

The Court further stated in *Rogers*, "We cannot simply look directly to an applicant's PSI to determine whether, under the facts contained therein, the elements or enumerated crimes clause is applicable. We must instead follow *Descamps* and other precedent that guide our analysis of the reach of those clauses." *Id.* at 5 n.7.

Page 5(c)

Here, as demonstrated below, "neither the record nor current binding precedent makes undeniably clear that, absent the residual clause, an enhanced sentence validly was entered." *Id.* at 5.

Aggravated Assault

It is respectfully submitted that the sole case relied upon to reject Mr. Parker's prior SOS Application as it related to aggravated assault, *Turner v. Warden,* is no longer good law. Moreover, although a divided Court initially denied Mr. Turner's application for leave to file a second or successive § 2255 motion, *see In re Turner*, No. 16-11914 (11th Cir. May 25, 2016), the Court unanimously granted his recent application, *see In re Turner*, No. 16-13012 (11th Cir. June 14, 2016). The interests in equal justice and fundamental fairness require the same result here.

In *Turner v. Warden*, the Court reasoned that aggravated assault is a violent felony because "by its definitional terms, the offense necessarily includes an assault which is 'an intentional, unlawful threat by word or act *to do violence* to the person of another, coupled with an apparent ability to do so." *Id.* at 1338 (emphasis in original). Therefore, the Court stated, "a conviction under section 784.021 will always include 'as an element the . . . threatened use of physical force against the person of another." *Id.* at 1338. The reasoning in *Turner*, however, is inconsistent with the strict, element-by-element comparison now required by the categorical approach as clarified in *Descamps* and *Howard*.

In *Howard*, the Court confirmed that sentencing courts conducting divisibility analysis "are bound to follow any state court decisions that define or interpret the statute's substantive elements because state law is what the state supreme court says it is"). 742 F.3d at 1346. And in *Turner*, the Court did not consider how Florida courts interpreted the *mens rea* element in the underlying assault statute, § 784.011.

Florida courts have held that a person may be convicted under § 784.021 upon a *mens rea* of "culpable negligence," which is akin to recklessness. *See LaValley v. State*, 633 So. 2d 1126 (Fla. 5th DCA 1995); *Kelly v. State*, 552 So. 2d 206 (Fla. 5th DCA 1989); *Green v. State*, 315 So. 2d 499 (4th DCA 1975); and *DuPree v. State*, 310 So. 2d 396 (Fla. 2d DCA 1975); *see generally United States v. Garcia-Perez*, 779 F.3d 278, 285 (5th Cir. 2015) (equating Florida's "culpable negligence" standard with "recklessness").

For an offense to be a violent felony within the ACCA's elements clause, however, it must have as an element the active and intentional employment of force, which requires more than negligence or recklessness. *See Leocal v. Ashcroft*, 543 U.S. 1, 9–10, 125 S. Ct. 377, 382 (2004) (the term "use" in the similarly-worded elements clause in 18 U.S.C. § 16(a) requires "active employment;" the

Page 5(e)

phrase "use . . . of physical force" in a crime of violence definition "most naturally suggests a higher degree of intent than negligent or merely accidental conduct"); *United States v. Palomino Garcia*, 606 F.3d 1317, 1334–36 (11th Cir. 2010) (ruling that because Arizona "aggravated assault" need not be committed intentionally, and could be committed recklessly, it did not "have as an element the use of physical force;" citing and following *Leocal*).

Based upon the Florida cases cited above, it is clear that the aggravated assault statute has been interpreted by the Florida courts to require no more than "culpable negligence," which is recklessness. Ergo, there is no "match" between the *mens rea* element in § 784.021 and an offense that "has as an element the use, attempted use, or threatened use of physical force against the person of another" as interpreted in *Leocal* and *Palomino Garcia*. As such, a conviction under § 784.021 is categorically overbroad and not a violent felony within the elements clause.

Although § 784.021 is "divisible," and one "alternative" under § 784.021 permits conviction for an assault "with a deadly weapon without intent to kill," § 784.021(a), the ultimate analysis does not change because the term "deadly weapon" is indeterminate and categorically overbroad vis-a-vis any offense within the elements clause. The term "deadly weapon," notably, is defined in the standard § 784.021 instruction to include anything "used or threatened to be used in a way likely to produce death or great bodily harm." And poison, anthrax, and chemical

Page 5(f)

weapons would each produce death or great bodily harm without the "use" of *any* "physical force." Other courts have declared convictions overbroad and outside the elements clause for precisely this reason. *See, e.g.*, *United States v. Perez-Vargas*, 414 F.3d 1282 (10th Cir. 2005); *United States v. Torres-Miguel*, 701 F.3d 165, 168–69 (4th Cir. 2012); *Matter of Guzman-Polanco*, 26 I & N Dec. 713, 717–18 (BIA Feb. 24, 2016).

Accordingly, this statute presents the precise scenario presaged in *Howard*, in which "none of the alternatives may match the elements of the generic crime." *Howard*, 742 F.3d at 1346. And in that scenario, *Howard* held, "the court can and should skip over any *Shepard* documents and simply declare that the prior conviction is not a predicate offense based on the statute itself." *Id.*

Since the elements clause analysis in *Turner* has been abrogated, *Turner* cannot serve as "current binding precedent [that] makes undeniably clear that, absent the residual clause, an enhanced sentence validly was entered." *In re Rogers*, Order at 5. Ergo, Mr. Parker should be allowed to file a § 2255 motion in the district court challenging his ACCA sentence based on the aggravated assault convictions.

Burglary

Likewise, Mr. Parker's prior Florida conviction for burglary warrants further review by the district court in a § 2255 motion, especially "[g]iven the unsettled state of the *Descamps* divisibility analysis as it applies" to Florida burglary. *See In re Rogers*, Order at 5.

The Court's conclusion that Mr. Parker failed to make the requisite prima facie showing conflicts with this Court's adjudication of numerous other identically-situated applications, including the applicant in the recently-published decision in *In re Adams*.[6]

Like the applicant in *In re Adams*, Mr. Parker is asserting a pure *Samuel Johnson* claim, and not a pure *Descamps* claim. As this Court recently explained:

> In this case, the sentencing court may have relied on the residual clause in imposing Mr. Adams' sentence based on his prior Florida burglary conviction. Thus, his sentence may be invalid under *Johnson*. In *Griffin*, *Johnson* was inapplicable because the petitioner was

---

[6] This Court has granted numerous successive *Johnson* applications in cases involving Florida burglary. *See, e.g.*, *In re Leone*, No. 16-12687 (June 15, 2016); *In re Jones*, No. 16-12696 (June 15, 2016); *In re Chancellor*, No. 16-12579 (June 10, 2016); *In re Brown*, No. 16-12602 (June 10, 2016); *In re Harris*, No. 16-12646 (June 10, 2016); *In re Davis*, No. 16-12662 (June 9, 2016); *In re Haugabook*, No. 16-12660 (June 8, 2016); *In re Higgins*, No. 16-12336 (June 6, 2016); *In re Sharp*, No. 16-12326 (June 3, 2016); *In re Sistrunk*, No. 16-12112 (June 2, 2016); *In re Brand*, No. 16-12231 (May 27, 2016); *In re Smith*, No. 16-12512 (May 25, 2016); *In re Dixon*, No. 16-12645 (May 24, 2016); *In re Kelly*, No. 16-11859 (May 19, 2016); *In re Jackson*, No. 16-11889 (May 13, 2016); *In re Landry*, No. 16-11614 (May 10, 2016); *In re Jackson*, No. 16-10895 (May 5, 2016); *In re Gomez*, No. 16-10516 (Mar. 3, 2016); *In re Barber*, No. 16-10107 (Feb. 10, 2016).

To ensure consistent rulings, the Court should grant this application as well. Such consistency is especially important given the inability of Mr. Parker to seek further review by way of a rehearing or certiorari petition. *See* 28 U.S.C. § 2244(b)(3)(E). Failing to grant this application would troublingly result in treating identically-situated individuals differently.

sentenced under the Guidelines, and in *Thomas*, *Johnson* was inapplicable because the district court clearly did not rely on the residual clause. Accordingly, the petitioners were forced to rely on *Descamps* as a standalone claim. In contrast, Mr. Adams's claim implicates *Johnson*, and the ambiguity surrounding the sentencing court's decision requires us to look to the text of the relevant statutes, including the ACCA, to determine which, if any, ACCA clauses Mr. Adams' prior convictions fall under. In fulfilling this duty, we should look to guiding precedent, such as *Descamps*, to ensure we apply the correct meaning of the ACCA's words. Although *Descamps* bears on this case, it is not an independent claim that is itself subject to the gatekeeping requirements.

In re Adams, __ F.3d __, slip op. at 8; *see also In re Chancellor*, No. 16-12579, Order at 5–6 (June 10, 2016) (similar). That same reasoning applies here.

Mr. Parker maintains that there is a "reasonable likelihood" that his *Johnson* claim has "possible merit" so as to "warrant fuller exploration by the district court." *In re Holladay*, 331 F.3d 1169, 1173–74 (2003) (citations omitted). A conviction for Florida burglary — regardless of whether its burglary of a dwelling or burglary of a structure — cannot qualify as a "violent felony" under any clause except the residual clause.

Under Florida law, "'burglary' means entering or remaining in a dwelling, a structure, or a conveyance with the intent to commit an offense therein . . . ." Fla. Stat. § 810.02. Critically, the statute defines the elements of "structure" and "dwelling" to include the curtilage thereof. *See* Fla. Stat. § 810.011(1)-(2). Accordingly, the Florida burglary statute is broader than generic burglary, which does not include burglary of the curtilage. *See James v. United States*, 550 U.S.

Page 5(i)

192, 212, 127 S. Ct. 1586, 1599 (2007); *see also In re Adams*, No. 16-12519, Order at 6-7 (citing *United States v. Matthews*, 466 F.3d 1271, 1275 (11th Cir. 2006) (holding that a Florida conviction for burglary of the curtilage constituted a violent felony under the ACCA's residual clause)).

The statute is also indivisible because "structure" and "dwelling" are defined to include the curtilage, and the Florida Supreme Court has made clear that burglary of the curtilage is not an alternative element or crime. *See Baker v. State*, 636 So.2d 1342, 1344 (Fla. 1994) ("There is no crime denominated burglary of a curtilage."). As explained in *In re Adams*:

> [T]he statute does not appear to be divisible such that it still could be violated in a way that comports with the generic definition of burglary. Rather than setting out the critical place-of-entry element in the alternative—i.e., "a building or its curtilage"—the place-of-entry element encompasses a "building of any kind, either temporary or permanent, which has a roof over it, together with the curtilage thereof." Fla. Stat. § 810.011(a)(1).

In re Adams, No. 16-12519, Order at 6-7.

Because the Florida burglary statute is overbroad and indivisible, convictions for burglary of a structure or dwelling can only qualify under the residual clause; they can never qualify as generic burglary, and the modified categorical approach does not apply. *See United States v. Howard*, 742 F.3d 1342, 1345–49 (11th Cir. 2014) (stating that where "none of the alternatives may match the elements of the generic crime . . . , the court can and should skip over any

Page 5(j)

Shepard documents and simply declare that the prior conviction is not a predicate offense based on the statute itself").

In denying Mr. Parker's application, the panel also relied on undisputed PSI facts. *In re Parker*, Order at 4-5. However, it is well-established that the Court may not look to *Shepard* documents where, as here, the statute is indivisible. *See In re Rogers*, No. 16-12626, Order at 5 n.7 (11th Cir. June 17, 2016). And, even where a statute is divisible, the Court may consider only *Shepard*-approved materials. A federal PSI is clearly not a *Shepard*-approved document: not only is it not a "conclusive record[ ] made or used in adjudicating guilty," *Shepard*, 544 U.S. at 21, but it was not a part of the underlying state proceedings. Thus, even if Mr. Parker did not object to the facts contained in the PSI during his federal sentencing, that has no constitutional significance. Instead, what matters is that he did not invoke or waive his constitutional right to a jury trial to find these facts during the earlier criminal proceeding. Thus, any use of PSI facts to enhance his sentence would violate his Sixth Amendment rights. *See Descamps v. United States*, 133 S. Ct. 2276 (2013).

While this Court has previously upheld guideline sentences based upon "undisputed PSI facts," all but one of those cases, pre-date *Descamps* and have been abrogated by the Supreme Court's Sixth Amendment discussion therein. Before *Descamps*, the constitutional problems with referring to PSI facts were not

Page 5(k)

clear because the Sixth Amendment discussion in Part III of the *Shepard* opinion was joined only by a plurality of the Court. The only post-*Descamps* Eleventh Circuit decision discussing whether the Court can uphold an ACCA sentence based upon "undisputed PSI facts" is *United States v. Ramirez-Flores*, 743 F.3d 816 (11th Cir. 2014). But that case – like the others – concerned an enhancement under the advisory Sentencing Guidelines, not the ACCA. Because the Court in *Ramirez-Flores* was not enhancing the defendant's sentence above the statutory maximum, as the Court did here in imposing the ACCA enhancement, the Sixth Amendment problems with considering non-*Shepard* documents did not exist and were not considered in *Ramirez-Flores*. That decision does not have persuasive value in an ACCA case, where Sixth Amendment concerns are present.

As a final matter, a thorough review of the merits is not required or possible at this stage of the proceedings, especially given the complexity of the merits analysis, the substantial number of successive applications before the Court, and the lack of counseled briefing, adversarial presentation, and oral argument. Addressing the merits under these sub-optimal conditions risks erroneous and inconsistent rulings, as this case demonstrates. *See* n.1, *supra*.

Accordingly, Mr. Parker respectfully requests that this Court grant him leave to brief and argue the merits of his ACCA challenge in the district court. That result is especially appropriate here because the record does not indicate which clause of the ACCA "violent felony" definition was relied upon at sentencing. Given that the residual clause is unconstitutional, and that Florida burglary cannot qualify under any clause except the residual clause, Mr. Parker has made a prima facie showing that his proposed claim for § 2255 relief comes under the rule announced by *Samuel Johnson,* and he should be allowed to present his claim to the district court.

Accordingly, Mr. Parker respectfully requests that the Court permit him to challenge his illegal ACCA sentence by filing a second § 2255 motion in the district court.

APPLICATION TO FILE SECOND OR SUCCESSIVE HABEAS CORPUS PETITION

Example Application #3—Leslie A. Parker (cont.)

Case: 16-13814   Date Filed: 06/21/2016   Page: 19 of 20

Does this claim rely on a "new rule of law?"   Yes ( )   No ( )
If "yes," state the new rule of law (give case name and citation):
n/a

Does this claim rely on "newly discovered evidence?"   Yes ( )   No ( )
If "yes," briefly state the newly discovered evidence, and why it was not previously available to you n/a

[Additional grounds may be asserted on additional pages if necessary]

11. Do you have any motion or appeal now pending in any court as to the judgment now under attack?   Yes ( )   No (X)
If "yes," name of court _____ Case number _____

Wherefore, applicant prays that the United States Court of Appeals for the Eleventh Circuit grant an Order Authorizing the District Court to Consider Applicant's Second or Successive Motion to Vacate under 28 U.S.C. § 2255.

/s/ Conrad Kahn

Conrad Kahn
Research and Writing Attorney
Florida Bar No. 104456
201 South Orange Avenue, Suite 300
Orlando, Florida 32801
Telephone: 407-648-6338
Facsimile: 407-648-6765
Email: Conrad_Kahn@fd.org

28 U.S.C. § 2255 Application   Page 6   *Revised 1/02/01*

APPLICATION TO FILE SECOND OR SUCCESSIVE HABEAS CORPUS PETITION

Example Application #3—Leslie A. Parker (cont.)

Case: 16-13814   Date Filed: 06/21/2016   Page: 20 of 20

PROOF OF SERVICE

Applicant must send a copy of this application and all attachments to the United States Attorney's office in the district in which you were convicted.

I certify that on June 20, 2016 [date], I mailed a copy of this Application and all attachments to Assistant United States Attorney David Rhodes

at the following address: United States Attorney's Office, 400 North Tampa Street, Suite 3200, Tampa, Florida 33602

Attorney's Signature

Pursuant to Fed.R.App.P. 25(a), "Papers filed by an inmate confined in an institution are timely filed if deposited in the institution's internal mail system on or before the last day of filing. Timely filing of papers by an inmate confined in an institution may be shown by a notarized statement or declaration (in compliance with 28 U.S.C. § 1746) setting forth the date of deposit and stating that first-class postage has been prepaid."

28 U.S.C. § 2255 Application   Page 7   Revised 1/02/01

APPLICATION TO FILE SECOND OR SUCCESSIVE HABEAS CORPUS PETITION

Example Application #4—Jasper Moore

Case: 16-13993 Date Filed: 06/24/2016 Page: 1 of 31

U.S. RECEIVED CLERK JUN 24 2016 ATLANTA, GA

UNITED STATES COURT OF APPEALS
ELEVENTH CIRCUIT

APPLICATION FOR LEAVE TO FILE A SECOND OR
SUCCESSIVE MOTION TO VACATE, SET ASIDE
OR CORRECT SENTENCE
28 U.S.C. § 2255
BY A PRISONER IN FEDERAL CUSTODY

Name **Jasper Moore**   Prisoner Number **65686-0044**

Institution **Colemlan Medium, FCI**

Street Address **846 NE 54th Terrace**

City **Sumterville**   State **FL**   Zip Code **33521**

INSTRUCTIONS--READ CAREFULLY

(1) This application must be legibly handwritten or typewritten and signed by the applicant under penalty of perjury. Any false statement of a material fact may serve as the basis for prosecution and conviction for perjury.

(2) All questions must be answered concisely in the proper space on the form.

(3) The Judicial Conference of the United States has adopted the 8½ x 11 inch paper size for use throughout the federal judiciary and directed the elimination of the use of legal size paper. All pleadings must be on 8½ x 11 inch paper, otherwise we cannot accept them.

(4) All applicants seeking leave to file a second or successive petition are required to use this form, except in capital cases. In capital cases only, the use of this form is optional.

(5) Additional pages are not permitted except with respect to additional grounds for relief and facts which you rely upon to support those grounds. DO NOT SUBMIT SEPARATE PETITIONS, MOTIONS, BRIEFS, ARGUMENTS, ETC., EXCEPT IN CAPITAL CASES.

28 U.S.C. § 2255 Application   Page 1   Revised 1/02/01

APPLICATION TO FILE SECOND OR SUCCESSIVE HABEAS CORPUS PETITION

Example Application #4 — Jasper Moore (cont.)

(6) In accordance with the "Antiterrorism and Effective Death Penalty Act of 1996," as codified at 28 U.S.C. § 2255, effective April 24, 1996, before leave to file a second or successive motion can be granted by the United States Court of Appeals, <u>it is the applicant's burden</u> to make a <u>prima facie</u> showing that he satisfies either of the two conditions stated below.

> A second or successive motion must be certified as provided in [28 U.S.C.] section 2255 by a panel of the appropriate court of appeals to contain—
>
> (1) newly discovered evidence that, if proven and viewed in light of the evidence as a whole, would be sufficient to establish by clear and convincing evidence that no reasonable factfinder would have found the movant guilty of the offense; or
>
> (2) a new rule of constitutional law, made retroactive to cases on collateral review by the Supreme Court, that was previously unavailable.

(7) When this application is fully completed, the original and three copies must be mailed to:

Clerk of Court
United States Court of Appeals for the Eleventh Circuit
56 Forsyth Street, N.W.
Atlanta, Georgia 30303

28 U.S.C. § 2255 Application   Page 2   *Revised 1/02/01*

APPLICATION TO FILE SECOND OR SUCCESSIVE HABEAS CORPUS PETITION

Example Application #4 — Jasper Moore (cont.)

Case: 16-13993   Date Filed: 06/24/2016   Page: 3 of 31

APPLICATION

1. (a) State and division of the United States District Court which entered the judgment of conviction under attack Southern District of Florida

    (b) Case number 05-20210-Cr-Lenard

2. Date of judgment of conviction September 7, 2005

3. Length of sentence 210 months   Sentencing Judge Honorable Joan A. Lenard

4. Nature of offense or offenses for which you were convicted: Possession of a firearm and ammunition by a convicted felon

5. Related to this conviction and sentence, have you ever filed a motion to vacate in any federal court?
    Yes (x) No ( )   If "yes", how many times? 1   (if more than one, complete 6 and 7 below as necessary)
    (a) Name of court US District Court, Southern District of Florida
    (b) Case number 08-20519-CV-Lenard
    (c) Nature of proceeding 28:2255- Motion to Vacate Sentence

    (d) Grounds raised (list all grounds; use extra pages if necessary)
    Defense counsel was ineffective for waiving the Defendant's right to require the government prove nexus of firearm to interstate Commerce or to allege in the indictment any connection to interstate commerce where such nexus was an element of the offense.

    (e) Did you receive an evidentiary hearing on your motion?   Yes ( ) No (x)
    (f) Result Motion to Vacate dismissed as time-barred, and denied on the merits

    (g) Date of result October 31, 2008

6. As to any second federal motion, give the same information:
    (a) Name of court
    (b) Case number
    (c) Nature of proceeding

28 U.S.C. § 2255 Application   Page 3   Revised 1/02/01

APPLICATION TO FILE SECOND OR SUCCESSIVE HABEAS CORPUS PETITION

Example Application #4 — Jasper Moore (cont.)

Case: 16-13993   Date Filed: 06/24/2016   Page: 4 of 31

      (d) Grounds raised (list <u>all</u> grounds; use extra pages if necessary) _____
_____
_____
_____

      (e) Did you receive an evidentiary hearing on your motion?   Yes ( )   No ( )
      (f) Result _____

      (g) Date of result _____

7.   As to any third federal motion, give the same information:
      (a) Name of court _____
      (b) Case number _____
      (c) Nature of proceeding _____
_____
_____

      (d) Grounds raised (list <u>all</u> grounds; use extra pages if necessary) _____
_____
_____
_____

      (e) Did you receive an evidentiary hearing on your motion?   Yes ( )   No ( )
      (f) Result _____

      (g) Date of result _____

8.   Did you appeal the result of any action taken on your federal motion? (Use extra pages to reflect additional petitions if necessary)
      (1) First motion   No (x)   Yes ( )   Appeal No. _____
      (2) Second motion   No ( )   Yes ( )   Appeal No. _____
      (3) Third motion   No ( )   Yes ( )   Appeal No. _____

9.   If you did <u>not</u> appeal from the adverse action on any motion, explain briefly why you did not: _____
_____
_____
_____

28 U.S.C. § 2255 Application   Page 4   Revised 1/02/01

APPLICATION TO FILE SECOND OR SUCCESSIVE HABEAS CORPUS PETITION

Example Application #4 — Jasper Moore (cont.)

Case: 16-13993   Date Filed: 06/24/2016   Page: 5 of 31

10. State concisely every ground on which you now claim that you are being held unlawfully. Summarize briefly the facts supporting each ground.

A. Ground one: _____

Supporting FACTS (tell your story briefly without citing cases or law):
The United States Supreme Court has declared the ACCA's residual clause to be unconstitutionally vague and has held that increasing a defendant's sentence under that clause violates due process. This ruling has been held to apply to enhanced sentences in cases similar to defendant's case. The enhanced sentence violated due process in this case and requires that the defendant be re-sentenced. See attached memo.

Was this claim raised in a prior motion?   Yes ( ) No (X)

Does this claim rely on a "new rule of law?"   Yes ( )   No ( )
If "yes," state the new rule of law (give case name and citation):
Johnson v. United States, 135 S.Ct. 2551 (2015)

Does this claim rely on "newly discovered evidence?"   Yes ( )   No (X)
If "yes," briefly state the newly discovered evidence, and why it was not previously available to you _____

B. Ground two: _____

Supporting FACTS (tell your story briefly without citing cases or law):
_____

Was this claim raised in a prior motion?   Yes ( ) No ( )

28 U.S.C. § 2255 Application   Page 5   *Revised 1/02/01*

APPLICATION TO FILE SECOND OR SUCCESSIVE HABEAS CORPUS PETITION

Example Application #4 — Jasper Moore (cont.)

Case: 16-13993   Date Filed: 06/24/2016   Page: 6 of 31

Does this claim rely on a "new rule of law?"   Yes ( )   No ( )
If "yes," state the new rule of law (give case name and citation): _____
_____
_____

Does this claim rely on "newly discovered evidence?"   Yes ( )   No ( )
If "yes," briefly state the newly discovered evidence, and why it was not previously available to you _____
_____
_____
_____
_____
_____
_____
_____

[Additional grounds may be asserted on additional pages if necessary]

11. Do you have any motion or appeal now pending in any court as to the judgment now under attack?   Yes ( )   No (X)
    If "yes," name of court _____ Case number _____

Wherefore, applicant prays that the United States Court of Appeals for the Eleventh Circuit grant an Order Authorizing the District Court to Consider Applicant's Second or Successive Motion to Vacate under 28 U.S.C. § 2255.

_____
Applicant's Signature

I declare under Penalty of Perjury that my answers to all the questions in this Application are true and correct.

Executed on 6/23/16
              [date]

_____
Applicant's Signature

28 U.S.C. § 2255 Application   Page 6   Revised 1/02/01

APPLICATION TO FILE SECOND OR SUCCESSIVE HABEAS CORPUS PETITION

Example Application #4 — Jasper Moore (cont.)

Case: 16-13993   Date Filed: 06/24/2016   Page: 7 of 31

PROOF OF SERVICE

Applicant must send a copy of this application and all attachments to the United States Attorney's office in the district in which you were convicted.

I certify that on __6/23/16__ [date], I mailed a copy of this Application* and all attachments to United States Attorney Office

at the following address:
99 NE 4th Street, Miami, Florida 33132

_____
Applicant's Signature

---

* Pursuant to Fed.R.App.P. 25(a), "Papers filed by an inmate confined in an institution are timely filed if deposited in the institution's internal mail system on or before the last day of filing. Timely filing of papers by an inmate confined in an institution may be shown by a notarized statement or declaration (in compliance with 28 U.S.C. § 1746) setting forth the date of deposit and stating that first-class postage has been prepaid."

28 U.S.C. § 2255 Application   Page 7   *Revised 1/02/01*

ADDITIONAL GROUNDS FOR RELIEF AND FACTS RELIED UPON TO SUPPORT THOSE GROUNDS FOR RELIEF

I. THE SCOPE OF REVIEW AT THIS STAGE IS STRICTLY CIRCUMSCRIBED

Authorization for leave to file a second or successive motion to vacate, correct, or set aside a federal sentence pursuant to 28 U.S.C. § 2255 may be granted where this Court certifies that the proposed motion "contain[s] . . . a new rule of constitutional law, made retroactive to cases on collateral review by the Supreme Court, that was previously unavailable." 28 U.S.C. § 2255(h)(2). This Court "may authorize the filing of a second or successive [motion] only if it determines that the [motion] makes a prima facie showing that [it] satisfies the requirements of this subsection." 28 U.S.C. § 2244(b)(3)(C).

In performing this "gatekeeping" function, the scope of review is strictly circumscribed. The plain language of the statute establishes that the only question at the authorization stage is whether the applicant has made a "prima facie showing" that the proposed § 2255 motion "contain[s] a new rule of constitutional law, made retroactive to cases on collateral review by the Supreme Court, that was previously unavailable." The underlying merits of the § 2255 motion are "not relevant." *In re Joshua*, 224 F.3d 1281, 1282 n.2 (11th Cir. 2000) (noting that it was "unnecessary for this Court to answer" questions about the merits of a proposed *Apprendi* claim, because the inquiry under § 2255(h)(2) "addresses only whether *Apprendi* has been made retroactive to cases on collateral review").[1] And, in that regard, "[a] prima facie showing is not a particularly high standard;" rather, "[a]n application need only show [a] sufficient likelihood of satisfying the strict standards of § 2255[h][2] to warrant a fuller exploration by the district court." *In re Holladay*, 331 F.3d 1169, 1173 (11th Cir. 2003) (quotation omitted).

In this case, the applicant wishes to bring a second or successive § 2255 motion based on the Supreme Court's decision in *Johnson v. United States*, 135 S. Ct. 2551 (2015). Thus, the only issue is whether he has made a "prima facie" showing that *Johnson* announced "a new rule of constitutional law, made retroactive to cases on collateral review by the Supreme Court, that was previously unavailable." 28 U.S.C. § 2255(h)(2). That issue is no longer in doubt following the Supreme Court's decision in *Welch v. United States*, 136 S. Ct. 1257 (Apr. 18, 2016). In *Welch*, the Court squarely held that "*Johnso*n announced a substantive rule that has retroactive effect in cases on collateral review." *Id.* at 1268. And in "making" *Johnson* retroactive for purposes of § 2255(h)(2), the Court also noted

---

[1] *See also* Hertz & Liebman, 2 *Federal Habeas Corpus Practice & Procedure* § 28.3[d], at 1615 (6th ed. 2011) ("lack of merit" is "irrelevant" at the authorization stage); *Ochoa v. Simmons*, 485 F.3d 538, 541 (10th Cir. 2007) ("This statutory mandate does not direct the appellate court to engage in a preliminary merits assessment. Rather, it focuses our inquiry solely on the conditions specified in § 2244(b) that justify raising a new habeas claim."); *In re Turner*, 267 F.3d 225, 228 n.2 (3d Cir. 2001) (noting the absence of "any specific language in the statute that would support" requiring the applicant to "make a 'prima facie' showing that he has a meritorious [new rule of constitutional law] claim in the first place").

2

APPLICATION TO FILE SECOND OR SUCCESSIVE HABEAS CORPUS PETITION

Example Application #4 — Jasper Moore (cont.)

that "*Johnson* announced a new rule" of constitutional law. *Id.* at 1264. Indeed, it overruled prior Supreme Court precedent. *See Sykes v. United States*, 564 U.S. 1, 15 (2011); *James v. United States*, 550 U.S. 192, 210 n.6 (2007). In light of *Welch*, the applicant here has done more than make the requisite "prima facie showing"; he has in fact satisfied the requirements of § 2255(h)(2). The statute requires nothing more.

Not only is that limited scope of review compelled by the plain statutory language, but it "is necessary for the proper implementation of the collateral review structure created by" Congress. *Tyler v. Cain*, 533 U.S. 656, 664 (2001). The statute requires this Court to adjudicate successive applications within 30 days, 28 U.S.C. § 2244(b)(3)(D), and "this stringent time limit thus suggests that the courts of appeals do not have to engage in the difficult legal analysis" that may be required to adjudicate the § 2255 motion, *Tyler*, 533 U.S. at 664. Rather, the statute leaves that analysis to the district court, which not only must adjudicate the merits of the § 2255 motion, but must also determine whether it in fact satisfies the gatekeeping requirements. *See In re Moss*, 703 F.3d 1301, 1303 (11th Cir. 2013) (stressing that the gatekeeping determination is "limited," and "the merits of the [§ 2255] motion, along with any defenses" are to be decided in the district court); 28 U.S.C. § 2244(b)(4).

3

APPLICATION TO FILE SECOND OR SUCCESSIVE HABEAS CORPUS PETITION

Example Application #4 — Jasper Moore (cont.)

The present context illustrates the point. Because *Johnson* invalidated the residual clause of the Armed Career Criminal Act ("ACCA"), 18 U.S.C. § 924(e), but left intact the ACCA's enumerated offenses and elements/force clause, 135 S. Ct. at 2563, *Johnson* claims will require the courts to determine whether prior convictions continue to qualify as "violent felonies" without the residual clause. That will inevitably present complex legal issues. Because the vast majority of previously-qualifying convictions satisfied the residual clause, there is now great uncertainty about whether they will continue to qualify after *Johnson*.

That inquiry will depend on intricacies and minutiae of state law, including hard-to-locate jury instructions. *See United States v. Howard*, 742 F.3d 1334, 1346 (11th Cir. 2014) (sentencing court is "bound to follow any state court decisions that define or interpret the statute's substantive elements). And, in each case, the Court must ascertain what state law provided at the time the specific conviction occurred. Thus, the very same offense may qualify as a violent felony if committed in one year but not the next. Difficulties will also arise regarding whether offenses constitute a felony "conviction," which is also a matter state law, and whether prior convictions occurred on "occasions different from one another." *See* 18 U.S.C. §§ 921(a)(20), 924(e)(1). In addition to such legal complexities, *Johnson* claims will often involve factual and procedural complexities. In many cases, it will not be clear from the record which prior convictions were relied upon or which state statutory provisions are involved.

Furthermore, the sheer number of successive applications based on *Johnson* will be substantial, and the vast majority of them will be filed by *pro se* inmates. This Court will seldom have the benefit of counseled briefing, let alone adversarial presentation and oral argument. Addressing the merits under these sub-optimal conditions will risk erroneous and inconsistent rulings. Yet the stakes could not be higher: meritorious *Johnson* claims will result in at least a five-year sentencing reduction; there is an ever-shortening statute of limitations, *see* 28 U.S.C. § 2255(f)(3); and unsuccessful applicants are unable to seek further review, *see* 28 U.S.C. § 2244(b)(3)(E). In short, it would be both impracticable and contrary to the administration of justice for the Court to resolve these myriad complexities on a limited record within 30 days. Fortunately, the statute does not require this Court to do so.

In any event, even if this Court were to consider the merits of the proposed *Johnson* claim, the applicant here has still made a "prima facie showing." This is so because there is, at the very least, a "reasonable likelihood" that his claim has "possible merit" "warrant[ing] fuller exploration by the district court." *Holladay*, 331 F.3d at 1173–74 (citations omitted). Again, "[a] prima facie showing is not a particularly high standard." *Id.* (citation omitted). Thus, at this stage, the applicant

APPLICATION TO FILE SECOND OR SUCCESSIVE HABEAS CORPUS PETITION

Example Application #4 — Jasper Moore (cont.)

need not establish that he will ultimately prevail on the merits. And any doubts in that regard should be resolved in the applicant's favor, lest he be forever barred from having his *Johnson* claim considered on the merits. Instead, the proper course is to permit the district court to consider the claim in the first instance based on a complete record, full briefing, and adversarial presentation, as the statute's plain language and structure contemplate.

APPLICATION TO FILE SECOND OR SUCCESSIVE HABEAS CORPUS PETITION

Example Application #4 — Jasper Moore (cont.)

II. THE CATEGORICAL AND MODIFIED CATEGORICAL APPROACHES

Although it would be inappropriate at this stage for the Court to scrutinize the merits of the applicant's *Johnson* claim, doing so would require a careful application of the methodology prescribed by the Supreme Court. That methodology, summarized below, was refined most recently in *Descamps v. United States*, 133 S. Ct. 2275 (2013), which this Court has recognized is "the law of the land" and "must be ... followed." *United States v. Howard*, 73 F.3d 1334, 1344 n.2 (11th Cir. 2014).[2]

In determining whether a prior conviction qualifies as a "violent felony," sentencing courts must apply the "categorical approach." Under that approach, "courts may 'look only to the statutory definitions'"—*i.e.*, the elements—of a defendant's prior offenses, and *not* 'to the particular facts underlying those convictions.'" *Descamps*, 133 S. Ct. at 2283 (quoting *Taylor v. United States*, 495 U.S. 575, 600 (1990)). In adopting this approach, the Court emphasized both Sixth Amendment concerns (explained below) and the need to avert "'the practical

---

[2] This Court has held that, because *Descamps* did not announce a "new" rule of law, but rather clarified existing precedent on the categorical approach, it applies to all *Johnson* claims on collateral review. *Mays v. United States*, __ F.3d __, 2016 WL 1211420, at *4–5 (11th Cir. Mar. 29, 2016). In that context, the constitutional error is the court's reliance on the residual clause. *Descamps* merely clarified the long-standing analytical framework that will determine whether the prior convictions continue to qualify as violet felonies absent the residual clause. Thus, it essentially goes to whether the *Johnson* error was prejudicial. It is not an independent claim that is itself subject to the gatekeeping requirements.

difficulties and potential unfairness of a [daunting] factual approach.'" *Id.* at 2287 (quoting *Taylor*, 495 U.S. at 601). As a result, courts "look no further than the statute and judgment of conviction." *United States v. Estrella*, 758 F.3d 1239, 1244 (11th Cir. 2014) (citation omitted). And, in doing so, they "must presume that the conviction 'rested upon nothing more than the least of the acts' criminalized." *Moncrieffe v. Holder*, 133 S. Ct. 1678, 1684 (2011) (quoting *Johnson v. United States*, 559 U.S. 133, 137 (2010)).

After *Johnson*, a conviction may qualify as a "violent felony" if it is one of the ACCA's enumerated offenses. In determining whether a prior conviction so qualifies, the court must ask whether "the relevant statute has the same elements as the 'generic' ACCA crime." *Descamps*, 133 S. Ct. at 2283. If so, "then the prior conviction can serve as an ACCA predicate; so too if the statute defines the crime more narrowly, because anyone convicted under that law is necessarily guilty of all the generic crime's elements." *Id.* (citation and ellipses omitted). However, "if the statute sweeps more broadly than the generic crime, a conviction under that law cannot count as an ACCA predicate, even if the Jasper Moore actually committed the offense in its generic form." *Id.* "The key . . . is elements, not facts." *Id.*

A prior conviction may also qualify as a "violent felony" if it satisfies the ACCA's elements/force clause. The categorical approach applies equally in that context. Again looking no further than the statute and judgment of conviction, a conviction will qualify as an ACCA predicate "only if the statute on its face requires the government to establish, beyond a reasonable doubt and without exception, an element involving the use, attempted use, or threatened use of physical force against a person for every charge brought under the statute." *Estrella*, 758 F.3d at 1244 (citation omitted). "Whether, in fact, the person suffering under this particular conviction actually used, attempted to use, or threatened to use physical force against a person is quite irrelevant. Instead, the categorical approach focuses on whether in every case a conviction under the statute *necessarily* involves proof of the element." *Id.* (citations omitted).

To implement the categorical approach, the Supreme Court has "recognized a narrow range of cases in which sentencing courts" may look beyond the statute and judgment of conviction and employ what it is referred to as the "modified categorical approach." *Descamps*, 133 S. Ct. at 2283–84. Those cases arise where the statute of conviction contains alternative elements, some constituting a violent felony and some not. In that scenario, "the statute is 'divisible,'" in that it "comprises multiple, alternative versions of the crime." *Id.* at 2284. As a result, "a later sentencing court cannot tell, without reviewing something more [than the statute and judgment of conviction], if the defendant's conviction" qualifies as violent felony. *Id.*

Two key points must be made about the modified categorical approach. First, *Descamps* made clear that "the modified categorical approach can be applied only when dealing with a divisible statute." *Howard*, 742 F.3d at 1344. Thus, where the statute of conviction "does not concern any list of alternative elements" that must be found by a jury, there is no ambiguity requiring clarification, and therefore the "modified approach . . . has no role to play." *Descamps*, 133 S. Ct. at 2285–86; *see Estrella*, 758 F.3d at 1245–46; *Howard*, 742 F.3d at 1345–46. "[I]f the modified categorical approach is inapplicable," then the court must limit its review to the statute and judgment of conviction. *Howard*, 742 F.3d at 1345. And, even if a statute is divisible, the court need not employ the modified categorical approach if none of the alternatives would qualify. *Id.* at 1346–47.

Second, even where the modified categorical approach does apply, it does not permit courts to consider the defendant's underlying conduct. Rather, "the modified approach merely helps implement the categorical approach when a Jasper Moore was convicted of violating a divisible statute. The modified approach thus acts not as an exception, but instead as a tool. It retains the categorical approach's central feature: a focus on the elements, rather than the facts, of a crime." *Descamps*, 133 S. Ct. at 2285. And, in order to ensure that the focus remains on the statutory elements rather than the defendant's underlying conduct, the court is restricted in what documents it may consider.

10

APPLICATION TO FILE SECOND OR SUCCESSIVE HABEAS CORPUS PETITION

Example Application #4 — Jasper Moore (cont.)

Case: 16-13993   Date Filed: 06/24/2016   Page: 18 of 31

In *Shepard v. United States*, 544 U.S. 13, 15 (2005), the Supreme Court held that courts are "limited to examining the statutory definition, charging document, written plea agreement, transcript of plea colloquy, and any explicit factual finding by the trial judge to which the Jasper Moore assented." What these *Shepard* documents have in common is that they are "conclusive records made or used in adjudicating guilt." *Id.* at 21; *see id.* at 23 ("confin[ing]" the class of permissible documents "to records of the convicting court approaching the certainty of the record of conviction"). That accords with their function in the modified categorical approach—namely, to permit the court to identify the elements for which the Jasper Moore was convicted. *Descamps*, 133 S. Ct. at 2284.

Importantly, that inexorable focus on the elements derives in large part from "the categorical approach's Sixth Amendment underpinnings." *Id.* at 2287–88. Other than the fact of a prior conviction, a jury must find beyond a reasonable doubt any fact that increases a defendant's sentence beyond the prescribed statutory maximum. *Id.* at 2288 (citing *Apprendi v. New Jersey*, 530 U.S. 466, 490 (2000)). The reason for the "prior conviction" exception is that, during the earlier criminal proceeding, the Jasper Moore either had a jury or waived his constitutional right to one. *See Apprendi*, 530 U.S. at 488.

As the Supreme Court made clear in *Descamps*, the use of *Shepard* documents "merely assists the sentencing court in identifying the defendant's

11

crime of conviction, as we have held the Sixth Amendment permits." 133 S. Ct. at 2288. This is so because "the only facts the court can be sure the jury . . . found [beyond a reasonable doubt] are those constituting elements of the offense;" and, similarly, "when a Jasper Moore pleads guilty to a crime, he waives his right to a jury determination of only that offense's elements." *Id.* But where a court relies on non-*Shepard* documents to increase a defendant's sentence, it "extend[s] judicial factfinding" "beyond merely identifying a prior conviction," violating the Sixth Amendment. *Id.*

In sum, in determining whether a conviction qualifies as a violent felony, a court must generally consider only the statute and judgment of conviction. Only if the statute is divisible may the court consider *Shepard* documents, and it may do so only for the sole purpose of ascertaining the statutory elements for which the Jasper Moore was convicted. Once those elements are identified, the court must determine whether the least of the acts prohibited thereby constitutes a generic offense enumerated in the ACCA or necessarily requires the use, attempted use, or threatened use of violent, physical force against another. In no case may a court rely on non-*Shepard* documents or analyze whether the defendant's underlying conduct constituted a violent felony.

III. THE APPLICANT HAS, AT THE VERY LEAST, MADE A PRIMA FACIE SHOWING THAT HE IS NO LONGER AN ARMED CAREER CRIMINAL

In this case, the record does not reflect which convictions the court relied on to enhance the applicant's sentence under the ACCA. However, the record reveals the following convictions that arguably could have qualified as "violent felonies" before *Johnson*: 1) Burglary of an Occupied Dwelling, PSI ¶ 20; 2) Burglary of a Conveyance with Assault, PSI ¶ 21; 3) Robbery with a Firearm, PSI ¶22; 4) Armed Robbery, PSI ¶ 23; 5) Attempted Robbery, Shooting or Throwing a Deadly Missile, PSI ¶ 24; 6) Robbery and Burglary with Assault, PSI ¶ 26; In light of *Johnson*, the applicant no longer has three qualifying "violent felonies" and is therefore no longer an armed career criminal, as explained below.

Under Florida law, "'burglary' means entering or remaining in a dwelling, a structure, or a conveyance with the intent to commit an offense therein . . . ." Fla. Stat. § 810.02. Critically, the statute defines the elements of "structure" and "dwelling" to include the curtilage thereof. Fla. Stat. § 810.011(1)-(2). Accordingly, the Florida burglary statute is broader than generic burglary, which does not include burglary of the curtilage. *See James v. United States*, 550 U.S. 192, 212 (2007). And the statute is also indivisible because "structure" and "dwelling" are defined to include the curtilage, and the Florida Supreme Court has made clear that burglary of the curtilage is not an alternative element or crime.

Baker v. State, 636 So.2d 1342, 1344 (Fla. 1994) ("There is no crime denominated burglary of a curtilage.").

Because the Florida burglary statute is overbroad and indivisible, convictions for burglary of a structure or dwelling can never qualify as generic burglary, and the modified categorical approach does not apply. *See United States v. Howard*, 742 F.3d 1342, 1345–49 (11th Cir. 2014) (where "none of the alternatives may match the elements of the generic crime . . . , the court can and should skip over any *Shepard* documents and simply declare that the prior conviction is not a predicate offense based on the statute itself"). Accordingly, this Court has granted several successive applications involving Florida burglary. *See, e.g., In re Gomez*, No. 16-10516, Order at 5 (Mar. 3, 2016) ("Convictions for burglary under Florida law do not qualify as 'violent felonies'" after *Johnson*); *In re Barber*, No. 16-10107, Order at 5–6 (Feb. 10, 2016) (observing that "the definition of 'burglary' under Florida law is broader than that of generic burglary" because it includes the curtilage, "the definitions of 'dwelling' and 'structure' under Fla. Stat. § 810.011 [are not] divisible," and therefore "burglary under [Fla. Stat.] § 810.02 can qualify as a 'violent felony' under only the residual clause"); *In re Urquhart*, No. 16-11460 (Apr. 29, 2016). The same outcome is warranted here.

The Supreme Court has made clear that a burglary of a conveyance is not "generic" burglary. *See James v. United States*, 550 U.S. 192, 197 (2007) (generic burglary is "'an unlawful or unprivileged entry into, or remaining in, a building or other structure, with intent to commit a crime'") (quoting *Taylor v. United States*, 495 U.S. 575, 598 (1990)).

According to *United States v. Welch*, 683 F.3d 1304 (11th Cir. 2012), a pre-1999 conviction for "strong-arm robbery" under Fla. Stat. §812.13(1) must be analyzed as a "robbery by sudden snatching," an offense for which "any degree of force" sufficed. In *Welch*, the Court distinguished *United States v. Lockley*, 632 F.3d 1238 (11th Cir. 2011) where it had found a 2001 conviction for attempted robbery was a "crime of violence" within both the elements and residual clauses of the Guidelines. Welch argued, and the Court agreed, that *Lockley* was not dispositive of whether his 1996 conviction under §812.13(1) was a violent felony, "because Lockley was convicted after Florida promulgated the 'sudden snatching' statute, *so snatching from the person might [have] furnish[ed] the basis for [the 1996] robbery conviction here but not in Lockley*." *Welch*, 683 F.3d at 1312 (emphasis added).

Although the language of §812.13(1) has never changed, what *did* change — quite significantly in 1999 (*after* both Welch and Jasper Moore were convicted) — was Florida's statutory scheme for robberies. In 1999, the Florida legislature enacted a separate "robbery by sudden snatching" statute, Fla. Stat. §812.131. But as of 1996 (before the enactment of that statute), the Court recognized in *Welch*, non-forceful snatching offenses were still being prosecuted as "strong-arm" robberies under §812.13(1) in many Florida DCAs – and importantly, in the Fourth DCA, the jurisdiction where both Welch and Jasper Moore were convicted. *See Welch*, 683 F.3d at 1311 and nn.28-38 (noting with significance that in 1996 when Welch was convicted, "the state courts of appeal were divided on whether a snatching, as of a purse, or cash from a person's hand, or jewelry on the person's body, amounted to robbery," and that in *Santiago v. State*, 497 So.2d 975, 976 (Fla. 4th DCA 1986), the 4th DCA had upheld a strong-arm robbery conviction for simply tearing a necklace off a victim's neck, explaining that evidence of force "*be it ever so little*" was sufficient). Only *after* Welch was convicted, the Court underscored, was §813.131 enacted, establishing a separate crime of "'robbery by sudden snatching,' in between larceny and robbery." 683 F.3d at 1311.

The Court recognized in *Welch* that the enactment of §812.131 "appear[ed] to have been a legislative response" to the Florida Supreme Court's decision in *Robinson v. State*, 692 So.2d 883, 886 (Fla. 1997), which clarified that "there must be resistance by the victim that is overcome by the physical force of the offender" to establish robbery, "so that the intermediate appellate decisions holding mere snatching to be sufficient were put in doubt." *Welch*, 683 F.3d at 1311.

16

APPLICATION TO FILE SECOND OR SUCCESSIVE HABEAS CORPUS PETITION

Example Application #4 — Jasper Moore (cont.)

Nonetheless, the *Welch* Court found *Robinson*'s clarification of the law irrelevant to whether the defendant's 1996 Florida robbery conviction qualified as an ACCA predicate, since "[i]n 'determining whether a Jasper Moore was convicted of a 'violent felony,'" the Court must apply "the version of the state law that the Jasper Moore was actually convicted of violating." *Welch*, 683 F.3d at 1311 (citing *McNeill v. United States*, 563 U.S. 816, 131 S.Ct. 2218, 2222 (2011)).

As this Court recognized in *Welch*, as of 1996 – and therefore, in [YEAR] when Jasper Moore was convicted as well – the "latest authoritative pronouncement" as to the elements of robbery under §812.13(1) was in *McCloud v. State*, 335 So.2d 257 (Fla. 1976). And in *McCloud*, the Florida Supreme Court expressly held that "any degree of force suffices" for robbery, including the minimal amount of force necessary to "extract" property from a victim's "grasp," so long as the taking is not by "stealth." *McCloud*, 335 So.2d 258-259 (what distinguished robbery from larceny is the victim's awareness of the taking). In *Santiago*, Florida's Fourth DCA specifically cited and strictly followed *McCloud*, in holding that "[t]he facts of this case [reaching into the victim's car and tearing two necklaces from around her neck], unlike picking a pocket or snatching a purse without any force or violence, shows sufficient force, *be it ever so little* to support robbery." 497 So.2d at 976 (emphasis added).

17

APPLICATION TO FILE SECOND OR SUCCESSIVE HABEAS CORPUS PETITION

Example Application #4 — Jasper Moore (cont.)

Like Welch, Jasper Moore pled guilty to robbery under §812.13 "at a time when mere snatching" with "any degree of force" sufficed for conviction under then-controlling Florida Supreme Court and Fourth DCA law. *Welch,* 683 F.3d at 1311-1312. Accordingly, for the same reason this Court assumed for its "violent felony" analysis that Welch's 1996 robbery conviction under §812.13(1) was for "robbery by sudden snatching," it should so assume for Jasper Moore's conviction here as well. The correctness of *Welch*'s "least culpable conduct" analysis, notably, has since been validated by the Supreme Court in *Moncrieffe v. Holder*, 133 S.Ct. 1678, 1684 (2013).

Admittedly, in *Welch* this Court did not follow its own "least culpable conduct" analysis to its logical conclusion under the ACCA's elements clause. However, it did agree with Welch that at least *"[a]rguably the elements clause would not apply to mere snatching." Id.* at 1312-1313 (emphasis added). Although the Court believed that question was "not cut and dried" at that time, it found it unnecessary to resolve definitively in 2012 since then-controlling precedent compelled a finding that even a non-forceful snatching was a "violent felony" within the residual clause. *Id.*

Now that the residual clause has been excised from the ACCA, however, and the Supreme Court has remanded in Welch's own §2255 case to definitively decide the elements clause question this Court left open in 2012, *see Welch v.*

United States, ___ U.S. ___, 136 S. Ct. 1257, 1268 (April 18, 2016), the Court will have to resolve it using the categorical approach as clarified by the Supreme Court in *Moncrieffe* and *Descamps*.

Based upon the foregoing argument, and the Supreme Court's holding in *Welch* that a certificate of appealability should issue in that case since "reasonable jurists could debate whether Welch is entitled to relief," 136 S.Ct. at 1268, Jasper Moore has made the requisite prima facie showing here.

That Jasper Moore was sentenced for "armed robbery" under Fla. Stat. §812.13(2) in 1985 does not change the above analysis. As a threshold matter, it is clear from the standard robbery instruction at the time of Jasper Moore's conviction, that in 1985 Fla. Stat. §812.13(2)(a) and (b) were simply penalty enhancement provisions, *not* separate enhanced "offenses" with additional "elements." Notably – and differently than today – juries were *not* instructed in 1985 that they needed to find that the state proved any of the "aggravating circumstances" in the statute ("carrying," of some "weapon," "in the course of committing a robbery") *beyond a reasonable doubt*. Therefore, according to *Descamps*, the fact that Jasper Moore's underlying robbery conviction under §812.13(1) was categorically overbroad, ends the ACCA elements clause inquiry. Jasper Moore's ACCA sentence cannot be upheld based upon judicial findings as

APPLICATION TO FILE SECOND OR SUCCESSIVE HABEAS CORPUS PETITION

Example Application #4 — Jasper Moore (cont.)

to facts on which he never had the protection of the Sixth Amendment. *Descamps*, 133 S.Ct. at 2289.

But notably, *even if* Jasper Moore's state court judge or a jury *had* been required to find the "aggravating circumstances" in §§812.13(2) beyond a reasonable doubt, that would not change the result now dictated by *Descamps* in any manner, since each of the "aggravating circumstances" in §812.13(2) is itself categorically overbroad vis-a-vis the ACCA's element clause.

First, §812.13(2) permits a sentence enhancement for "armed robbery" simply for "*carrying*" a weapon, which does *not* necessitate either using it, brandishing it in a threatening manner, or even visibly displaying it. According to *State v. Baker*, 452 So.2d 927 (Fla. 1984), it simply requires "possessing" it. *See id.* at 929 ("The victim may never even be aware that a robber is armed, so long as the perpetrator has the weapon in his possession during the offense."). In *United States v. Archer*, 531 F.3d 1347 (2008), this Court expressly held that the mere act of "carrying" a weapon, and specifically a firearm, "does *not* involve the use, attempted use, or threatened use of force, and so is *not* a crime of violence under [the elements clause." *Id.* at 1349 (emphasis added).

Second, the word "weapon" in §812.13(2)(b) [or "deadly weapon" in §812.13(2)(a)] is not only indeterminate but categorically overbroad vis-a-vis any offense within the elements clause. Poison, anthrax, and chemical weapons are

20

"weapons" that may easily cause death without the "use" of *any* "physical force." Other courts, notably, have declared convictions overbroad and outside the elements clause for precisely this reason. *See, e.g.,* *United States v. Perez-Vargas*, 414 F.3d 1282 (10th Cir. 2005); *United States v. Torres-Miguel*, 701 F.3d 165, 168-169 (4th Cir. 2012); *Matter of Guzman-Polanco*, 26 I & N Dec. 713, 717-718 (BIA Feb. 24, 2016). And although the Florida legislature has expressly defined the term "weapon" in Fla. Stat. §790.001(13) to include a "chemical weapon," under Florida law, the list of "weapons" in §790.001(13) has never limited the universe of items that may qualify a Florida Jasper Moore for an "armed robbery" enhancement. Juries and courts have always been permitted to use the much broader, open-ended definition of "weapon" in the standard §812.13 instruction, pursuant to which "any object that could be used to cause death or inflict serious bodily injury" qualifies as a "weapon." Significantly, that definition creates an "objective test," pursuant to which any item could qualify as a "weapon," if it caused great bodily harm to the victim "during the course of the robbery," even if that was *not* the defendant's intent. *See Williams v. State*, 651 So.2d 1242, 1243 (Fla. 2nd DCA 1995)(under this "objective test," even coffee could trigger enhanced penalty for "armed robbery," if it caused great bodily harm).

Finally, the phrase "in the course of committing the robbery" in §§812.13(2), is itself broadly defined in a separate provision, §812.13(3)(a), which

21

APPLICATION TO FILE SECOND OR SUCCESSIVE HABEAS CORPUS PETITION

Example Application #4 — Jasper Moore (cont.)

explains: "An act shall be deemed 'in the course of committing the robbery" *if it occurs in an attempt to commit a robbery or in flight after the attempt or commission*." Because of that expansive definition, Florida courts have upheld an enhanced penalty for "armed robbery" upon evidence that a Jasper Moore simply stole a gun *after* robbing a victim of money and other property, and fled with the gun as part of the "loot." *State v. Brown*, 496 So.2d 194 (Fla. 3rd DCA 1986) (defendant's conduct "fell within the unequivocal reach of the armed robbery provision," even if he did not "carry" the firearm during the "taking of the proceeds" from the cash register, because he then stole a gun from under the cash register, and fled the scene with it). Such conduct plainly involves no more than knowing, illegal "possession" of a firearm, which this Court has held is *not* a "violent felony" under the ACCA. *United States v. McGill*, 618 F.3d 1273, 1279 (11th Cir. 2010).

Although a panel of this Court noted in 2006 that it had "conclud[ed] without difficulty," that a Florida armed robbery conviction was "undeniably a conviction for a violent felony," *United States v. Dowd*, 451 F.3d 1244, 1255 (11th Cir. 2006), it offered nothing beyond "[s]ee 18 U.S.C. §924(e)(2)(B)(i)" to support that "undeniable" conclusion. There is no stated analysis in the opinion, and it is therefore unclear what the panel relied upon to reach that conclusion.

Moreover, *Dowd* was decided prior to *Archer* (in 2010); *Curtis Johnson v. United States*, 559 U.S. 133 (2010) (*Johnson I*); *United States v. Welch*, 683 F.3d 1304 (11th Cir. 2012); *Moncrieffe* (in 2013); and *Descamps* (in 2013 as well). And the *Dowd* panel's presumption that a 1975 Florida "armed robbery" conviction was "undeniably" an offense within the ACCA's elements clause cannot be squared with the strict, element-by-element comparison now required by the categorical approach.

This Court has long recognized that its "first duty" is always "to follow the dictates of the United States Supreme Court," and it "*must consider*" whether intervening Supreme Court decisions have "effectively overruled" a prior precedent. *United States v. Contreras*, 667 F.2d 976, 979 (11th Cir. 1982). In similar circumstances, the Court has easily declared prior precedents "effectively overruled." *See Dawson v. Scott*, 50 F.3d 884, 892 n. 20 (11th Cir. 1995); *Archer*, 531 F.3d at 1352; *United States v. Howard*, 742 F.3d 1334, 1337, 1343-1345 (11th Cir. 2014); *see also* Scalia, Antonin, J., *The Rule of Law as a Law of Rules*, 56 U. Chi. L. Rev. 1175, 1177 (1989) (lower courts are not only bound by the narrow "holdings" of higher court decisions, but also by their "mode of analysis"). Based upon the different "mode of analysis" now dictated by *Archer*, *Curtis Johnson*, *Welch*, *Moncrieffe*, and *Descamps*, *Dowd* has been effectively overruled at this time.

APPLICATION TO FILE SECOND OR SUCCESSIVE HABEAS CORPUS PETITION

Example Application #4 — Jasper Moore (cont.)

Case: 16-13993   Date Filed: 06/24/2016   Page: 31 of 31

Although a panel of this Court recently found after reviewing a *pro se* inmate's application to file a second or successive §2255 motion in light of *Johnson*, that a Florida "armed robbery" conviction "appears to contain 'as an element the use, attempted use, or threatened use of physical force against the person of another," and that "[n]either *Johnson* nor any other case" suggests that such a conviction did not count as an ACCA predicate," *In re Robinson*, ___ F.3d ___, 2016 WL 1583616 (11th Cir. April 19, 2016), none of the above-cited cases were cited by Mr. Robinson, nor did he make any of the above arguments in his *pro se* application. However, even assuming Mr. Robinson did not show a "reasonable likelihood" that his *pro se* challenge to a Florida armed robbery conviction had "possible merit," Jasper Moore here has made a completely different, much stronger showing sufficient to "warrant fuller exploration by the district court. *Holladay*, 331 F.3d at 1173-74.

<6> PREPARATION OF APPENDIX FOR ACCOMPANYING EXHIBITS

Organization of Appendix

As stated in the previous chapter, and in *Smith's Guide to State Habeas Corpus Relief for State Prisoners*, it may be more practical to prepare your appendix before preparing your application. In doing so, the appendix can be used as an aid when preparing your application, enabling you to cite the specific exhibit that proves each material fact you set forth in your application, as well as that exhibit's location in the appendix.

The appendix of accompanying exhibits should have a caption and a title, followed by a list of all exhibits in support of your application. These exhibits should be listed alphabetically unless there are more then twenty-six of them. In that instance, use numbers instead of letters. (See the example appendix of accompanying exhibits at the end of this chapter.)

Page Numbering (Optional)

If you have a lot of exhibits, you may number the pages of the appendix, starting at the first exhibit. Just use a pen or pencil and write the page number at the bottom right corner of each page. You can then refer to an actual page number when citing an exhibit establishing material fact. (Note: do not mark your original exhibits; mark *only* copies.)

Binding

Most courts today use electronic filing, so it is unnecessary to staple your pleadings. In fact, some United States courts of appeal specifically ask you not to staple your pleadings. It is best to leave your pleadings unbound.

Affidavits

If your testimony is necessary to make a prima facie showing in order to meet the newly discovered evidence requirement for filing a second or successive petition, then your affidavit should be the first exhibit listed in the appendix. That is, of course, unless the United States court of appeals in your circuit requires you to provide specific legal pleadings with your application. (See Appendix A, at the end of this book.) In such instance, those pleadings should be listed first, then your affidavit, followed by any other exhibits.

At the end of this chapter you can find example affidavits to help you in preparing your own. The examples may also be useful when preparing affidavits for other witnesses whose testimony may be necessary to prove your claim(s).

German psychologists developed a system they called *"Statement Validity Assessment"* (SVA) which is now used to determine the credibility of children in sexual abuse cases. The system can also be used in assessing the credibility of adults. The SVA is a list of nineteen indicators to look for when determining whether a story someone is telling is true or false.

Aldert Vrij, the author of *Detecting Lies and Deceit*, discusses how the SVA system can be used in everyday situations to help spot liars and deceivers. SVA is widely known and used by law enforcement, including police officers, detectives, prosecutors, defense attorneys, judges, etc.

Below are thirteen of the most notable and applicable indicators, which can be embedded in your own affidavit, and the affidavits of other witnesses, lending them more credibility.

1. Unstructured Production

True stories tend to jump around in time, moving forward and backward, when being told. For example, the person telling the story may start with the reason for the story and what he or she wants to convey first before giving the narrative, providing more details as the story progresses. The less likely a story was rehearsed, the more likely it is true, especially when it is of a serious incident.

2. Quantity of Details

When a person lies, he or she may not give a lot of details. Instead, that person will likely just continue to repeat what was already said, when asked for more specific details. The more detailed a story is, the more likely it is true. Usually when a person makes up a story, he or she is only concerned with telling a basic outline, something easy to remember and deliver, especially when under pressure. Of course, if the person has a sufficient amount of time to make the story up and then rehearse it, he or she can tell a very convincing lie.

3. Contextual Embedding

"I was talking to Mike about coming over to take me to the store. And it being a nice day, I thought I'd wait outside for him. As I walked to the door, I heard three gunshots and saw a green Chevy speed off." This is contextual embedding, injecting information about the speaker's daily life before describing some other event. Contextual embedding doesn't usually happen when the story is made up.

4. Descriptions of Interactions

When a story is true, the person telling it will usually provide details about what other people said and did. For example, "When I went back to the Jackson County

Detention Center to await my third trial, Fred asked me, 'Let's cut the shit, what plea would you take?' I answered, 'I'll take ten years.' Fred grinned and said, 'I bet you would. I can't take the State an offer like that. It's *highly* unlikely they would agree to it.'"

5. Reproduction of Speech

Liars do not usually reproduce parts of dialogue between them or other people in their story. For example, he or she would say something like, "I told him to stop and put his hands up, but he didn't do it. I was afraid. I fired seventeen warning shots. I didn't mean to kill him." This example sounds extreme, but the point is that when someone is telling the truth he or she wants to give the listener a play-by-play of everything that was said and done by everyone in the story.

6. Unusual Details

"Between the dates of July 17 and July 19, 2004, I personally visited the above listed address on three (3) occasions. At my first attempt, on July 17, 2004, no one answered the door. At my second attempt, on July 18, 2004, a woman answered the door. She indicated that Mr. Franco did not reside at that location, nor did she know a Daniel Franco or where I might locate him. At my third attempt, on July 19, 2004, a second woman answered the door. She indicated that she is Daniel Franco's sister and that my earlier contact was with Mr. Franco's mother. The woman indicated that Mr. Franco previously resided at this location; however, he no longer resides there. She was not able to provide an address at which Mr. Franco could be contacted." The more unusual the details, the more credible the story is. In this example, it is the context of the statements made by the two women that make the situation unusual, pointing out the untruthful statements by the first woman.

7. Accurately Reported Details Misunderstood

This happens in contexts where a person is describing a situation about which he or she doesn't have all the facts to fully understand, but the person listening does. This indicator is mostly applicable to the telling of a story by a child, in naive terms, of a sexual situation he or she was put in by a pedophile. But it can be powerful evidence in a case where a witness provides testimony that fills in the gaps of other evidence.

8. Accounts of Subjective Mental State

Truthful accounts generally include the thoughts and feelings of the person telling them. For example, "the gunshots were so close that I grabbed my chest and fell to the ground. I was scared I was hit."

9. Attribution of the Perpetrator's Mental State

This is when a person describes what he or she believes another person was feeling. For example, "He was jittery, pacing back and forth, looking around the room as if he knew something was about to happen."

10. Spontaneous Corrections

If a person is excited when telling a true story, he or she may make corrections and add facts during their account, as if reliving it and recalling events clearer as the story being told progresses.

11. Admitting Lack of Memory

Sometimes things happen so fast or appear to be so inconsequential that certain details don't get stored in the person's long-term memory. A person telling the truth will usually admit a lack of memory if the story is true. But when a person says, "I can't remember," or, "I don't recall," to a direct question, the person is likely being evasive and doesn't want to incriminate themselves or someone else.

12. Raising Doubts About One's Own Testimony

When someone is being truthful, he or she may admit to being wrong about something he or she heard or witnessed. This doesn't mean the person is lying, it just shows that the person isn't sure and doesn't want to provide misinformation.

13. Self-deprecation

When someone is telling the truth, he or she will give information that may be incriminating or make him or her look foolish. For example, "When those guys started arguing at the party, I left because I didn't want to get beat up in front of the girls from my neighborhood."

The above is not an all-inclusive list of how an account can reveal itself as true or false, but it is a useful guide. Look for these indicators in the example affidavits and implement them in your own affidavit and those of any witnesses you may have.

PREPARATION OF APPENDIX FOR ACCOMPANYING EXHIBITS

Example—Appendix for Exhibits in Support of Application

UNITED STATES COURT OF APPEALS
FOR THE EIGHTH CIRCUIT

In re: Zachary A. Smith,)
)
       Petitioner.)
)
) Cause No. 16-2250
)

EXHIBITS IN SUPPORT OF APPLICATION TO FILE

SECOND OR SUCCESSIVE PETITION FOR A WRIT OF HABEAS CORPUS

1. Affidavit of Zachary A. Smith, Petitioner's Exhibit A.

2. First trial transcript page, Petitioner's Exhibit B.

3. Fax by Bronwyn E. Werner, Petitioner's Exhibit C.

4. Docket sheet entries: State v. Smith, Petitioner's Exhibit D.

5. Elizabeth Carlyle letter, Petitioner's Exhibit E.

6. Memo to case file, Petitioner's Exhibit F.

7. Nancy Wiebe affidavit, Petitioner's Exhibit G.

8. Chief Disciplinary Counsel's Report and Recommendation, Petitioner's Exhibit H.

9. Daniel Franco's Application to Surrender License, Petitioner's Exhibit I.

10. In re: Daniel L. Franco, Supreme Court of Kansas, Petitioner's Exhibit J.

11. Affidavit of Zachary A. Smith, Petitioner's Exhibit K.

12. Andrew Schroeder letter (Oct. 23, 2002), Petitioner's Exhibit L.

13. Andrew Schroeder letter (Oct. 23, 2002), Petitioner's Exhibit M.

14. State's Response to Request for Discovery, Petitioner's Exhibit N.

PREPARATION OF APPENDIX FOR ACCOMPANYING EXHIBITS

Example—Appendix for Exhibits in Support of Application (cont.)

15. State's Supplemental Response to Defendant's Request for Discovery, Petitioner's Exhibit O.

16. Rule 26(a) Disclosure of Defendants in Smith v. Roger Lewis, et al., Petitioner's Exhibit P.

17. John R. Pierson statement, Petitioner's Exhibit Q.

18. KCPD booking sheet for Cynthia J. Frost, Petitioner's Exhibit R.

19. Nancy Wiebe letter, Petitioner's Exhibit S.

20. Jim Miller affidavit, Petitioner's Exhibit T.

21. George A. Halterman affidavit, Petitioner's Exhibit U.

22. Steven J. Pietroforte, Petitioner's Exhibit V.

23. Findings of Fact, Conclusions of Law and Judgment in Matthew Davis v. State of Missouri, Petitioner's Exhibit W.

24. Letter and stipulation for dismissal in Smith v. Lewis, et al., Petitioner's Exhibit X.

25. KCPD Procedural Instruction 91-12B, 91-12A, Annex E, Search of Premises, Petitioner's Exhibit Y.

26. Stanley v. Bartley, 465 F.3d 810 (7th Cir. 2006), Petitioner's Exhibit Z.

Respectfully Submitted,

ZA Smith
Zachary A. Smith,
Reg. No. 521163
Crossroads Corr. Center
1115 E. Pence Road
Cameron, Missouri 64429

Petitioner

CERTIFICATE OF SERVICE

I hereby certify that on this 12th day of May, 2016, a true

2

Example—*Appendix for Exhibits in Support of Application (cont.)*

and correct copy of the foregoing was mailed, postage prepaid, to: Chris Koster, Attorney General, P.O. Box 899, Jefferson City, MO 65102.

Z. A. Smith
Zachary A. Smith

PREPARATION OF APPENDIX FOR ACCOMPANYING EXHIBITS

Example—Affidavit of Zachary A Smith

IN THE CIRCUIT COURT OF DEKALB COUNTY, MISSOURI
AT MAYSVILLE

ZACHARY A. SMITH,)
)
        Petitioner,)
)
  v.) Case No. _____
)
RHONDA PASH, WARDEN,)
)
        Respondent.)

AFFIDAVIT OF ZACHARY A. SMITH

My name is Zachary A. Smith. I am over eighteen years of age, of sound mind, and capable of executing this affidavit. Being duly sworn, I depose and state, to the best of my knowledge and belief, the following.

1. In 1998, I filed a 1983 Civil Rights Action, Zachary A. Smith v. Roger Lewis, et al., Case No. 98-0721-CV-DW, United States District Court, Western District. Prior to my third criminal trial, I filed a motion to stay the proceedings in Smith v. Lewis, et al., until after the criminal trial.

2. The criminal trial started April 24, 2000, and ended May 1, 2000. I was convicted and sentenced June 16, 2000.

3. When I returned to Crossroads Corr. Center, the stay in Smith v. Lewis, et al., was lifted. During the discovery phase, I received two documents that I was never provided during the discovery in State v. Smith, Case No. CR95-4292, a statement by John R. Pierson (Petitioner's Exhibit G) and a booking sheet for Cynthia J. Frost (Petitioner's Exhibit H).

4. On November 15, 2002, a settlement was reached in Smith v. Lewis, et al., and the civil case was dismissed with prejudice (Petitioner's Exhibit N).

1

PREPARATION OF APPENDIX FOR ACCOMPANYING EXHIBITS

Example—Affidavit of Zachary A Smith (cont.)

5. I wrote letters and made phone calls to appellate attorney, Andrew Schroeder, asking him to search my trial file for the Pierson statement (Petitioner's Exhibit G) and the booking sheet (Petitioner's Exhibit C). Mr. Schroeder told me that he would have Nancy Wiebe look through the file; I never received a definite answer from either one of them. Instead, they sent the entire trial file to me. And when I received it, I searched through it--the Pierson statement and booking sheet was not in the trial file; my trial attorneys never received them as part of the state's discovery disclosure.

6. Because I never received the Pierson statement and booking sheet of Cynthia Frost from the state, I made a Brady claim (PCR L.F. 8, 54-55). However, Fredrick Duchardt said that he could not remember whether he ever saw the Pierson statement and booking sheet of Cynthia Frost as part of the discovery provided by the state; Daniel Franco could not be found to question him about the undisclosed documents.

7. As a result, I was forced to drop the Brady claim because I could not meet the factual and legal basis of the claim by proving the Brady violation by a preponderance of the evidence. In 2003, Daniel Miller was a respected assistant prosecuting attorney and his credibility outweighed mine, a convicted felon--as far as meeting the legal standard of a preponderance of evidence.

8. However, I have since discovered new evidence, enabling me to now meet my burden of proof, proving that the state, through Daniel C. Miller, withheld favorable evidence from me throughout three first degree murder trials.

2

PREPARATION OF APPENDIX FOR ACCOMPANYING EXHIBITS

Example—Affidavit of Zachary A Smith (cont.)

Zachary A. Smith
Zachary A. Smith

 Subscribed and sworn to before me, a Notary Public, this 13 day of February, 2015.

Notary Public

My Commission Expires:

```
          VINCENT NEGUS
     Notary Public - Notary Seal
        STATE OF MISSOURI
          DeKalb County
       Commission # 13898623
   My Commission Expires: 11-18-2017
```

3

PREPARATION OF APPENDIX FOR ACCOMPANYING EXHIBITS

Example—Affidavit of Jim Miller

IN THE CIRCUIT COURT OF JACKSON COUNTY, MISSOURI
STATE OF MISSOURI

ZACHARY SMITH, §
§
Plaintiff §
§
vs. § Cause No. 03CV204050
§
STATE OF MISSOURI, § Division 13
§
Defendant §

EXHIBIT 5

Affidavit of Jim Miller

My name is Jim Miller. I am over the age of eighteen years and am fully competent to make this affidavit.

I am an investigator located in Springfield, Missouri. Elizabeth Carlyle retained me to locate Daniel Franco.

Ms. Carlyle provided two (2) social security numbers for Mr. Franco (515-61-0497 and 515-62-0497), a date of birth of December 9, 1955 and a Missouri bar number of 42232. I was also aware that Mr. Franco had been disbarred.

On January 2, 2004, my initial investigation indicated that as of July 2003, Mr. Franco was employing three different aliases with no hard addresses for any of the names. I also determined that Mr. Franco had relatives in the state of California. No current phone numbers were available for any of those relatives.

By January 28, 2004, I had determined that Mr. Franco was not residing in California and determined that he might possibly be incarcerated based on an initial check of his name and known aliases. I began a search of institutions to determine whether or not he was incarcerated.

<u>AFFIDAVIT OF JIM MILLER</u> – Page 1

Example—*Affidavit of Jim Miller (cont.)*

I located a Daniel Franco, age 49, at USP Allenwood with a release date of 2007. It was later determined that this was not the Daniel Franco I was attempting to locate.

By March 23, 2004, I was able to acquire additional dates of birth of 12-9-55 and 12-9-53 and an accurate name of Luis D. Franco. Information was received from the Department of Treasury indicating that Dan Franco had possibly traveled to Bogota, Columbia and not returned from that trip, flagging him as having a passport infraction.

On March 28, 2004, I again ran all known aliases, which included David L. Franco, Daniel Franco and Luis D. Franco. I attempted to locate him through who I believed to be his ex-wife in that she appeared on all of his federal tax liens and judgments. I was unsuccessful in locating Ms. Lana Jo Franco.

I then returned to the California connection and was able to determine that his father's name is Dr. Sergio Franco with a home address of 441 Ramona Avenue, Sierra Madre, California, 91024. I located a home phone number of 626-836-3782 and a fax number of 626-294-2966.

On March 28, 2004, I contacted the residence at that above-listed phone number and made contact with a female who represented herself as Daniel Franco's mother. I confirmed with her that her son was formerly an attorney in the Kansas City, Missouri area to be sure that I had the correct relatives. I identified myself and indicated that I was attempting to get in contact with Daniel. She responded that he lives with them. At that point, a male picked up a second telephone in the house, identified himself as Dr. Franco and expressed agitation at my phone call and what he considered an invasion of privacy. His mother then indicated that Daniel was at church and she would relay a message to him upon his return. I did not receive a return phone call from Daniel Franco.

<u>AFFIDAVIT OF JIM MILLER</u> – Page 2

PREPARATION OF APPENDIX FOR ACCOMPANYING EXHIBITS

Example—Affidavit of Jim Miller (cont.)

On March 28, 2004, I detailed my findings to Ms. Carlyle, including the contact information I had discovered for Daniel Franco.

_____
Jim Miller

Subscribed and sworn to before me this 15th day of ~~December, 2004~~ June, 2005

_____
Notary Public

My Commission Expires:

> Katherine L. Armstrong – Notary Public
> Notary Seal For State of
> Missouri – Greene County
> My Commission Expires 10/18/2007

AFFIDAVIT OF JIM MILLER – Page 3

Example—Affidavit of George A. Haltermann, III

IN THE CIRCUIT COURT OF JACKSON COUNTY, MISSOURI
STATE OF MISSOURI

ZACHARY SMITH,	§ § § §	
Plaintiff	§ §	
vs.	§ §	Cause No. 03CV204050
STATE OF MISSOURI,	§ §	Division 13
Defendant	§ §	

AFFIDAVIT OF GEORGE A. HALTERMAN, III

My name is George A. Halterman. I am over 18 years of age and am fully competent to make this affidavit.

I am an attorney practicing in Sierra Madre, California. I was retained by Elizabeth Carlyle to obtain and serve a subpoena for a deposition to a Mr. Daniel Franco.

The address Ms. Carlyle provided for Daniel Franco was 441 Ramona Avenue, Sierre Madre, California, 91024.

My agreement with Ms. Carlyle was to file a Petition for Issuance of Deposition Subpoena re Deposition for Use Outside of California with the Court in California. I was also to attempt to serve the subpoena on Mr. Franco for the deposition scheduled August 6, 2004. I filed the petition and received an order that the subpoena be issued. A copy of the petition and order are attached hereto.

Between the dates of July 16 and July 23, 2004, I personally visited the above listed address on three (3) occasions. On each occasion, it appeared that no one was home at the time.

AFFIDAVIT OF GEORGE HALTERMAN, III – Page 1

Example—Affidavit of George A. Haltermann, III (cont.)

Following those attempts, a certified letter was sent to Mr. Franco at the same address marked "Do Not Forward – Address Correction Requested." No response was received, and therefore a substituted service was not possible.

[signature]
George A. Halterman, III

Subscribed and sworn to before me this 11th day of December, 2004.

[Notary seal: Nancy Sue Shollenberger, COMM. # 1299517, NOTARY PUBLIC • CALIFORNIA, LOS ANGELES COUNTY, Comm. Exp. MARCH 31, 2005]

[signature] Nancy Sue Shollenberger
Notary Public

My commission expires: 3/31/05

AFFIDAVIT OF GEORGE HALTERMAN, III – Page 2

IN THE CIRCUIT COURT OF JACKSON COUNTY, MISSOURI
STATE OF MISSOURI

ZACHARY SMITH,	§	
Plaintiff	§	
vs.	§	Cause No. 03CV204050
STATE OF MISSOURI,	§	Division 13
Defendant	§	

No. 07-06068-CV-SJ-ODS
Smith v. Kemna
Petitioner's Exhibit H

AFFIDAVIT OF STEVEN J. PIETROFORTE

My name is Steven J. Pietroforte. I am over 18 years of age and am fully competent to make this affidavit.

I am an attorney practicing in Los Angeles, California. My partner, George A. Halterman, III, was retained by Elizabeth Carlyle to obtain and serve a subpoena for a deposition to a Mr. Daniel Franco.

The address Ms. Carlyle provided for Daniel Franco was 441 Ramona Avenue, Sierre Madre, California, 91024.

Between the dates of July 17 and July 19, 2004, I personally visited the above listed address on three (3) occasions. At my first attempt on July 17, 2004, no one answered the door.

At my second attempt on July 18, 2004, a woman answered the door. She indicated that Mr. Franco did not reside at that location, nor did she know a Daniel Franco or where I might locate him.

At my third attempt on July 19, 2004, a second woman answered the door. She indicated that she is Daniel Franco's sister and that my earlier contact was with Mr.

AFFIDAVIT OF STEVEN J. PIETROFORTE– Page 1

Example—Affidavit of Steven J. Pietroforte (cont.)

Franco's mother. The woman indicated that Mr. Franco previously resided at this location; however, he no longer resides there. She was not able to provide an address at which Mr. Franco could be contacted.

At this time, I informed Mr. Halterman of my findings and we ceased our attempts to physically serve the Deposition Subpoena at that location.

Steven J. Pietroforte

Subscribed and sworn to before me this 11th day of December, 2004.

Nancy Sue Shollenberger
COMM. # 1299517
NOTARY PUBLIC • CALIFORNIA
LOS ANGELES COUNTY
Comm. Exp. MARCH 31, 2005

Nancy Sue Shollenberger
Notary Public

My commission expires: 3/31/05

AFFIDAVIT OF STEVEN J. PIETROFORTE – Page 2

PREPARATION OF APPENDIX FOR ACCOMPANYING EXHIBITS

<7> FILING APPLICATION AND ACCOMPANYING EXHIBITS WITH THE COURT

Filing Requirements

Most United States courts of appeal only require the petitioner to file the original application, along with any exhibits and other required pleadings. However, the Eleventh Circuit requires a petitioner to file the original and three copies. To be sure, check Appendix A for the correct number of copies to include when filing with the United States court of appeals in your circuit.

After the court clerk receives your application, he or she will send you a notice stating the filing date, the case number issued, and an order of any action taken. (See the example letter from the clerk for the Eighth Circuit at the end of this chapter.) If you are required to provide further information, to comply with a local rule or practice, an order will be issued. In such instance the court will grant you additional time to comply with the order, usually fourteen days. If you need more time, you may ask the court for an extension of time, to comply with its order.

Filing Fee

The District of Columbia Circuit Court of Appeals is the only court that requires the petitioner to pay a filing fee: fifty dollars. There is no filing fee requirement for any of the other United States courts of appeal.

Mailing Application and Exhibits

When everything is in proper order, sign, date, and mail your application, its accompanying exhibits, and any other required pleading, to the clerk for the United States court of appeals in your circuit. (See Appendix A for addresses.)

Also send a copy of your application and any other pleadings to the respondent, if required to do so by your circuit. (See Appendix A for specific instructions.)

FILING APPLICATION AND ACCOMPANYING EXHIBITS WITH THE COURT

Example—Letter from Clerk for the Eighth Court

United States Court of Appeals
For The Eighth Circuit
Thomas F. Eagleton U.S. Courthouse
111 South 10th Street, Room 24.329
St. Louis, Missouri 63102

Michael E. Gans
Clerk of Court

VOICE (314) 244-2400
FAX (314) 244-2780
www.ca8.uscourts.gov

May 19, 2016

Mr. Michael Joseph Spillane
ATTORNEY GENERAL'S OFFICE
207 W. High Street
P.O. Box 899
Jefferson City, MO 65102-0000

    RE: 16-2250 Zachary Smith v. Ronda Pash

Dear Counsel:

    An application for permission to file a successive habeas has been filed and assigned the caption and case number shown above. A copy of the application is attached.

    Counsel in the case must supply the clerk with an Appearance Form. Counsel may download or fill out an Appearance Form on the "Forms" page on our web site at www.ca8.uscourts.gov.

    Your response to the application is due within fourteen days of your receipt of this letter. Please serve a copy of your response on petitioner. Further information about the court's procedures in successive habeas proceedings is contained in Eighth Circuit Rule 22B "Second or Successive Habeas Corpus and Section 2255 Proceedings."

    Upon receipt of your response, the matter will be referred to the court for a ruling.

    Please note that service by pro se parties is governed by Eighth Circuit Rule 25B. A copy of the rule and additional information is attached to the pro se party's copy of this notice.

    Please contact this office if you have any questions.

                                Michael E. Gans
                                Clerk of Court

PSA

Enclosure(s)

cc: Mr. Zachary A. Smith

<8> RESPONDENT'S RESPONSE TO PETITIONER'S APPLICATION

Respondent's Response

In a typical case, the court of appeals will direct the respondent to file a response, usually within fourteen days after the filing of an application to file a second or successive habeas petition. Some circuits only require the respondent to file a response if ordered to do so. Other circuits allow the respondent to waive the opportunity to respond to an application altogether. (See Appendix A to determine which is the preference of the circuit in which you are applying.)

In an opposing response to an application to file a second or successive habeas petition, the respondent will be limited to arguing that the petitioner failed to meet the statutory requirements. Below are four affirmative defenses the respondent may raise.

1. Claim presented in Prior Application

A claim presented in a second or successive habeas corpus application that was presented in a prior application will be dismissed, per 28 U.S.C. § 2244(b)(1).

2. Supreme Court Case Not Retroactive

A claim made based on a new rule of constitutional law, must rely on a case made retroactive to cases on collateral review by the United States Supreme Court. (See Chapter 2)

3. Facts Not Newly Discovered

A petitioner asking for permission to file a second or successive habeas petition must show good reason why he or she was unable to discover the facts supporting the application before filing the first habeas petition. See *Felker v. Turpin 101 F.3d 657 (11th Cir. 1996)*, in which the petitioner's application was denied for providing no "reason why [the means of discovering the facts underlying his application] would not have been just as available before he filed his first habeas petition as it was after he had unsuccessfully litigated that petition."

4. Claim Fails to Show Actual Innocence

A petitioner must make a prima facie showing that "the facts underlying the claim, if proven and viewed in light of the evidence as a whole, would be sufficient to establish by clear and convincing evidence that, but for constitutional error, no reasonable factfinder would have found the [petitioner] guilty of the underlying offense." 28 U.S.C. § 2244(2)(B)(ii).

Petitioner's Reply

Once a response to the application is filed, the petitioner is usually given fourteen days to file a reply. Any reply filed should be brief, concise, and to the point, attacking only the respondent's contentions that can be disputed with documentation (such as affidavits, exhibits, etc.) or with case law.

A reply should not be repetitive, merely restating all the facts and legal arguments set forth in the application. Instead, the reply should only contain a caption, a title, and an argument disputing the respondent's contentions, and correcting any misstatements of fact or law.

Case Submission

Once the response and reply have been filed, the case will be submitted to a three-judge panel for a decision.

RESPONDENT'S RESPONSE TO PETITIONER'S APPLICATION

Example Petitioner's Reply—Robert James Campbell

Case: 14-20293 Document: 00512627380 Page: 1 Date Filed: 05/13/2014

No. 14-20293

IN THE
UNITED STATES COURT OF APPEALS
FOR THE FIFTH CIRCUIT

———————————

In re ROBERT JAMES CAMPBELL,

Movant.

———————————

REPLY TO RESPONSE IN OPPOSITION TO MOTION FOR
AUTHORIZATION AND MOTION FOR STAY OF EXECUTION

THIS IS A DEATH PENALTY CASE

ROBERT C. OWEN	**RAOUL D. SCHONEMANN**
Texas Bar No. 15371950	Texas Bar No. 00786233
BLUHM LEGAL CLINIC	**CAPITAL PUNISHMENT CLINIC**
Northwestern University	The University of Texas at Austin
School of Law	School of Law
375 East Chicago Ave.	727 East Dean Keeton St.
Chicago, IL 60611	Austin, Texas 78705-3224
(312) 503-0135 Telephone	(512) 232-9391 Telephone
(312) 503-8977 Facsimile	(512) 232-9171 Facsimile
robert.owen@law.northwestern.edu	rschonemann@law.utexas.edu

TABLE OF CONTENTS

I. The issues Respondent seeks to litigate are beyond the scope of this proceeding 1

    A. Even if the statute of limitations is appropriately considered in an authorization proceeding, resolving the fact-bound question of equitable tolling in this case is a matter for the district court 3

    B. Respondent's assertion of a procedural default is both beyond the scope of these proceedings and frivolous in light of Circuit precedent squarely rejecting the same argument 11

    C. Until this Court authorizes further proceedings on Mr. Campbell's *Atkins* claim, this Court is without jurisdiction to consider Respondent's arguments challenging the merits of the claim. Mr. Campbell has met the only applicable requirement: he has made a sufficient *prima facie* showing of each element of an *Atkins* claim 14

        1. Significant limitation in intellectual functioning 15

        2. Significant limitation in adaptive behavior and functioning 18

        3. Onset of these limitations before the age of 18 22

II. This Court can and should recall the mandate 24

III. Mr. Campbell is entitled to a stay of execution 26

PRAYER FOR RELIEF 28

CERTIFICATE OF SERVICE 29

i

Case: 14-20293   Document: 00512627380   Page: 3   Date Filed: 05/13/2014

I. The issues Respondent seeks to litigate are beyond the scope of this proceeding.

To obtain authorization for merits review of an *Atkins*[1] claim in a successive habeas corpus proceeding, this Court requires a *prima facie* showing that:

> (1) the claims to be presented in the proposed successive habeas corpus application have not previously been presented in any prior application to this Court;
>
> (2) the claim to be presented in the proposed successive habeas corpus application relies on a new rule of constitutional law, made retroactive to cases on collateral review by the Supreme Court, that was previously unavailable . . . ; and
>
> (3) applicant should be categorized as "mentally retarded" as defined in these cases.

In re Morris, 328 F.3d 739, 740–41 (5th Cir. 2003).

Respondent offers no opposition to Mr. Campbell's motion on any of these three grounds, choosing instead to raise three arguments outside the scope of a 28 U.S.C. § 2244(b) inquiry. First, Respondent argues that Mr. Campbell's *Atkins* claim is barred by the statute of limitations and should not be subject to equitable tolling. Opp. at 17–24. Second, Respondent raises a procedural default defense to

---

[1] *Atkins v. Virginia*, 536 U.S. 304 (2002).

Case: 14-20293   Document: 00512627380   Page: 4   Date Filed: 05/13/2014

consideration of the merits of Mr. Campbell's *Atkins* claim, a defense that he would presumably invoke if and when this case proceeds beyond this authorization proceeding. Opp. at 24–26. Third, Respondent—without contesting that Mr. Campbell has made a *prima facie* showing that he has mental retardation—urges this Court to reach the merits of Mr. Campbell's *Atkins* claim and deny it. Opp. at 27–39.

Each of the defenses invoked by Respondent is beyond the scope of proceedings pursuant to 28 U.S.C. § 2244(b):

> The statute limits the scope of review at this stage to the specific question whether the motion makes a *prima facie* showing that any of the claims in the petition satisfy AEDPA's substantive successive petition standards, thereby evidently rendering irrelevant other possible grounds for dismissal such as ultimate lack of merit, nonexhaustion, procedural default, and the like.

Hertz & Leibman, FEDERAL HABEAS CORPUS PRACTICE AND PROCEDURE, Sixth Edition § 28.3(d). Mr. Campbell will address why Respondent's arguments are premature in this proceeding.

2

A. **Even if the statute of limitations is appropriately considered in an authorization proceeding, resolving the fact-bound question of equitable tolling in this case is a matter for the district court.**

Respondent urges this Court to impose a time-bar against Mr. Campbell's *Atkins* claim. Opp. 17–24. He notes that this Court "has examined the statute of limitations issue and the availability of equitable tolling in the very same context of a . . . motion for authorization to file a successive . . . petition," and asserts that the Court has "authority to determine whether the limitations period in § 2244(d)(1) bars consideration of Campbell's" claim. *Id.* 20–21. Respondent omits that whether a court of appeals can even address the time-bar issue in an authorization proceeding is a question that presently divides the Circuits.[2] Mr. Campbell respectfully submits

---

[2] The circuits disagree about whether a panel should consider a statute of limitations defense when deciding whether to authorize review of a successive habeas corpus application. The Fourth Circuit is the most recent court to choose a side on this question. *In re Vassell*, ___ F.3d ___, 2014 WL 1779039, at *4 (4th Cir. May 6, 2014). Mr. Vassell "argue[d] that any consideration of the statute of limitations is premature at this stage when [the court is] applying only the standard applicable for *authorizing* a successive § 2255 motion." *Id.* Mr. Vassell relied on the Sixth Circuit's decisional law which precludes reaching the statute of limitations issue in authorization proceedings:

[I]nvestigating compliance with the one-year statute of limitations outlined in 28 U.S.C. § 2244(d)—clearly a separate subsection from 28 U.S.C. § 2244(b)—is not within the purview of the court of appeals'

3

that, for the reasons articulated by the Sixth and Tenth Circuits, the statute of limitations is beyond the proper scope of these authorization proceedings. But even if this Court *could* reach the time-bar question, it should not do so here, where Mr. Campbell has not had a fair opportunity to develop the record in support of equitable tolling and, even at this early stage, there are many controverted issues of material fact relevant to whether equitable tolling is appropriate.

If Mr. Campbell's claim is indeed time-barred, he will have a compelling argument for equitable tolling. The State of Texas withheld *two* pre-*Atkins* IQ scores when Mr. Campbell was attempting to timely

---

consideration of applications requesting authorization to file a second or successive *habeas corpus* petition pursuant to 28 U.S.C. § 2244(b).

In re McDonald, 514 F.3d 539, 543 (6th Cir. 2008); *accord Ochoa v. Sirmons*, 485 F.3d 538, 544 (10th Cir. 2007) (same).

Acknowledging this split in the circuits, the Fourth Circuit rejected the Sixth Circuit's approach:

> [W]e join other courts of appeals that have recognized as appropriate consideration of the timeliness of a successive petition for collateral review when deciding whether to authorize its filing. *See In re Lewis*, 484 F.3d 793, 795–96 (5th Cir. 2007) (per curiam); *In re Hill*, 437 F.3d 1080, 1083 (11th Cir. 2006) (per curiam); *Johnson v. Robert*, 431 F.3d 992, 993 (7th Cir. 2005) (per curiam) (concluding that "there [was] no point in authorizing [the petitioner] to file another collateral attack" "[b]ecause he waited too long"). *But see In re McDonald*, 514 F.3d at 543; *Ochoa v. Sirmons*, 485 F.3d 538, 543–44 (10th Cir. 2007) (per curiam).

Vassell, 2014 WL 1779039 at *4.

4

Case: 14-20293   Document: 00512627380   Page: 7   Date Filed: 05/13/2014

raise his *Atkins* claim. Motion for Authorization at 20–21. Respondent gamely tries to minimize the State's conduct in this case, protesting that officials only failed to turn over "one test score." Opp. at 40. With respect to the one IQ score Respondent acknowledges having withheld, he now faults Mr. Campbell for not having had himself IQ-tested and offering no explanation for that shortcoming now. This argument misstates the facts; Mr. Campbell has explained precisely how Respondent's actions short-circuited the prior *Atkins* proceedings:

> In fairness, the Court must assume that *had TDCJ informed Mr. Waggoner of the existence of this record, Mr. Waggoner would have brought it to this Court's attention, providing the "individualized, fact specific [showing] … that a movant must make in order to have a motion for leave to file a successive habeas petition granted by this Court."* Campbell, 82 Fed. Appx. at 351. Instead, by falsely informing Mr. Waggoner that no such intelligence testing was conducted on incoming death row inmates (and thus that he need not pursue the issue further), TDCJ officials contributed to this Court's decision to deny Mr. Campbell's motion for authorization to [raise the] *Atkins* claim on the basis of an incomplete and misleading factual record. This unfairness deserves correction, and the most direct path to that correction is for the Court to grant Mr. Campbell's motion for authorization.

Motion for Authorization at 9–10 (emphasis added).

After Mr. Campbell moved for authorization, the four CCA judges who voted to reopen Mr. Campbell's original *Atkins* proceeding

5

confirmed this point, identifying Respondent's withholding of evidence as the "but for" cause that slammed the courthouse door on Mr. Campbell's *Atkins* claim:

> Had TDCJ not misinformed former habeas counsel regarding applicant's available IQ test scores, then this Court would have had IQ testing supportive of applicant's mental-retardation claim during the earlier habeas proceeding, and *applicant would have been able to make out a prima facie case of mental retardation at that time.*

Ex parte Campbell, No. WR-44,551-05, slip op. at 3 (Alcala, Price, Johnson, and Cochran, JJ., dissenting) (emphasis added).

Only after securing a berth for his *Atkins* claim in state or federal court could Mr. Campbell, who is penniless, have secured the resources necessary to hire an expert to evaluate him. Respondent's complaint that Mr. Campbell's "last minute claim is the antithesis of diligence," Opp. at 22, is particularly offensive because Mr. Campbell *did* try to secure the resources to hire an expert in 2003, and Respondent—capitalizing on having "misinformed" Mr. Campbell's counsel—was able to defeat that request. *See* Respondent Dretke's Response in Opposition to Campbell's Motion for Authorization of Funds for Intellectual Function Testing, Docket #43, *Campbell v. Dretke*, No. 00-3844 (S.D. Tex. 2003).

6

Example Petitioner's Reply—Robert James Campbell (cont.)

Case: 14-20293 Document: 00512627380 Page: 9 Date Filed: 05/13/2014

Respondent's withholding of IQ test scores that were specifically requested by Mr. Campbell's counsel in 2003 could justify equitable tolling on its own, but that is not Mr. Campbell's whole case. Respondent fails to even *mention* that the Houston school system measured Mr. Campbell's IQ at 68 when he was nine years old. This document provides compelling evidence of Mr. Campbell's significantly sub-average intellectual functioning prior to the age of 18. But, by the time *Atkins* was decided, this document had been lost or destroyed by the school system and thus was not furnished to Mr. Campbell's counsel in response to his 2003 request for Houston Independent School District ("HISD") records. Thus, Mr. Campbell proceeded to litigate his *Atkins* claim with partial school records that made no mention of his IQ. The Harris County District Attorney's Office, however, had in its file a copy of the record reflecting Mr. Campbell's IQ score of 68. The State nonetheless opposed Mr. Campbell's 2003 attempt to raise the *Atkins* claim in state court, arguing that while Mr. Campbell's "sparse school records ... show that [he] made failing grades in middle school," they failed to establish that he met the criteria to establish mental retardation. Respondent's Motion to Dismiss Applicant's Subsequent

7

RESPONDENT'S RESPONSE TO PETITIONER'S APPLICATION

Example Petitioner's Reply—Robert James Campbell (cont.)

Case: 14-20293   Document: 00512627380   Page: 10   Date Filed: 05/13/2014

Application for Writ of Habeas Corpus at 20. The State asserted that "there [wa]s no credible evidence of mental retardation and no credible basis for believing that the applicant [wa]s a mentally retarded person [under] prevailing diagnostic standards." *Id.* at 21. This assertion was contradicted by compelling evidence in the State's own file. Having specifically targeted Mr. Campbell's school records for subpoena prior to his capital trial, the State's representations in 2003 about the absence of "credible evidence" of his intellectual functioning were at best recklessly false, and at worst intentionally so.

Mr. Campbell is aware of no other case with such an extraordinary set of circumstances weighing in favor of equitable tolling, and Respondent cites no authority for the desperate claim that the State's unclean hands, in having withheld compelling evidence of mental retardation, are irrelevant to whether Mr. Campbell ought to be afforded the equitable remedy of tolling the limitations period. HISD measured Mr. Campbell's IQ at 68 when he was nine years old. The State of Texas knew this fact, but failed to acknowledge it at the same time it was arguing to the courts that no credible evidence supported Mr. Campbell's *Atkins* claim. Any fair assessment of Mr. Campbell's

Case: 14-20293   Document: 00512627380   Page: 11   Date Filed: 05/13/2014

potential case for equitable tolling would have discussed these facts, but Respondent ignores them altogether.

Respondent also fails to acknowledge controlling Fifth Circuit precedent governing the application of equitable tolling to *Atkins* claims. This Court has held that

> the merits [of an *Atkins* claim] blend inseparably into the question of equitable tolling here. The bases for equitable tolling that prompt us to remand—in particular the relationship between Rivera's retardation and his ability to pursue habeas relief—are made the more compelling precisely because Rivera has been adjudicated to be retarded. *That is, answering whether Rivera is retarded is logically antecedent—if not a core element itself—to determining whether equitable tolling is available.*

Rivera v. Quarterman, 505 F.3d 349, 355 (5th Cir. 2007) (emphasis added). Mr. Campbell asserts that his mental retardation is likewise "logically antecedent" to, if not a "core element" of, resolving any equitable tolling issues in this case.

Having succeeded in withholding compelling evidence of Mr. Campbell's mental retardation for years, Respondent now seeks to block all access to the courts because Mr. Campbell did not discover the State's chicanery within the limitations period. There is nothing equitable about that outcome. Even if this Court is empowered to go

9

Case: 14-20293   Document: 00512627380   Page: 12   Date Filed: 05/13/2014

beyond the authorization issue and consider the statute of limitations defense raised by Respondent, it should decline to do so here because "[t]he record before the court is not sufficiently developed for [the Court] to engage in the fact-intensive determination of whether equitable tolling is appropriate." *Id.* at 354. *See also Vassell*, 2014 WL 1779039 at *5 ("Our conclusion does not mean that we always should reach the question of the successive motion's timeliness at the gatekeeping stage. In many cases, the record might not be adequately developed to enable us to resolve disputed factual issues or to determine whether equitable tolling should apply. We also recognize that it would be inappropriate to deny authorization based on a finding that the successive § 2255 motion would be time-barred without 'accord[ing] the parties fair notice and an opportunity to present their positions' on whether the limitation period has elapsed.") (quoting *Day v. McDonough*, 547 U.S. 198, 210 (2006)).

If this Court needed an additional reason to conclude that any equitable tolling issue should be resolved by the district court, Respondent's pleading supplies it. Here, even basic historical facts are disputed by the parties, such as how many pre-*Atkins* IQ scores the

10

State withheld from Mr. Campbell during his timely attempt to raise his *Atkins* claim in 2003. Thus, if Mr. Campbell's claim is time-barred, this case must be remanded to the district court so that Mr. Campbell will have a fair opportunity to adequately develop the record on whether equitable tolling is appropriate.

> **B. Respondent's assertion of a procedural default is both beyond the scope of these proceedings and frivolous in light of Circuit precedent squarely rejecting the same argument.**

Respondent next argues that Mr. Campbell's *Atkins* claim is procedurally defaulted because both state court rejections of the claim were based on Texas's abuse-of-the-writ rule. Opp. at 24–26. Respondent's procedural defenses to Mr. Campbell's claim, such as default and exhaustion, are beyond the scope of these authorization proceedings.[3] Respondent cites no authority from any Circuit that

---

[3] Hertz & Leibman, FEDERAL HABEAS CORPUS PRACTICE AND PROCEDURE § 28.3(d) ("The statute limits the scope of review at this stage to the specific question whether the motion makes a *prima facie* showing that any of the claims in the petition satisfy AEDPA's substantive successive petition standards, thereby evidently rendering irrelevant other possible grounds for dismissal such as . . . procedural default . . . ."); *see also In re McDonald*, 514 F.3d 539, 544 n. 3 (6th Cir. 2008) ("this court need not consider at this stage whether the petitioner's claims have been exhausted"); *Hatch v. Oklahoma*, 92 F.3d 1012, 1016 (10th Cir. 1996) ("Exhaustion is not, however, a precondition to our consideration of this Application for Order Authorizing a Successive Petition for Habeas Corpus Relief. Were we to grant this application, the district court would then have before it the merits of Hatch's habeas petition, and in that context the district court would need to decide whether the

would permit consideration of the State's procedural defenses in initial authorization proceedings before the court of appeals.

Even if Respondent's attempt to litigate his defenses to consideration of the merits of Mr. Campbell's claim were proper at this preliminary stage, his procedural default argument was squarely rejected by this Court in *Rivera*:

> The CCA denied both of Rivera's *Atkins* petitions as abuses of the writ, concluding that neither the first petition nor the second supplemented petition made a *prima facie* showing of retardation. In granting Rivera's motion to file a successive petition after the CCA denied his second petition, this court explained that "characterizing the failure to meet the threshold requirement as an abuse of the writ does not foot the ruling on an independent state ground. This is a determination on the merits."

Rivera, 505 F.3d at 355 (quoting *In re Rivera*, No. 03-41069 (5th Cir. Aug. 6, 2003)). This Court has never wavered from its approach to the CCA's application of the abuse-of-the-writ rule to *Atkins* claims; indeed, the Court recently reaffirmed that such rulings are merits determinations:

> Although the CCA dismissed this successive petition ostensibly as an abuse of the writ, we have explained that "in the *Atkins* context, Texas courts have imported an

---

claim was exhausted or whether waiver of the exhaustion requirement is warranted."), *overruled on other grounds by Daniel v. United States*, 254 F.3d 1180, 1188 (10th Cir. 2001).

12

antecedent showing of 'sufficient specific facts' to merit further review, rendering dismissal of such claims [as abuse of the writ] a decision on the merits . . . . Thus, a decision that an *Atkins* petition does not make a *prima facie* showing—and is, therefore, an abuse of the writ—is not an independent state law ground."

Ladd v. Stephens, ___ F.3d ___, 2014 WL 1379110, at *2 n. 10 (5th Cir. April 8, 2014) (citing *Rivera*, 505 F.3d at 359).

In fact, the law of this Circuit is so well-established in this regard that Respondent has abandoned its assertion of procedural default in another similarly-situated case. *See Blue v. Thaler*, 665 F.3d 647, 653–54 (5th Cir. 2011) (after CCA dismissed Blue's successive application as an abuse of the writ, "[t]he State unsuccessfully argued to the district court that Blue had procedurally defaulted his *Atkins* claim, and did not re-urge procedural default in its response to Blue's motion for a COA. In short, the state accept[ed] that the CCA decided the merits of Blue's *Atkins* claim.").

Respondent's assertion that Mr. Campbell's claim is procedurally defaulted is both premature and frivolous. That Respondent failed to mention, much less attempt to distinguish, this Court's long line of decisions foreclosing such an argument is a troubling omission that

13

should cause this Court to hesitate before relying on any of Respondent's briefing in this matter.

> C. **Until this Court authorizes further proceedings on Mr. Campbell's *Atkins* claim, this Court is without jurisdiction to consider Respondent's arguments challenging the merits of the claim. Mr. Campbell has met the only applicable requirement: he has made a sufficient *prima facie* showing of each element of an *Atkins* claim.**

Respondent's only other argument against authorizing review of Mr. Campbell's claim is that "[w]ere this Court to review Campbell's mental retardation claim on the merits, the Court would not find him entitled to relief." Opp. at 27; *see also id.* at 39 ("Campbell is not mentally retarded for purposes of *Atkins*."). It should go without saying, but the merits of Mr. Campbell's *Atkins* claim are not before this Court. Instead, at the authorization stage, this Court assesses only whether Mr. Campbell has made a *prima facie* showing of mental retardation. *In re Hearn*, 418 F.3d 444, 444–45 (5th Cir. 2005). "A *prima facie* showing of mental retardation is 'simply a sufficient showing of possible merit to warrant a fuller [exploration] by the district court.'" *Id.* at 445 (quoting *Morris*, 328 F.3d at 740) (internal quotation marks omitted). Respondent does not dispute that Mr.

Example Petitioner's Reply—Robert James Campbell (cont.)

Case: 14-20293   Document: 00512627380   Page: 17   Date Filed: 05/13/2014

Campbell has satisfied his burden in this regard, nor could he credibly do so.

This Court has said that whether a prima facie showing of mental retardation has been made is judged with respect to the American Association of Mental Retardation's definition and associated factors:

> Mental retardation is a disability characterized by three criteria: significant limitation in intellectual functioning, significant limitation in adaptive behavior and functioning, and onset of these limitations before the age of 18.

In re Mathis, 483 F.3d 395, 397 (5th Cir. 2007); *Hearn*, 418 F.3d at 445. Taking each of these in turn:

1. Significant limitation in intellectual functioning.

With respect to the first prong – "significant limitation in intellectual functioning" – Mr. Campbell has presented evidence of three IQ scores, as well as other standardized test results of intellectual functioning, all of which place him within the range for a diagnosis of mental retardation under prevailing clinical standards.

First, Mr. Campbell's elementary school records indicate that when he was 9 years old and in the third grade, he was measured with a "deviation IQ" of 68 on the Otis-Lennon Mental Ability Test ("OLMAT"). *See* Exhibit 3 (school records). *Id.* Second, previously undisclosed TDCJ medical records indicate that a state-employed prison psychologist assessed Mr. Campbell with an IQ of 71 on the WAIS-R short form, a score that is statistically indistinguishable from the childhood 68 IQ score on the OLMAT. *See* Exhibit 5 (excerpt from TDCJ medical records). Third, a comprehensive evaluation undertaken in the past month, which included administration of the Wechsler Adult Intelligence Scale IV (WAIS-IV)—the "gold standard" testing instrument for intellectual functioning—measured Mr. Campbell's IQ as 69, fully consistent with the prior scores. *See* Exhibit 2 (Dr. Rosenstein report).[4] The level of intellectual functioning measured on each of these tests is two standard deviations below the mean and is squarely in the range of significantly subaverage intellectual functioning necessary for a diagnosis of mental retardation under the AAMR definition.

Moreover, Mr. Campbell's 68 IQ score on the OLMAT, which placed him in the bottom four percent of his peers nationwide, is consistent with the results of other standardized tests reflected in his

---

[4] Indeed, Dr. Rosenstein's report of her comprehensive assessment alone provides "significant, if not necessarily conclusive, prima facie support" for Mr. Campbell's *Atkins* claim. *See Mathis*, 483 F.3d at 399 (psychiatric evidence as to mental retardation "provides significant, if not necessarily conclusive, prima facie support for an *Atkins* claim").

school records. For example, in 1979, when Mr. Campbell was 7 years old and in the first grade, he was given the Metropolitan Readiness Test, on which he similarly scored at the 4th percentile. *See* Exhibit 3 (school records). The school records also showed that Mr. Campbell's composite scores on the annually administered Iowa Test of Basic Skills placed him in the 5th percentile in 1981 (second grade), the 2nd percentile in 1982 (third grade), the 11th percentile in 1983 (while repeating the third grade), the 4th percentile in 1984 (fourth grade), the 8th percentile in 1985 (fifth grade), and the 1st percentile in 1986 (sixth grade). *Id.*

Respondent concedes that Mr. Campbell offers three scores "showing IQs at or near the cut off of 70," Opp. at 30, yet counters that "an IQ evaluation made by the Texas Department of Criminal Justice when Campbell first entered the state prison system gave Campbell an IQ score of 84." *Id.* As this Court has recognized in other cases, Respondent's argument is without merit. *See, e.g., Mathis*, 483 F.3d at 399 (finding prima facie case of mental retardation notwithstanding "varying measures of Mathis's IQ"); *In re Henderson*, 462 F.3d 413, 415-17 (finding prima facie case of subaverage intellectual functioning based

Case: 14-20293   Document: 00512627380   Page: 20   Date Filed: 05/13/2014

on IQ score of 66 and grade school achievement tests, and implicitly rejecting State's argument that prima facie case was undermined by a TDCJ IQ score); *Rivera v. Quarterman*, 505 F.3d at 361–62 (this Court authorized successive proceedings, and ultimately upheld the district court's finding that Rivera has mental retardation, despite three pre-*Atkins* IQ scores of 85, 92, and 80 on TDCJ IQ tests).

2. Significant limitation in adaptive behavior and functioning.

With respect to the second prong, Mr. Campbell has proffered substantial evidence of significant limitation in adaptive behavior and functioning.

First, as part of her comprehensive evaluation, Dr. Rosenstein assessed Mr. Campbell's *functional academic skills* by administering the Woodcock-Johnson-II-NU Tests of Achievement: Passage Comprehension, Applied Problems, Writing Samples. *See* Exhibit 2 (Dr. Rosenstein report) at 1. In combination with Mr. Campbell's academic history as revealed by his available school records, his performance on the academic achievement test revealed significant deficits, *i.e.*, "applied academic skills consistent with an individual midway through the fifth grade." *Id.* at 2.

18

RESPONDENT'S RESPONSE TO PETITIONER'S APPLICATION

Example Petitioner's Reply—Robert James Campbell (cont.)

Case: 14-20293   Document: 00512627380   Page: 21   Date Filed: 05/13/2014

As Dr. Rosenstein noted, Mr. Campbell manifested difficulties in *conceptual skills* such reading and in written communication: he "failed to consistently write complete sentences," and although "[h]e was able to read and comprehend short sentences and short passages," he "sometimes missed the gist of the sentence completely," as indicated by his "filling in blanks with a word or phrase [that was] opposite [to] the correct response." *Id.* "Some of his responses involved simply offering words or phrases from the reading passage or completing the sentence with a common phrase that did not match the context or meaning of the sentence." *Id.* Queried about the meaning of some of the words he used, he "often ... could not explain the meaning of the word or phrase correctly." *Id.*

Second, Mr. Campbell demonstrated significantly impaired *practical skills* in that he had difficulty performing ordinary monetary calculations ("he was able to count and add change," but "was not consistently accurate in calculating change from a purchase," and "could not answer simple questions about ... money savings"). *Id.* Mr. Campbell also had to ask a friend to read the time on his [Mr. Campbell's] non-digital watch. Exhibit 8 (declaration of Otha Lee

19

RESPONDENT'S RESPONSE TO PETITIONER'S APPLICATION

Example Petitioner's Reply—Robert James Campbell (cont.)

Case: 14-20293   Document: 00512627380   Page: 22   Date Filed: 05/13/2014

Norton) at 1. In addition, Mr. Campbell never obtained a driver's license, and that although he was known to drive, he experienced a number of minor driving incidents that suggested a degree of difficulty with his driving skill. *See, e.g.* 65 RR 1722 (testimony that while driving a stolen car, Mr. Campbell "hit a mailbox" and "ran [the car] into the ditch;" *see also* 64 RR 1503 (testimony that when driving a different car, Mr. Campbell "seemed to be having trouble driving [a] stick shift"). Another informant states that Mr. Campbell could not read the gas gauge on a car, and always had to ask others whether there was enough fuel to get to the destination. Exhibit 8 (declaration of Otha Lee Norton dec) at 1.

In addition, Mr. Campbell never obtained any gainful employment beyond physical labor (*i.e.*, mowing lawns) or which resulted in, *e.g.*, IRS W-2 filings. *See also, e.g.*, 65 RR 1791 (trial testimony of Mr. Campbell's cousin Marcus Arvey that he and Mr. Campbell had "cut yards" from the time that Arvey was "about five years old" until Mr. Campbell was eighteen or so); 65 RR 1797 (Mr. Campbell went around "cutting people's yards"); 65 RR 1792-93 (trial testimony that Mr.

RESPONDENT'S RESPONSE TO PETITIONER'S APPLICATION

Example Petitioner's Reply—Robert James Campbell (cont.)

Case: 14-20293   Document: 00512627380   Page: 23   Date Filed: 05/13/2014

Campbell had tried to find a job "[d]owntown" in Houston, applying at "Kroger's ... Rice and ... Family Dollar," but no one would hire him).

Finally, Dr. Rosenstein found other adaptive functioning deficits with respect to *social skills*. Dr. Rosenstein observed that "individuals who knew Mr. Campbell in childhood and adolescence" described him as "small and mentally slow / impaired," and noted that he was teased by others about his size and behavior, and (perhaps as a consequence) that he spent time with children much younger than he. Exhibit 2 (Dr. Rosenstein First Addendum). These informants also "noted that [Mr. Campbell] was a follower, and not a leader." *Id.*

Respondent asserts that Mr. Campbell has not established a *prima facie* case because he "offers no standardized tests results to support a finding that he possesses adaptive deficits sufficient to support a retardation finding." Opp. at 35. Respondent's argument fails because standardized test results of adaptive functioning are not required to establish a prima facie case. *See, e.g.*, *Mathis*, 483 F.3d at 398 (finding a prima facie case of adaptive functioning deficits on the basis of "affidavits of several lay witnesses"). Respondent further argues that the record contains "ample evidence that Campbell did not

21

exhibit 'significant limitations' in adaptive functioning at the time of the murder" because he was described by a family member as an "average child," could drive a stick-shift car, enjoyed playing sports and singing in the church choir, mowed yards for money, and "[m]ost impressively," was "entrusted to babysit." Opp. at 37–38. None of these relatively simple abilities undermines Mr. Campbell's prima facie showing of adaptive functioning deficits. *Compare, e.g., Henderson*, 462 F.3d 413, 417 (finding prima facie case of adaptive functioning deficits notwithstanding evidence that Henderson "had a very good vocabulary and an ability to form concepts and comprehend procedures and rules"; "had ordered paperback and hardcover books, and had copies of Tom Clancy and Stephen King novels in his cell"; and "was not a follower, was always aware of what he did and why he did it, and wrote rational letters of restitution to his crime victims").

3. Onset of these limitations before the age of 18.

Finally, with respect to the third prong – "onset of these limitations before the age of 18" – Dr. Rosenstein has noted that Mr. Campbell performed more than two standard deviations below the population mean on a measure of mental ability "as early as age 9," *see*

Example Petitioner's Reply—Robert James Campbell (cont.)

Case: 14-20293   Document: 00512627380   Page: 25   Date Filed: 05/13/2014

Exhibit 2 (Dr. Rosenstein report) at 3, and that he had "a long history *throughout childhood* of academic failures, poor test performances, inability to live independently, inability to obtain gainful employment, and inability to stay out of trouble." *Id.* (emphasis added). Considering that Mr. Campbell has been incarcerated since he was just a few months over 18 years old, all of the observations of adaptive limitations reported by lay witnesses were within the developmental period. These facts establish that Mr. Campbell's intellectual disability manifested itself during the developmental period (*i.e.*, prior to age 18).

In response, Respondent complains that Mr. Campbell "offers no contemporaneous records suggesting that he was other than a poor student," and "offers no pre-eighteen Wechsler or Stanford-Binet score." Opp. at 39. This remarkable assertion ignores the standardized test scores reflected in Mr. Campbell's elementary school records, including an IQ score of 68 dating from when Mr. Campbell was 9 years old. *See* Exhibit 3 (school records). Again, Mr. Campbell's evidence substantially exceeds the showing that this Court has deemed sufficient in other capital cases. *Compare, e.g., Mathis*, 483 F.3d at 399 (finding a

23

prima facie showing notwithstanding the fact that "[n]either party entered much evidence specifically on the point of pre-eighteen onset").

II. This Court can and should recall the mandate.

The four judges of the Texas Court of Criminal Appeals who addressed the merits of Mr. Campbell's recent application found that

> the current application provides evidence that [Respondent] *misinformed applicant about the existence of records that would have supported his mental retardation claim when he first raised it in 2003.* Though, perhaps, a habeas attorney could have uncovered the misinformation from [the Respondent] earlier than the present application, *it would be unjust to penalize an applicant for not uncovering such a falsehood previously when he had no basis to believe that a falsehood had been conveyed to him.*

Ex parte Campbell, No. WR-44,551-05, slip op. at 4 (Alcala, Price, Johnson, and Cochran, JJ., dissenting) (emphasis added). As a result of Respondent's "falsehood," the rejection of Mr. Campbell's attempt to bring his *Atkins* claim was based on "misinformation or wholly inadequate information." *Id.* This is the gravamen of Mr. Campbell's complaint about the 2003 proceedings before this Court on the *Atkins* claim. Mr. Campbell is not asking this Court to revisit the merits of its prior determination. This Court's prior review of Mr. Campbell's *Atkins* claim was, like the state court's, "based on misinformation or wholly

Example Petitioner's Reply—Robert James Campbell (cont.)

Case: 14-20293   Document: 00512627380   Page: 27   Date Filed: 05/13/2014

inadequate information." *Id.* Mr. Campbell is asking for an extraordinary remedy because he hopes that these circumstances – where Respondent has been responsible for shameful gamesmanship and misrepresentation of the facts – are truly extraordinary. Indeed, Respondent does not suggest that he ordinarily withholds critical evidence of mental retardation while simultaneously representing to the courts that no such evidence exists. Instead, Respondent attacks Mr. Campbell for being "dilatory." Opp. at 40.

This is not a game of hide-and-seek. It is worse. Mr. Campbell sought the relevant evidence in a timely manner, and Respondent replied with the "falsehood" that no such evidence existed and then argued to the courts that the absence of such evidence required denial of Mr. Campbell's *Atkins* claim. Respondent is playing hide-and-seek with critical evidence *and* cheating. Notwithstanding Respondent's mischaracterization of Mr. Campbell's pleading to the contrary, Opp. at 40, Mr. Campbell is attacking the integrity of the process that followed. Nothing in *Calderon v. Thompson*, 523 U.S. 538 (1998), or the AEDPA prevents this Court from withdrawing its mandate under these extraordinary circumstances.

25

Case: 14-20293   Document: 00512627380   Page: 28   Date Filed: 05/13/2014

III. Mr. Campbell is entitled to a stay of execution.

Respondent identifies the correct standard for assessing requests for a stay of execution. Opp. at 42 ("(1) whether the stay applicant has made a strong showing that he is likely to succeed on the merits; (2) whether the applicant will be irreparably injured absent a stay; (3) whether issuance of the stay will substantially injure the other parties interested in the proceedings; and (4) where the public interest lies."). But Respondent fails to address the arguments in Mr. Campbell's stay motion, and instead asserts only that Mr. Campbell's claim is "untimely and unmeritorious," and that Mr. Campbell has "wholly failed to meet any of the required elements for a stay." *Id.* at 43. Mr. Campbell has already addressed, *supra*, why the merits of the *Atkins* claim are not yet before this Court, and the urgent need to make a complete record on the issue of equitable tolling if Mr. Campbell's claim is deemed out-of-time. Respondent's claim that Mr. Campbell has "wholly failed to meet any of the required elements for a stay" is baseless.

First, as described above, Mr. Campbell has come forward with more than enough evidence to make a *prima facie* case for authorizing review of an *Atkins* claim. Second, it is hard to fathom a definition of

26

Case: 14-20293   Document: 00512627380   Page: 29   Date Filed: 05/13/2014

"irreparable injury" that excludes execution without access to judicial review. Third, Respondent identifies no interest of his that will be harmed if Mr. Campbell's execution is stayed pending the resolution of this claim. Fourth and finally, the public interest lies in a fair administration system of justice:

> It would offend the sense of justice if . . . federal appeals courts allowed [Mr. Campbell's] execution to proceed.
>
> The question is . . . one of honestly complying with constitutional prohibitions against executing mentally limited criminals. It's one of making sure capital punishment is reserved for the worst of the worst in a transparent, evenhanded process that doesn't elevate procedure over fundamental questions of justice.

Editorial: "Getting the death penalty right," THE DALLAS MORNING NEWS (May 10, 2014) (http://www.dallasnews.com/opinion/editorials/20140509-justice-offended.ece).

As described above, Respondent has distorted the record in this case, misrepresented Mr. Campbell's arguments, and failed to acknowledge legal precedent that squarely forecloses his argument. He now seeks to capitalize on the "misinformation" he fed to Mr. Campbell's counsel in 2003—misinformation that, as four judges of the Court of Criminal Appeals correctly note, changed the course of this

27

case by thwarting review at the earliest opportunity of Mr. Campbell's *Atkins* claim. *Ex parte Campbell, supra*, slip op. at 5 (Alcala, Price, Johnson, and Cochran, JJ., dissenting) ("the current application provides evidence that TDCJ misinformed applicant about the existence of records that would have supported his mental retardation claim when he first raised it in 2003."). What Respondent has *not* done is rebut Mr. Campbell's argument that the extraordinary circumstances of this case warrant a stay of execution.

PRAYER FOR RELIEF

ACCORDINGLY, Mr. Campbell asks this Court to:

1. Authorize the district court to consider the merits of his *Atkins* claim;

2. Stay Mr. Campbell's execution;

3. Grant such other relief as law and justice require.

Respectfully submitted,

/s/ Robert C. Owen
ROBERT C. OWEN
Texas Bar No. 15371950
Bluhm Legal Clinic
Northwestern University
   School of Law
375 East Chicago Ave.
Chicago, Illinois 60611

28

Case: 14-20293   Document: 00512627380   Page: 31   Date Filed: 05/13/2014

(312) 503-0135 voice
(312) 503-8977 facsimile
robert.owen@law.northwestern.edu

RAOUL D. SCHONEMANN
Texas Bar No. 00786233
Capital Punishment Clinic
School of Law
The University of Texas at Austin
727 East Dean Keeton Street
Austin, Texas 78705-3224
(512) 232-9391 voice
(512) 232-9171 facsimile

Attorneys for Robert James Campbell

CERTIFICATE OF SERVICE

On May 13, 2014, I electronically submitted the foregoing document to the Clerk of Court for the United States Court of Appeals for the Fifth Circuit, using the electronic case filing system of the court. I hereby certify that I have served all counsel and/or *pro se* parties of record electronically or by another manner authorized by Federal Rule of Civil Procedure 5 (b)(2).

/s/ *Robert C. Owen*
Robert C. Owen

Example Petitioner's Reply—Robert James Campbell (cont.)

Case: 14-20293   Document: 00512627380   Page: 32   Date Filed: 05/13/2014

CERTIFICATE OF COMPLIANCE

Pursuant to 5th Cir. R. 32.2.7(c), the undersigned certifies this brief complies with the type-volume limitations of 5th Cir. R. 32.2.7(b).

1. EXCLUSIVE OF THE EXEMPTED PORTIONS IN 5th Cir. R. 32.2.7(b)(3), THE BRIEF CONTAINS (select one):

A. 5,864 words.

2. THE BRIEF HAS BEEN PREPARED (select one):

A. in proportionally spaced typeface using:

Microsoft Word 2003 for Windows; with 14-point proportionally-spaced Century Schoolbook font in the text, and 12-point proportionally-spaced Century Schoolbook font in the footnotes.

3. IF THE COURT SO REQUESTS, THE UNDERSIGNED WILL PROVIDE AN ELECTRONIC VERSION OF THE BRIEF AND/OR A COPY OF THE WORD OR LINE PRINTOUT.

4. THE UNDERSIGNED UNDERSTANDS A MATERIAL MISREPRESENTATION IN COMPLETING THIS CERTIFICATE, OR CIRCUMVENTION OF THE TYPE- VOLUME LIMITS IN 5th Cir. R. 32.2.7, MAY RESULT IN THE COURT'S STRIKING THE BRIEF AND IMPOSING SANCTIONS AGAINST THE PERSON SIGNING THE BRIEF.

/s/ *Robert C. Owen*
Signature of filing party

30

<9> COURT OF APPEALS' DECISION

Grant or Denial of Leave to File Second or Successive Habeas Petition

As stated in Chapter One, once a panel of a United States court of appeals grants or denies a petitioner leave to file a second or successive § 2254 petition or § 2255 motion, 28 U.S.C. § 2244(b)(3)(E) prohibits any party (petitioner or respondent) from seeking further review of that court's decision, whether from the original three-judge panel, from the court en banc, or from the United States Supreme Court.

Court of Appeals' Decision

A written opinion is usually only issued when the court of appeals grants an application for leave to file a second or successive § 2254 petition or § 2255 motion. (See examples in which leave was granted, at the end of this chapter.)

When an application for leave to file a second or successive § 2254 petition or § 2255 motion is denied, the court of appeals will usually issue a one-page judgment and mandate. (See example at the end of this chapter.)

Conclusion

As stated in *Smith's Guide to State Habeas Corpus Relief for State Prisoners*, obtaining relief from a conviction is often a very long and arduous endeavor, requiring extreme patience and focused attention on the task until the desired results are achieved. Do not allow a denial of relief by the court to discourage you from pursuing other options, such an application for clemency.

COURT OF APPEALS' DECISION

Example—Decision Granting Application (In Re: Jackson Stallings)

Case: 12-16244   Date Filed: 12/06/2012   Page: 16 of 33

IN THE UNITED STATES COURT OF APPEALS

FOR THE ELEVENTH CIRCUIT

FILED
U.S. COURT OF APPEALS
ELEVENTH CIRCUIT
JUL 21 2011
JOHN LEY
CLERK

No. 11-13016-I

IN RE: JACKSON STALLINGS,

                                       Petitioner.

Application for Leave to File a Second or Successive
Habeas Corpus Petition, 28 U.S.C. § 2244(b)

Before HULL, WILSON and MARTIN, Circuit Judges.

BY THE PANEL:

Pursuant to 28 U.S.C. § 2244(b)(3)(A), Jackson Stallings has filed an application seeking an order authorizing the district court to consider a second or successive petition for a writ of habeas corpus. Such authorization may be granted only if:

    (A) the applicant shows that the claim relies on a new rule of constitutional law, made retroactive to cases on collateral review by the Supreme Court, that was previously unavailable; or

    (B)(i) the factual predicate for the claim could not have been discovered previously through the exercise of due diligence; and

COURT OF APPEALS' DECISION

Example—Decision Granting Application (In Re: Jackson Stallings) (cont.)

> (ii) the facts underlying the claim, if proven and viewed in light of the evidence as a whole, would be sufficient to establish by clear and convincing evidence that, but for constitutional error, no reasonable factfinder would have found the applicant guilty of the underlying offense.

28 U.S.C. § 2244(b)(2). "The court of appeals may authorize the filing of a second or successive application only if it determines that the application makes a prima facie showing that the application satisfies the requirements of this subsection." *Id.* § 2244(b)(3)(C).

In his application, Stallings indicates that he wishes to raise one claim in a second or successive § 2254 petition. Stallings argues that his life sentence, which was for non-homicidal crimes he committed as a juvenile, violated his Eighth Amendment right to be free from cruel and unusual punishment. Stalling alleges that: (1) he was 17 years old when he committed the crimes that resulted in his life sentence; and (2) under Florida law, he is ineligible for parole. Stallings asserts that his claim relies upon a new rule of constitutional law, namely *Graham v. Florida*, 560 U.S. __, 130 S. Ct. 2011 (2010). In *Graham*, the Supreme Court held that the Eighth Amendment "prohibits the imposition of a life without parole sentence on a juvenile offender who did not commit homicide." *Graham*, 560 U.S. at __, 130 S. Ct. at 2034. In doing so, the *Graham* Court stated that the "case implicates a particular type

Example—Decision Granting Application (In Re: Jackson Stallings) (cont.)

of sentence as it applies to an entire class of offenders who have committed a range of crimes." *Id.* at __, 130 S. Ct. at 2022-23.

In *Tyler v. Cain*, 533 U.S. 656, 121 S. Ct. 2478 (2001), the Supreme Court stated that a new rule of constitutional law satisfies § 2244(b)(2)(A) only when the Supreme Court itself "has held that the new rule is retroactively applicable to cases on collateral review." *Tyler*, 533 U.S. at 662, 121 S. Ct. at 2482. The Supreme Court has not expressly stated, in *Graham* or later, that *Graham* is retroactively applicable to cases on collateral review.

However, the Supreme Court acknowledged in *Tyler* that it can make a rule retroactive not only with a single express statement, but "with the right combination of holdings." *Tyler*, 533 U.S. at 666, 121 S. Ct. at 2484. In *In re Holladay*, 331 F.3d 1169, 1172-73 (11th Cir. 2003), this Court employed this "retroactivity by logical necessity" mechanism to conclude the Eighth Amendment prohibition on executing mentally retarded persons announced in *Atkins v. Virginia*, 536 U.S. 304, 122 S. Ct. 2242 (2002), was made retroactive to collateral review cases by the Supreme Court.

Thus, there is an argument that the *Graham* rule may be retroactive to cases on collateral review even though the Supreme Court has not expressly so stated. Accordingly, we conclude that Stallings has met his burden of making a prima facie showing that his application satisfies § 2244(b)(2)(A). *See* 28 U.S.C. §

3

Example—Decision Granting Application (In Re: Jackson Stallings) (cont.)

2244(b)(3)(C). Whether the argument is ultimately correct is an issue we leave to the district court. *See id.* § 2244(b)(4) ("A district court shall dismiss any claim presented in a second or successive application that the court of appeals has authorized to be filed unless the applicant shows that the claim satisfies the requirements of this section."). If the district court concludes that Stallings has satisfied the § 2244 requirements for filing a second or successive petition, it shall proceed to consider the merits of the petition, along with any defenses the respondent may raise.

Stallings's application for leave to file a second or successive habeas corpus petition is GRANTED.

COURT OF APPEALS' DECISION

Example—Decision Granting Application (In Re: Ralph Brazel, Jr.)

Case: 12-16244   Date Filed: 12/06/2012   Page: 25 of 33

IN THE UNITED STATES COURT OF APPEALS

FOR THE ELEVENTH CIRCUIT

No. 11-15691-E

FILED
U.S. COURT OF APPEALS
ELEVENTH CIRCUIT
JAN 03 2012
JOHN LEY
CLERK

IN RE: RALPH BRAZEL JR.,

　　　　　　　　　　　　　　　　　　　　　　　　Petitioner.

Application for Leave to File a Second or Successive
Motion to Vacate, Set Aside,
or Correct Sentence, 28 U.S.C. § 2255(h)

Before CARNES, HULL and MARTIN, Circuit Judges:

BY THE PANEL:

Pursuant to 28 U.S.C. §§ 2255(h) and 2244(b)(3)(A), Ralph Brazel Jr., has filed an application seeking an order authorizing the district court to consider a second or successive motion to vacate, set aside, or correct his federal sentence, 28 U.S.C. § 2255. Such authorization may be granted only if this Court certifies that the second or successive motion contains a claim involving:

　　　(1) newly discovered evidence that, if proven and viewed in light of the evidence as a whole, would be sufficient to establish by clear and convincing evidence that no reasonable factfinder would have found the movant guilty of the offense; or

Case: 11-15691   Date Filed: 01/03/2012   Page: 1 of 4

Example—Decision Granting Application (In Re: Ralph Brazel, Jr.) (cont.)

(2) a new rule of constitutional law, made retroactive to cases on collateral review by the Supreme Court, that was previously unavailable.

28 U.S.C. § 2255(h). "The court of appeals may authorize the filing of a second or successive application only if it determines that the application makes a prima facie showing that the application satisfies the requirements of this subsection." *Id.* § 2244(b)(3)(C).

In his application, Brazel indicates that he wishes to raise one claim in a second or successive § 2254 petition. Specifically, Brazel asserts that he was a juvenile when he was sentenced to life without parole for a non-homicide offense, which he contends violates the Eighth Amendment. He contends further that this claim relies on a new rule of constitutional law, established in Graham v. Florida, 560 U.S. ___, 130 S. Ct. 2011 (2010). In Graham, the Supreme court held that the Eighth Amendment "prohibits the imposition of a life without parole sentence on a juvenile offender who did not commit homicide." Graham, 560 U.S. at ___, 130 S. Ct. at 2034. In doing so, the Court explained that the "case implicates a particular type of sentence as it applies to an entire class of offenders who have committed a range of crimes." Id. at ___, 130 S. Ct. at 2022–23.

In Tyler v. Cain, 533 U.S. 656, 121 S. Ct. 2478 (2001), the Supreme Court stated that a new rule of constitutional law satisfies § 2244(b)(2)(A) when the

COURT OF APPEALS' DECISION

Example—Decision Granting Application (In Re: Ralph Brazel, Jr.) (cont.)

Case: 12-16244　Date Filed: 12/06/2012　Page: 27 of 33

Court itself "has held that the new rule is retroactively applicable to cases on collateral review." Tyler, 533 U.S. at 662, 121 S. Ct. at 2482. But in so doing, the Court acknowledged that such an express holding may be found in a single statement, or "with the right combination of holdings." Id. at 666, 121 S. Ct. at 2484. This Court, in turn, applied this latter "retroactivity by logical necessity" framework to conclude that the Eighth Amendment rule announced in Atkins v. Virginia, 536 U.S. 304, 122 S. Ct. 2242 (2002), was made retroactive by the Supreme Court to cases on collateral review, despite the absence of an explicit statement to that end. In re Holladay, 331 F.3d 1169, 1172–73 (11th Cir. 2003).

Thus, there is an argument that the Graham rule may be retroactive to cases on collateral review even though the Supreme Court has not said so in an explicit statement. Therefore, we conclude that Brazel has met his burden of making a prima facie showing that his application satisfies § 2244(b)(2)(A). See 28 U.S.C. § 2244(b)(3)(C). This is of course a limited determination on our part, and as we have explained, "[t]he district court is to decide the § 2244(b)(1) & (2) issues fresh, or in the legal vernacular, de novo." Jordan v. Secretary, DOC, 485 F.3d 1351, 1358 (11th Cir. 2007); see also id. at 1357–58 (setting forth limited scope of prima facie determination); 28 U.S.C. § 2244(b)(4). If the district court concludes that Brazel has satisfied the § 2244 requirements for filing a second or successive

3

Case: 11-15691　Date Filed: 01/03/2012　Page: 3 of 4

Example—Decision Granting Application (In Re: Ralph Brazel, Jr.) (cont.)

petition, it shall proceed to consider the merits of the petition, along with any defenses the respondent may raise. Any determination that the district court makes about whether Brazel has satisfied the requirements for filing a second or successive petition, and any determination it makes on the merits, if it reaches the merits, is subject to review on appeal from a final judgment or order if an appeal is filed. And if an appeal is filed from the district court's determination, nothing herein shall bind the appellate panel in that appeal.

Brazel's application for leave to file a second or successive habeas corpus petition is GRANTED.

COURT OF APPEALS' DECISION

Example—Decision Granting Application (In Re: Jasper Moore)

Case: 16-14361   Date Filed: 07/27/2016   Page: 1 of 8

[PUBLISH]

IN THE UNITED STATES COURT OF APPEALS

FOR THE ELEVENTH CIRCUIT

_____

Nos. 16-13993-J, 16-14361-J

_____

IN RE: JASPER MOORE,

　　　　　　　　　　　　　　　　　　　　　　　　　　Petitioner.

_____

Application for Leave to File a Second or Successive
Motion to Vacate, Set Aside,
or Correct Sentence, 28 U.S.C. § 2255(h)

_____

Before HULL, MARCUS, and JULIE CARNES, Circuit Judges.

B Y T H E P A N E L :

Pursuant to 28 U.S.C. §§ 2255(h) and 2244(b)(3)(A), Jasper Moore has filed two applications—one counseled and one *pro se*—seeking an order authorizing the district court to consider a second or successive motion to vacate, set aside, or correct his federal sentence, 28 U.S.C. § 2255. Such authorization may be granted only if this Court certifies that the second or successive motion contains a claim involving:

　　(1) newly discovered evidence that, if proven and viewed in light of the evidence as a whole, would be sufficient to establish by clear and convincing evidence that no reasonable factfinder would have found the movant guilty of the offense; or

　　(2) a new rule of constitutional law, made retroactive to cases on collateral review by the Supreme Court, that was previously unavailable.

Case: 16-14361   Date Filed: 07/27/2016   Page: 2 of 8

28 U.S.C. § 2255(h). "The court of appeals may authorize the filing of a second or successive application only if it determines that the application makes a prima facie showing that the application satisfies the requirements of this subsection." *Id.* § 2244(b)(3)(C); *see also Jordan v. Sec'y, Dep't of Corrs.*, 485 F.3d 1351, 1357-58 (11th Cir. 2007) (explaining that this Court's determination that an applicant has made a *prima facie* showing that the statutory criteria have been met is simply a threshold determination).

In his counseled application, Moore indicates that he wishes to raise one claim in a second or successive § 2255 motion. Moore asserts that his claim relies upon a new rule of constitutional law announced in *Johnson v. United States*, 576 U.S. ___, 135 S. Ct. 2551, 192 L. Ed. 2d 569 (2015). He argues that his sentence was unconstitutionally enhanced under the residual clause of the Armed Career Criminal Act ("ACCA"). Moore specifically argues that his prior Florida convictions for burglary, robbery, and armed robbery no longer qualify as violent felonies. Moore filed supplemental authority, arguing that the Supreme Court's grant of *certiorari* in *Beckles v. United States*, 15-8544 (U.S. June 27, 2016), could directly impact this case. Moore's *pro se* application raises the same claim as his counseled application, namely that his prior convictions are no longer violent felonies after *Johnson*. Because Moore's two applications raise the same claims, they are hereby consolidated and are considered his first *Johnson*-based application.

The ACCA defines the term "violent felony" as any crime punishable by a term of imprisonment exceeding one year that:

(i)   has as an element the use, attempted use, or threatened use of physical force against the person of another; or

Case: 16-14361   Date Filed: 07/27/2016   Page: 3 of 8

(ii) is burglary, arson, or extortion, involves use of explosives, or otherwise involves conduct that presents a serious potential risk of physical injury to another.

18 U.S.C. § 924(e)(2)(B). The first prong of this definition is sometimes referred to as the "elements clause," while the second prong contains the "enumerated crimes" and, finally, what is commonly called the "residual clause." *United States v. Owens*, 672 F.3d 966, 968 (11th Cir. 2012).

On June 26, 2015, the Supreme Court in *Johnson* held that the residual clause of the ACCA is unconstitutionally vague because it creates uncertainty about how to evaluate the risks posed by a crime and how much risk it takes to qualify as a violent felony. *Johnson*, 576 U.S. at ___, ___, 135 S. Ct. at 2557-58, 2563. The Supreme Court clarified that, in holding that the residual clause is void, it did not call into question the application of the elements clause and the enumerated crimes of the ACCA's definition of a violent felony. *Id.* at ___, 135 S. Ct. at 2563. On April 18, 2016, the Supreme Court held in *Welch* that *Johnson* announced a new substantive rule that applies retroactively to cases on collateral review. *Welch v. United States* 578 U.S. ___, ___, ___, 136 S. Ct. 1257, 1264-65, 1268, 194 L. Ed. 2d 387 (2016).

In light of the Supreme Court's holdings in *Johnson* and *Welch*, federal prisoners who can make a *prima facie* showing that they previously were sentenced, at least in part, in reliance on the ACCA's now-voided residual clause are entitled to file a second or successive § 2255 motion in the district court. *See In re Robinson*, 822 F.3d 1196, 1197 (11th Cir. 2016). However, merely alleging a basis that meets § 2255(h)'s requirements in the abstract only "represent[s] the minimum showing" necessary to file a successive § 2255 motion because, under § 2244(b)(3)(C), the applicant also must make "a *prima facie* showing that the application satisfies the requirements

3

COURT OF APPEALS' DECISION

Example—Decision Granting Application (In Re: Jasper Moore) (cont.)

Case: 16-14361   Date Filed: 07/27/2016   Page: 4 of 8

of this subsection." *In re Holladay*, 331 F.3d 1169, 1173 (11th Cir. 2003). Accordingly, it appears that it is not enough for a federal prisoner to simply identify *Johnson* as the basis for the claim or claims he seeks to raise in a second or successive § 2255 motion, as he also must show that he falls within the scope of the new substantive rule announced in *Johnson*. *See, e.g., id.*; 28 U.S.C. § 2244(b)(3)(C).

Moore has made a *prima facie* case that he falls within the scope of the new substantive rule announced in *Johnson*. Moore's two Florida robbery-with-a-firearm convictions (which count as one predicate conviction because they were not committed on occasions different from one another) and his separate armed robbery conviction qualify as violent felonies under our binding precedent. *In re Thomas*, ___ F.3d ___, ___, Nos. 16-12065, 16-12649, 2016 WL 3000325, at *3 (11th Cir. May 25, 2016); *United States v. Dowd*, 451 F.3d 1244, 1255 (11th Cir. 2006). It is not clear, however, which of Moore's other felony convictions were used by the district court as the third ACCA predicate offense and why. It is also not clear whether the district court relied on the residual clause or the other ACCA clauses not implicated by *Johnson*. Whether at the time of his September 2005 sentencing hearing any of Moore's other felony convictions qualified as violent felonies within the statutory meaning is a matter we leave to the district court in the first instance.

It is important to note that our threshold determination that an applicant has made a *prima facie* showing that he has met the statutory criteria of § 2255(h), thus warranting our authorization to file a second or successive § 2255 motion, does not conclusively resolve that § 2255(h) requirement issue. *See Jordan*, 485 F.3d at 1357 (involving the functionally equivalent § 2244(b)(2) successive application standard applicable to state prisoners). In *Jordan*, we

4

COURT OF APPEALS' DECISION

Example—Decision Granting Application (In Re: Jasper Moore) (cont.)

Case: 16-14361   Date Filed: 07/27/2016   Page: 5 of 8

emphasized that, once the prisoner files his authorized § 2255 motion in the district court, "the district court not only can, but must, determine for itself whether those [§ 2255(h)] requirements are met." *Id.* Notably, the statutory language of § 2244, which is cross referenced in § 2255(h), expressly provides that "[a] district court shall dismiss any claim presented in a second or successive application that the court of appeals has authorized to be filed unless the applicant shows that the claim satisfies the requirements of this section." *Id.* (quoting 28 U.S.C. § 2244(b)(4)). We rejected the assertion that the district court owes "some deference to a court of appeals' prima facie finding that the requirements have been met." *Id.* at 1357. We explained that, after the district court looks at the § 2255(h) requirements *de novo*, "[o]ur first hard look at whether the § [2255(h)] requirements actually have been met will come, if at all, on appeal from the district court's decision . . . ." *Id.* at 1358; *see also In re Moss*, 703 F.3d 1301, 1303 (11th Cir. 2013) (reiterating that our threshold conclusion in granting a successive application that a *prima facie* showing has been made is necessarily a "limited determination," as the district court then must also decide "fresh" the issue of whether § 2255(h)'s criteria are met, and, if so, proceed to considering the merits of the § 2255 motion). Furthermore, the Supreme Court instructed in *Welch* that even if a defendant's prior conviction was counted under the residual clause, courts can now consider whether that conviction counted under another clause of the ACCA. *See Welch*, 578 U.S. at ___, 136 S. Ct. at 1268.

Stated another way, this grant is a limited determination on our part, and, as we have explained before, "[t]he district court is to decide the [§ 2255(h)] issues fresh, or in the legal vernacular, *de novo*." *Jordan*, 485 F.3d at 1358. The district court must decide whether or not Moore was sentenced under the residual clause in 2005, whether the new rule in *Johnson* is

5

COURT OF APPEALS' DECISION

Example—Decision Granting Application (In Re: Jasper Moore) (cont.)

Case: 16-14361   Date Filed: 07/27/2016   Page: 6 of 8

implicated as to Moore's third predicate conviction, and whether the § 2255(h) "applicant has established the [§ 2255(h)] statutory requirements for filing a second or successive motion." *In re Moss*, 703 F.3d at 1303. Only then should the district court "proceed to consider the merits of the motion, along with any defenses and arguments the respondent may raise." *Id.* We repeat what we have said before:

> Any determination that the district court makes about whether [the § 2255(h) applicant] has satisfied the requirements for filing a second or successive motion, and any determination it makes on the merits, if it reaches the merits, is subject to review on appeal from a final judgment or order if an appeal is filed. Should an appeal be filed from the district court's determination, nothing in this order shall bind the merits panel in that appeal.

Id.

We add one further thought. We grant this application because it is unclear whether the district court relied on the residual clause or other ACCA clauses in sentencing Moore, so Moore met his burden of making out a *prima facie* case that he is entitled to file a successive § 2255 motion raising his *Johnson* claim. There in the district court though, a movant has the burden of showing that he is entitled to relief in a § 2255 motion — not just a *prima facie* showing that he meets the requirements of § 2255(h)(2), but a showing of actual entitlement to relief on his *Johnson* claim. *See Rivers v. United States*, 777 F.3d 1306, 1316 (11th Cir. 2015) ("In making [the] determination [whether the district court correctly denied the § 2255 motion], we note that [the movant] bears the burden to prove the claims in his § 2255 motion."); *LeCroy v. United States*, 739 F.3d 1297, 1321 (11th Cir. 2014) ("[O]n a § 2255 [motion, the burden of proof] belongs to the [movant]."); *see also United States v. Pettiford*, 612 F.3d 270, 277 (4th Cir. 2010) ("[T]he district court must determine whether the [§ 2255 movant] has met his burden of showing that his sentence is unlawful on one of the specified grounds."); *United States v. DiCarlo*, 575 F.2d 952, 954 (1st

COURT OF APPEALS' DECISION

Example—Decision Granting Application (In Re: Jasper Moore) (cont.)

Case: 16-14361   Date Filed: 07/27/2016   Page: 7 of 8

Cir. 1978) ("In seeking collaterally to attack their convictions under section 2255, defendants bear the burden of establishing by a preponderance of the evidence that they are entitled to relief."); *Coon v. United States*, 441 F.2d 279, 280 (5th Cir. 1971) ("A movant in a collateral attack upon a judgment has the burden to allege and prove facts which would entitle him to relief."); *Zovluck v. United States*, 448 F.2d 339, 341 (2d Cir. 1971) (stating, in the context of an appeal from the denial of a § 2255 motion, that "[t]here is no doubt but that appellant had the burden of proof"); *Taylor v. United States*, 229 F.2d 826, 832 (8th Cir. 1956) ("Because the statutory proceeding is a collateral attack upon the judgment of conviction, the burden is on the [movant] to establish a basis for relief under some one or more of the grounds set forth in [§ 2255]."); *United States v. Trumblay*, 234 F.2d 273, 273 (7th Cir. 1956) ("On a motion to vacate, set aside or correct a sentence, a movant has the burden of proof."). There are many reasons why one who files a collateral proceeding has the burden of proof and persuasion on all of the elements of his claim. Chief among them is the principle that "direct appeal is the primary avenue for review of a conviction or sentence . . . . When the process of direct review . . . comes to an end, a presumption of finality and legality attaches to the conviction and sentence." *Barefoot v. Estelle*, 463 U.S. 880, 887, 103 S. Ct. 3383, 3391–92 (1983); *see also Jones v. United States*, 304 F.3d 1035, 1039 (11th Cir. 2002) ("A fundamental purpose for the [Antiterrorism and Effective Death Penalty Act] was to establish finality in post-conviction proceedings.") (citations omitted).

In other words, the district court cannot grant relief in a § 2255 proceeding unless the movant meets his burden of showing that he is entitled to relief, and in this context the movant cannot meet that burden unless he proves that he was sentenced using the residual clause and that the use of that clause made a difference in the sentence. If the district court cannot determine whether the residual clause was used in sentencing and affected the final sentence — if the court cannot tell one way or the other — the district court must deny the § 2255 motion. It must do so because the movant will have failed to carry his burden of showing all that is necessary to warrant § 2255 relief.

Accordingly, because Moore has made a *prima facie* showing of the existence of either of the grounds set forth in 28 U.S.C. § 2255, his application for leave to file a second or successive motion is hereby GRANTED.

COURT OF APPEALS' DECISION

Example—Judgment and Mandate Denying Application

UNITED STATES COURT OF APPEALS
FOR THE EIGHTH CIRCUIT

No: 16-2250

Zachary A. Smith

Petitioner

v.

Ronda Pash, Warden

Respondent

Petition for Permission to file a Successive Habeas Petition

JUDGMENT

Before LOKEN, BOWMAN and COLLOTON, Circuit Judges.

The petition for authorization to file a successive habeas application in the district court is denied. Mandate shall issue forthwith.

August 22, 2016

Order Entered at the Direction of the Court:
Clerk, U.S. Court of Appeals, Eighth Circuit.

/s/ Michael E. Gans

COURT OF APPEALS' DECISION

Example—Judgment and Mandate Denying Application (cont.)

**UNITED STATES COURT OF APPEALS
FOR THE EIGHTH CIRCUIT**

No: 16-2250

Zachary A. Smith

Petitioner

v.

Ronda Pash, Warden

Respondent

Petition for Permission to file a Successive Habeas Petition

MANDATE

In accordance with the judgment of 08/22/2016, and pursuant to the provisions of Federal Rule of Appellate Procedure 41(a), the formal mandate is hereby issued in the above-styled matter.

August 22, 2016

Clerk, U.S. Court of Appeals, Eighth Circuit

COURT OF APPEALS' DECISION

APPENDIX A
APPLICATION PROCESS

District of Columbia Circuit Court of Appeals 266

First Circuit Court of Appeals 267
(Maine, Massachusetts, New Hampshire, Rhode Island, Puerto Rico)

Second Circuit Court of Appeals 269
(Connecticut, New York, Vermont)

Third Circuit Court of Appeals 271
(Delaware, New Jersey, Pennsylvania, Virgin Islands)

Fourth Circuit Court of Appeals 273
(Maryland, North Carolina, South Carolina, Virginia, West Virginia)

Fifth Circuit Court of Appeals 275
(Louisiana, Mississippi, Texas)

Sixth Circuit Court of Appeals 277
(Kentucky, Michigan, Ohio, Tennessee)

Seventh Circuit Court of Appeals 279
(Illinois, Indiana, Wisconsin)

Eighth Circuit Court of Appeals 281
(Arkansas, Iowa, Minnesota, Missouri, Nebraska, North Dakota, South Dakota)

Ninth Circuit Court of Appeals 283
(Alaska, Arizona, California, Guam, Hawaii, Idaho, Montana, Nevada, Northern Mariana Islands, Oregon, Washington)

Tenth Circuit Court of Appeals 285
(Colorado, Kansas, New Mexico, Oklahoma, Utah, Wyoming)

Eleventh Circuit Court of Appeals 287
(Alabama, Florida, Georgia)

DISTRICT OF COLUMBIA CIRCUIT COURT OF APPEALS

Application Process

There is no application form for leave to file a second or successive petition in the District of Columbia Circuit. An application must only meet the statutory requirement of 28 USCS § 2255(h).

A copy of the application, together with all attachments, must be served on the United States Attorney General at the same time as the application is filed with the court.

Mail the original application, along with attachments, to the address below.

Clerk of the Court
District of Columbia Circuit Court of Appeals
United States Courthouse
333 Avenue NW, Room 5205
Washington, DC 20001
(202) 216-7000

APPENDIX A—APPLICATION PROCESS

FIRST CIRCUIT COURT OF APPEALS

Application Process

The rule governing successive habeas corpus petitions to the First Circuit (Rule 22.1) reads as follows:

(a) Motion for Authorization. Any prisoner seeking to file a second or successive petition for relief pursuant to 28 U.S.C. §§ 2254 or 2255 must first file a motion with this court for authorization. A motion for authorization to file a second or successive § 2254 or § 2255 petition must be sufficiently complete on filing to allow the court to assess whether the standard set forth in 28 U.S.C. §§ 2244(b) or 2255, as applicable, has been satisfied. The motion must be accompanied by both:

(1) a completed application form, available from this court, stating the new claim(s) presented and addressing how Section 2244(b) or Section 2255's standard is satisfied; and

(2) copies of all relevant portions of earlier court proceedings, which must ordinarily include:

(A) copies of all § 2254 or § 2255 petitions earlier filed;

(B) the respondent's answer to the earlier petitions (including any portion of the state record the respondent submitted to the district court);

(C) any magistrate-judge's report and recommendation in the earlier § 2254 or § 2255 proceedings;

(D) the district court's decision in the earlier proceedings;

and

(E) the portions of the state court record needed to evaluate the claims presented and to show that movant has exhausted state court remedies.

(b) Incomplete Motion. Failure to provide the requisite application and attachments may result in the denial of the motion for authorization with or without prejudice to refiling. At its discretion, the court may instead treat the motion as lodged, the filing being deemed complete when the deficiency is remedied.

(c) Service. The movant shall serve a copy of the motion to file a second or successive petition and all accompanying attachments on the state attorney general (§ 2254 cases) or United States Attorney (§ 2255 cases) is requested to file a response within 14 days of the filing of the motion.

(e) Transfer. If a second or successive § 2254 or § 2255 petition is filed in a district court without the requisite authorization by the court of appeals pursuant to 28 U.S.C. § 2244(b)(3), the district court will transfer the petition to the court of appeals pursuant to 28 U.S.C. § 1631 or dismiss the petition. If the petition is transferred, the petitioner must file a motion meeting the substantive requirements of Loc. R. 22.1 (a) within 45 days of the date of notice from the clerk of the court of appeals that said motion is required. If the motion is not timely filed, the court will enter an order denying authorization for the § 2254 or § 2255 petition.

You may request authorization forms to file a second or successive § 2254 or § 2255 petition from the address below.

Clerk of the Court
United States Court of Appeals for the First Circuit
John Joseph Moakley Courthouse
1 Courthouse Way, Suite #2500
Boston, MA 02210
(617) 748-9057

APPENDIX A—APPLICATION PROCESS

SECOND CIRCUIT COURT OF APPEALS

Application Process

A prisoner who either has filed in the district court a § 2255 motion challenging a federal conviction or sentence, or a § 2254 petition challenging a state conviction or sentence, may not subsequently file a § 2255 motion or § 2254 petition again challenging the same conviction or sentence unless certain conditions are met.

Before filing in the district court a second or successive § 2255 motion or § 2254 petition, the prisoner must file a motion for an order authorizing the district court to consider the second or successive habeas application. The motion must be made on a form the Second Circuit has authorized for this purpose. There is one form for challenging a state court conviction or sentence, and a separate form for challenging a federal court conviction or sentence. Forms are available upon request from the court clerk. No fee is charged for filing the motion.

The motion must be decided within thirty days after it is filed, in accordance with 28 U.S.C. § 2244(b)(3); § 2255(h).

If this court grants the motion, the prisoner may file a second or successive motion or petition in the district court. If the motion is denied, the prisoner is barred from filing in the district court. The grant or denial of an authorization to file a second or successive application is not appealable, and it cannot be the subject of a petition for rehearing or motion for reconsideration. See 28 U.S.C. § 2244(b)(3)(E).

The Second Circuit Local Rule 22.2, governing second or successive applications under § 2254 or § 2255, reads:

- **(a) Transfer Required.** When an unauthorized second or successive application under 28 U.S.C. § 2254 or § 2255 is filed in district court, the district court will transfer it to the circuit court in accordance with 28 U.S.C. § 1631.

- **(b) Notice to Applicant.** Upon transfer under (a), this Court will send a notice to the applicant that the applicant must, within 45 days after the notice date, move in the circuit court for authorization under 28 U.S.C. § 2244 to file a second or successive application.

- **(c) Motion Contents.** Any motion for authorization to file a second or successive application under 28 U.S.C. § 2254 or § 2255 must (1) use the appropriate Second Circuit form, and (2) attach copies of all prior applications for § 2254 or § 2255 relief and any resulting district court decisions, including any written opinions.

- **(d) Failure to Comply.** Failure to comply with any of these requirements may result in denial of the motion.

APPENDIX A—APPLICATION PROCESS

You may request authorization forms to file a second or successive § 2254 or § 2255 petition from the address below.

Clerk of the Court
United States Court of Appeals for the Second Circuit
Thurgood Marshall U.S. Courthouse
40 Foley Square
New York, NY 10007
(212) 857-8500

APPENDIX A—APPLICATION PROCESS

THIRD CIRCUIT COURT OF APPEALS

Application Process

Permission must be obtained from the Court of Appeals before filing a second or successive habeas corpus petition under 28 U.S.C. § 2254, or a motion to vacate under 28 U.S.C. § 2255.

Use the form provided to file a "Motion Under 28 U.S.C. § 2244 for Order Authorizing District Court to Consider Second or Successive Application for Relief Under 28 U.S.C. § 2254 or § 2255."

Answer completely all the questions on the form provided. Failure to provide complete answers may result in the court denying your motion.

Include copies of the following documents with your motion:

1. The § 2254 or § 2255 application you want to file in the district court if the Court of Appeals grants your motion.

2. All § 2254 or § 2255 applications previously filed in federal court, challenging the judgment of conviction or sentence, which you now want to challenge.

3. All court opinions and orders, final and interlocutory, disposing of the claims in previous § 2254 or § 2255 applications that challenged the judgment of conviction or sentence that you now want to challenge.

4. All magistrate judges' reports and recommendations issued in all previous § 2254 or § 2255 applications that challenged the judgment of conviction or sentence that you now want to challenge.

You must sign the motion in two places at the end of page 5. Failure to sign the motion or to complete the Proof of Service on page 7 may result in the court denying you motion.

You must file with the Court of Appeals the original motion and all documents attached to it. Keep a copy for your records.

If your motion seeks relief under 28 U.S.C. § 2254, you must serve a copy of the motion, and all documents attached to it, on the attorney general of the state in which you are confined or the district attorney for the county in which you were convicted. If you do not serve the attorney general, your motion may be denied.

If your motion seeks relief under 28 U.S.C. § 2255, you must serve a copy of the motion, and all documents attached to it, on the United States Attorney for the federal judicial district in which you were convicted. The court may deny your motion if you fail to serve the United States Attorney.

APPENDIX A—APPLICATION PROCESS

You may request authorization forms to file a second or successive § 2254 or § 2255 from the address below.

Clerk of the Court
United States Court of Appeals for the Third Circuit
United States Courthouse
601 Market Street, Room 21400
Philadelphia, PA 19106
(215) 597-2995

APPENDIX A—APPLICATION PROCESS

FOURTH CIRCUIT COURT OF APPEALS

Application Process

Permission must be obtained from the Court of Appeals before filing a second or successive habeas corpus petition under 28 U.S.C. § 2254, or a motion to vacate under 28 U.S.C. § 2255.

Use the form provided by the court to file a "Motion Under 28 U.S.C. § 2244 for Order Authorizing District Court to Consider Second or Successive Application for Relief Under 28 U.S.C. §§ 2254 or 2255."

Answer completely all the questions on the form provided. Failure to provide complete answers may result in the court denying your motion.

Include copies of the following documents with your motion:

1. The § 2254 or § 2255 application you want to file in the district court if the Court of Appeals grants your motion.

2. All § 2254 or § 2255 applications previously filed in federal court, challenging the judgment of conviction or sentence, which you now want to challenge.

3. All court opinions and orders, final and interlocutory, disposing of the claims in previous § 2254 or § 2255 applications that challenged the judgment of conviction or sentence that you now want to challenge.

4. All magistrate judges' reports and recommendations issued in all previous § 2254 or § 2255 applications that challenged the judgment of conviction or sentence that you now want to challenge.

You must sign the motion in three places at the end of page 4. Failure to sign the motion or to complete the Proof of Service may result in the court denying your motion.

You must file with the Court of Appeals the original motion and all documents attached to it. Keep a copy for your records.

If your motion seeks relief under 28 U.S.C. § 2254, you must serve a copy of the motion, and all documents attached to it, on the attorney general of the state in which you are confined. If you do not serve the attorney general, your motion may be denied.

If your motion seeks relief under 28 U.S.C. § 2255, you must serve a copy of the motion, and all documents attached to it, on the United States Attorney for the federal judicial district in which you were convicted. The court may deny your motion if you fail to serve the United States Attorney.

Documents are scanned into electronic form by the clerk and posted to the docket. Therefore, do not use staples, tape, or binding.

You may request authorization forms to file a second or successive § 2254 or § 2255 from the address below.

Clerk of the Court
United States Court of Appeals for the Fourth Circuit
Lewis F. Powell Jr. United States Courthouse Annex
1100 E. Main Street, Room 501
Richmond, VA 23219
(804) 916-2700

APPENDIX A—APPLICATION PROCESS

FIFTH CIRCUIT COURT OF APPEALS

Application Process

Permission must be obtained from the Court of Appeals before filing a second or successive habeas corpus petition under 28 U.S.C. § 2254, or a motion to vacate under 28 U.S.C. § 2255.

Use the form provided by the court to file a "Motion Under 28 U.S.C. § 2244 for Order Authorizing District Court to Consider Second or Successive Application for Relief Under 28 U.S.C. §§ 2254 or 2255."

Answer completely all the questions on the form provided. Failure to provide complete answers may result in the court denying your motion.

Include copies of the following documents with your motion:

1. The § 2254 or § 2255 application you want to file in the district court if the Court of Appeals grants your motion.

2. All § 2254 or § 2255 applications previously filed in federal court, challenging the judgment of conviction or sentence, which you now want to challenge.

3. All court opinions and orders, final and interlocutory, disposing of the claims in previous § 2254 or § 2255 applications that challenged the judgment of conviction or sentence that you now want to challenge.

4. All magistrate judges' reports and recommendations issued in all previous § 2254 or § 2255 applications that challenged the judgment of conviction or sentence that you now want to challenge.

You must sign the motion in three places at the end of page 4. Failure to sign the motion or to complete the Proof of Service may result in the court denying your motion.

You must file with the Court of Appeals the original motion and all documents attached to it. Keep a copy for your records.

If your motion seeks relief under 28 U.S.C. § 2254, you must serve a copy of the motion, and all documents attached to it, on the attorney general of the state in which you are confined. If you do not serve the attorney general your motion may be denied.

If your motion seeks relief under 28 U.S.C. § 2255, you must serve a copy of the motion, and all documents attached to it, on the United States Attorney for the federal judicial district in which you were convicted. The court may deny your motion if you fail to serve the United States Attorney.

Documents are scanned into electronic form by the clerk and posted to the docket. Therefore, do not use staples, tape, or binding.

APPENDIX A—APPLICATION PROCESS

You may request authorization forms to file a second or successive § 2254 or § 2255 from the address below.

Clerk of the Court
United States Court of Appeals for the Fifth Circuit
600 S. Maestri Place
New Orleans, LA 70130
(504) 310-7700
(504) 310-7705, Deputy Clerk

APPENDIX A—APPLICATION PROCESS

SIXTH CIRCUIT COURT OF APPEALS

Application Process

Permission must be obtained from the Court of Appeals before filing a second or successive habeas corpus petition under 28 U.S.C. § 2254, or a motion to vacate under 28 U.S.C. § 2255.

Use the form provided by the court to file a "Motion Under 28 U.S.C. § 2244 for Order Authorizing District Court to Consider Second or Successive Application for Relief Under 28 U.S.C. §§ 2254 or 2255."

Answer completely all the questions on the form provided. Failure to provide complete answers may result in the court denying your motion.

Include copies of the following documents with your motion:

1. The § 2254 or § 2255 application you want to file in the district court if the Court of Appeals grants your motion.

2. All § 2254 or § 2255 application previously filed in federal court, challenging the judgment of conviction or sentence, which you now want to challenge.

3. All court opinions and orders, final and interlocutory, disposing of the claims in previous § 2254 or § 2255 applications that challenged the judgment of conviction or sentence that you now want to challenge.

4. All magistrate judges' reports and recommendation issued in all previous § 2254 or § 2255 applications that challenged the judgment of conviction or sentence that you now want to challenge.

You must sign the motion in three places at the end of page 4. Failure to sign the motion or to complete the Proof of Service may result in the court denying your motion.

You must file with the Court of Appeals the original motion and all documents attached to it. Keep a copy for your records.

If your motion seeks relief under 28 U.S.C. § 2254, you must serve a copy of the motion, and all documents attached to it, on the attorney general of the state in which you are confined. If you do not serve the attorney general, your motion may be denied.

If your motion seeks relief under 28 U.S.C. § 2255, you must serve a copy of the motion, and all documents attached to it, on the United States Attorney for the federal judicial district in which you were convicted. The court may deny your motion if you fail to serve the United States Attorney.

Documents are scanned into electronic form by the clerk and posted to the docket. Therefore, do not use staples, tape, or binding.

APPENDIX A—APPLICATION PROCESS

You may request authorization forms to file a second or successive § 2254 or § 2255 from the address below.

Clerk of the Court
United States Court of Appeals for the Sixth Circuit
Potter Stewart United States Courthouse
100 E. Fifth Street, Room 540
Cincinnati, OH 45202
(513) 564-7000

APPENDIX A—APPLICATION PROCESS

SEVENTH CIRCUIT COURT OF APPEALS

Application Process

There is no application form for leave to file a second or successive petition under 28 U.S.C. § 2254 or§ 2255. An application must only conform to Seventh Circuit Rule 22.2:

(a) A request under 28 U.S.C. § 2244(b) or the final paragraph of 28 U.S.C. § 2255 for leave to file a second or successive petition must include the following information and attachments, in this order:

(1) A disclosure statement, if required by Circuit Rule 27.1.

(2) A short narrative statement of all claims the person wishes to present for decision. This statement must disclose whether any of these claims has been presented previously to any state or federal court and, if it was, how each court to which it was presented resolved it. If the claim has not previously been presented to a federal court, the applicant must state either:

(A) That the claim depends on a new rule of constitutional law, made retroactive to cases on collateral review by the Supreme Court; or

(B) That the factual predicate for the claim could not have been discovered previously through the exercise of due diligence and that the facts, if proven and viewed in light of the evidence as a whole, would be sufficient to establish by clear and convincing evidence that no reasonable fact-finder would have found the applicant guilty of the crime, had there been no constitutional error.

(3) A short narrative statement explaining how the person proposes to establish the requirements mentioned above. An applicant who relies on a new rule of constitutional law must identify the new rule, the case that establishes that rule, and the decision of the Supreme Court that holds this new rule applicable to cases on collateral review.

(4) Copies of all opinions rendered by any state or federal court previously rendered in the criminal prosecution, any appeal, and any collateral attack.

(5) Copies of all prior petitions or motions for collateral review.

(b) A copy of the application, together with all attachments, must be served on the attorney for the appropriate government agency at the same time as the application is filed with the court. The application must include a certificate stating who was served, by what means, and when. If the application is made by a prisoner who is not represented by counsel, filing and service may be made under the terms of Fed. R. App. P. 4(c).

(c) Except in capitol cases in which execution is imminent, the attorney for the custodian (in state cases) or the United States Attorney (in federal cases) may file a response within 14 days. When an execution is imminent, the court will not wait for a response. A response must include copies of any petitions or opinions that the applicant omitted from the papers.

APPENDIX A—APPLICATION PROCESS

(d) The applicant may file a reply memorandum within 14 days of the response, after which the request will be submitted to a panel of the court for decision.

(e) An applicant's failure to supply the information and documents required by this rule lead the court to dismiss the application, but without prejudice to its renewal in proper form.

Upon the completion of your application, mail the original, along with attached documents, to the address below.

Clerk of the Court
United States Court of Appeals for the Seventh Circuit
Everett McKinley Dirksen U.S. Courthouse
219 S. Dearborn Street, Room 2722
Chicago, IL 60604
(312) 435-5850

APPENDIX A—APPLICATION PROCESS

EIGHTH CIRCUIT COURT OF APPEALS

Application Process

There is no application form for leave to file a second or successive petition under 28 U.S.C. § 2254 or § 2255. An application must only meet the statutory requirements of 28 U.S.C. § 2244{b) and § 2255{h).

The Eighth Circuit has amended its local rules to provide that pro se litigants can use the CM/ECF {electronic filing) system to serve their documents on opposing counsel. Rule 25B details the new procedure as follows:

- **(a) General Provisions.** Pro se litigants who are not registered users of the CM/ECF system may use CM/ECF to serve their pleadings on registered users of the system. When the case is docketed, the clerk will provide the pro se litigant with a listing of the parties to the case which will show whether a party can be served electronically by the clerk or must be served by mail by the pro se litigant. If a party to the appeal is a registered CM/ECF user or is represented by a registered user, the clerk will perform service on the party pursuant to the provisions of these rules, and the pro se litigant is not required to serve a paper copy of the pleading on the registered user. If a party to the appeal is not a registered user or is not represented by a registered user, the pro se litigant must serve a paper copy of the document on the party in accordance with the provisions of FRAP 25 at the same time he files the document with the clerk.

- **(b) Duties of the Clerk and Service on Parties to the Appeal.** When a pro se litigant files a paper document with the clerk's office, the clerk will scan the document into the CM/ECF system and create a docket entry for the pleading showing its filing date. The clerk will then provide every registered user with an electronic Notice of Docket Activity. This electronic Notice of Docket Activity will constitute service of the document on the registered user for purposes of FRAP 26, and the date of the electronic Notice of Docket Activity will serve as the date of service for purposes of FRAP 26(c). Response or reply times for non-registered users who receive their service by mail will be calculated in accordance with the provisions of FRAP 26(c).

- **(c) Pro Se Certificate of Service.** Every document filed by a pro se litigant shall include a certificate of service which provides the date the party mailed the document to the clerk, together with the names of any parties or attorneys the pro se party served by mail. A sample pro se certificate of service can be found at Appendix B to these rules.

- **(d) Clerk to Provide Copy of Notice of Docket Activity.** The clerk will provide the pro se filer with a paper copy of the Notice of Docket Activity showing the date the document was filed and the names of the persons the clerk served electronically.

APPENDIX A—APPLICATION PROCESS

Upon the completion of your application, mail the original, along with attachments, to the address below.

Clerk of the Clerk
Eighth Circuit Court of Appeals
111 W. 10th Street, Room 24.329
St. Louis, MO 63102
(314) 244-2400

APPENDIX A—APPLICATION PROCESS

NINTH CIRCUIT COURT OF APPEALS

Application Process

Ninth Circuit Rule 22-3, which governs applications for leave to file a second or successive 28 U.S.C. § 2254 petition or § 2255 motion, states:

(a) Application. An applicant seeking authorization to file a second or successive 28 U.S.C. § 2254 petition or 28 U.S.C. § 2255 motion in the district court must file an application in the Court of Appeals demonstrating entitlement to such leave under sections 2254 or 2255. See Form 12. An original in paper format of the application must be filed with the Clerk of the Court of Appeals unless the application is submitted via Appellate CM/ECF. No filing fee is required. If an application for authorization to file a second or successive section 2254 petition or 2255 motion is mistakenly submitted to the district court, the district court shall refer it to the Court of Appeals. If an unauthorized second or successive section 2254 petition or section 2255 motion is submitted to the district court, the district court may, in the interests of justice, refer it to the Court of Appeals. (Rev. 12/1/09; Rev. 7/1/13; Rev. 7/1/16)

The applicant must:

(1) include Form 12 if submitted by an applicant not represented by counsel;

(2) include the proposed section 2254 petition or section 2255 motion that the applicant seeks to file in the district court;

(3) state as to each claim presented whether it previously has been raised in any state or federal court and, if so, the name of the court and the date of the order disposing of such claim(s); and

(4) state how the requirements of sections 2244(b) or 2255 have been satisfied.

(b) Attachments. If reasonably available to the applicant, the application must include copies of all relevant state court orders and decisions. (Rev. 12/1/09; Rev. 7/1/16)

(c) Service.

(1) Capital Cases: In capital cases, the applicant must serve a copy of the application, attachments, and proposed section 2254 petition/section 2255 motion on the respondent, and must attach a certificate of service to the application filed with the Court. (Rev. 7/1/16)

(2) Noncapital Cases: In noncapital cases, service of the application on the respondent is not required. (New 7/1/16)

(d) Response.

(1) Capital Cases: In capital cases where an execution date is scheduled and no stay is in place, respondent shall respond to the application and file supplemental attachments as soon as practicable. Otherwise, in capital cases, respondent shall respond and file supplemental attachments within 14 days of the date the application is served. (Rev. 12/1/09)

(e) Decision. The application will be determined by a three-judge panel. In capital cases where an execution date is scheduled and no stay is in place, the Court will grant or deny the application, and state its reasons therefore, as soon as practicable.

(f) Stays of Execution. If an execution date is scheduled and no stay is in place, any judge may, if necessary, enter a stay of execution, see Circuit Rule 22-2(e), but the question will be presented to the panel as soon as practicable. If the Court grants leave to file a second or successive application, the Court shall stay the applicant's execution pending disposition of the second or successive petition by the district court.

Mistakenly filed applications that appear to be unauthorized section 2254 petitions or 2255 motions facially alleging a claim based on a new rule of constitutional law or newly discovered evidence of actual innocence may be transferred to the Court of Appeals, in the interests of justice. The district court may, alternatively, dismiss the filing without prejudice.

Rule 22-3 requires applicants to provide the Ninth Circuit Court with their proposed petition or motion. Pro se applicants are encouraged to use the form petition or motion.

You may request a Form 12 to file a second or successive § 2254 petition or § 2255 motion from the address below.

Clerk of the Court
United States Court of Appeals for the Ninth Circuit
P.O. Box 193939
San Francisco, CA 94119
(415) 355-8000

APPENDIX A—APPLICATION PROCESS

TENTH CIRCUIT COURT OF APPEALS

Application Process

Permission must be obtained from the Court of Appeals before filing a second or successive habeas corpus petition under 28 U.S.C. § 2254, or a motion to vacate under 28 U.S.C. § 2255.

Use the form provided by the court to file a "Motion Under 28 U.S.C. § 2244 for Order Authorizing District Court to Consider Second or Successive Application for Relief Under 28 U.S.C. §§ 2254 or 2255."

Answer completely all the questions on the form provided. Failure to provide complete answers may result in the court denying your motion.

Include copies of the following documents with your motion:

1. The § 2254 or § 2255 application you want to file in the district court if the Court of Appeals grants your motion.

2. All § 2254 or § 2255 applications previously filed in federal court, challenging the judgment of conviction or sentence, which you now want to challenge.

3. All court opinions and orders, final and interlocutory, disposing of the claims in previous § 2254 or § 2255 applications that challenged the judgment of conviction or sentence that you now want to challenge.

4. All magistrate judges' reports and recommendations issued in all previous § 2254 or § 2255 applications that challenged the judgment of conviction or sentence that you now want to challenge.

You must sign the motion in three places at the end of page 4. Failure to sign the motion or to complete the Proof of Service may result in the court denying your motion.

You must file with the Court of Appeals the original motion and all documents attached to it. Keep a copy for your records.

If your motion seeks relief under 28 U.S.C. § 2254, you must serve a copy of the motion, and all documents attached to it, on the attorney general of the state in which you are confined. If you do not serve the attorney general, your motion may be denied.

If your motion seeks relief under 28 U.S.C. § 2255, you must serve a copy of the motion, and all documents attached to it, on the United States Attorney for the federal judicial district in which you were convicted. The court may deny your motion if you fail to serve the United States Attorney.

Documents are scanned into electronic form by the clerk and posted to the docket. Therefore, do not use staples, tape, or binding.

APPENDIX A—APPLICATION PROCESS

You may request authorization forms to file a second or successive § 2254 or § 2255 from the address below.

Clerk of the Court
United States Court of Appeals for the Tenth Circuit
Byron White United States Courthouse
1823 Stout Street
Denver, CO 80257
(303) 844-3157

APPENDIX A—APPLICATION PROCESS

ELEVENTH CIRCUIT COURT OF APPEALS

Application Process

Permission must be obtained from the Court of Appeals before filing a second or successive habeas corpus petition under 28 U.S.C. § 2254, or a motion to vacate under 28 U.S.C. § 2255.

Use the form provided by the court to file a "Motion Under 28 U.S.C. § 2244 for Order Authorizing District Court to Consider Second or Successive Application for Relief Under 28 U.S.C. §§ 2254 or 2255."

Answer completely all the questions on the form provided. Failure to provide complete answers may result in the court denying your motion.

You must sign the motion in three places at the end of page 7. Failure to provide complete answers, to sign the motion, or to complete the Proof of Service may result in the court denying your motion.

Include three copies and the original motion when you file. Keep another copy for your records.

If your motion seeks relief under 28 U.S.C. § 2254, you must serve a copy of the motion, and all documents attached to it, on the attorney general of the state in which you are confined. If you do not serve the attorney general, your motion may be denied.

If your motion seeks relief under 28 U.S.C. § 2255, You must serve a copy of the motion, and all documents attached to it, on the United States Attorney for the federal judicial district in which you were convicted. The court may deny your motion if you fail to serve the United States Attorney.

Documents are scanned into electronic form by the clerk and posted to the docket. Therefore, do not use staples, tape, or binding.

You may request authorization forms to file a second or successive § 2254 or § 2255 from the address below.

Clerk of the Court
United States Court of Appeals for the Eleventh Circuit
56 Forsyth Street NW
Atlanta, GA 30303
(404) 335-6100

APPENDIX A—APPLICATION PROCESS

APPENDIX B
ATTORNEYS GENERAL OFFICES

STATE ATTORNEYS GENERAL OFFICES

ALABAMA ATTORNEY GENERAL OFFICE

11 S. Union Street, 3rd Floor
Montgomery, AL 36130
(334) 242-7300

ALASKA ATTORNEY GENERAL OFFICE

P.O. Box 110300
Juneau, AK 99811
(907) 465-3600

ARIZONA ATTORNEY GENERAL OFFICE

1275 W. Washington Street
Phoenix, AZ 85007
(602) 542-5025

ARKANSAS ATTORNEY GENERAL OFFICE

200 Catlett-Prien Tower
323 Center Street, Suite 200
Little Rock, AR 72201
(501) 682-2007

CALIFORNIA ATTORNEY GENERAL OFFICE

P.O. Box 944255
Sacramento, CA 94244-2550
(916) 445-9555

APPENDIX B— *STATE ATTORNEYS GENERAL OFFICES*

COLORADO ATTORNEY GENERAL OFFICE

1525 Sherman Street, 5th Floor
Denver, CO 80203
(303) 866-4494

CONNECTICUT ATTORNEY GENERAL OFFICE

55 Elm Street
Hartford, CT 06106
(860) 808-5318

DELAWARE ATTORNEY GENERAL OFFICE

820 N. French Street
Wilmington, DE 19801
(302) 577-8400

FLORIDA ATTORNEY GENERAL OFFICE

State Capitol, PL-01
Tallahassee, FL 32399
(850) 487-1963

GEORGIA ATTORNEY GENERAL OFFICE

40 Capitol Square SW
Atlanta, GA 30334
(404) 656-3300

HAWAII ATTORNEY GENERAL OFFICE

425 Queen Street
Honolulu, HI 96813
(808) 586-1500

IDAHO ATTORNEY GENERAL OFFICE

P.O. Box 83720
Boise, ID 83720
(208) 334-2400

ILLINOIS ATTORNEY GENERAL OFFICE

500 S. Second Street
Springfield, IL 62706
(217) 782-1090

APPENDIX B— *STATE ATTORNEYS GENERAL OFFICES*

INDIANA ATTORNEY GENERAL OFFICE

302 W. Washington Street, 5th Floor
Indianapolis, IN 46204
(317) 232-6201

IOWA ATTORNEY GENERAL OFFICE

1305 E. Walnut Street, 2nd Floor
Des Moines, IA 50319
(515) 281-8373

KANSAS ATTORNEY GENERAL OFFICE

120 SW Tenth Avenue, 2nd Foor
Topeka, KS 66612
(785) 296-2215

KENTUCKY ATTORNEY GENERAL OFFICE

State Capitol Building
700 Capitol Avenue, Suite 120
Frankfort, KY 40601
(502) 696-5614

LOUISIANA ATTORNEY GENERAL OFFICE

P.O. Box 94005
Baton Rouge, LA 70804
(225) 326-6705

MAINE ATTORNEY GENERAL OFFICE

6 State House Station
Augusta, ME 04333
(207) 626-8800

MARYLAND ATTORNEY GENERAL OFFICE

200 St. Paul Place, 16th Floor
Baltimore, MD 21202
(410) 576-6300

MASSACHUSETTS ATTORNEY GENERAL OFFICE

1 Ashburton Place, Suite 2010
Boston, MA 02108
(617) 727-2200

MICHIGAN ATTORNEY GENERAL OFFICE

525 W. Ottawa Street
Lansing, MI 48933
(517) 373-1110

MINNESOTA ATTORNEY GENERAL OFFICE

1400 Bremer Tower
445 Minnesota Street
Saint Paul, MN 55101
(651) 296-3353

MISSISSIPPI ATTORNEY GENERAL OFFICE

P.O. Box 220
Jackson, MS 39205
(601) 359-3680

MISSOURI ATTORNEY GENERAL OFFICE

P.O. Box 899
Jefferson City, MO 65102
(573) 751-3321

MONTANA ATTORNEY GENERAL OFFICE

215 N. Sanders Street
Helena, MT 59601
(406) 444-2026

NEBRASKA ATTORNEY GENERAL OFFICE

1445 K Street, Suite 2115
Lincoln, NE 68508
(402) 471-2682

NEVADA ATTORNEY GENERAL OFFICE

100 N. Carson Street
Carson City, NV 89701
(775) 684-1100

NEW HAMPSHIRE ATTORNEY GENERAL OFFICE

33 Capitol Street
Concord, NH 03301
(603) 271-3658

NEW JERSEY ATTORNEY GENERAL OFFICE

P.O. Box 080
25 Market Street
Trenton, NJ 08625
(609) 292-4925

NEW MEXICO ATTORNEY GENERAL OFFICE

P.O. Drawer 1508
Santa Fe, NM 87504
(505) 827-6000

NEW YORK ATTORNEY GENERAL OFFICE

State Capitol
Albany, NY 12224
(518) 474-7330

NORTH CAROLINA ATTORNEY GENERAL OFFICE

114 W. Edenton Street
Raleigh, NC 27603
(919) 716-6400

NORTH DAKOTA ATTORNEY GENERAL OFFICE

600 E. Boulevard Avenue, Department 125
Bismarck, ND 58505
(701) 328-2210

OHIO ATTORNEY GENERAL OFFICE

30 E. Broad Street, 17th Floor
Columbus, OH 43215
(614) 466-4320

OKLAHOMA ATTORNEY GENERAL OFFICE

313 NE 21st Street
Oklahoma City, OK 73105
(405) 521-3921

OREGON ATTORNEY GENERAL OFFICE

Justice Building
1162 Court Street NE
Salem, OR 97301
(503) 378-4400

PENNSYLVANIA ATTORNEY GENERAL OFFICE

Strawberry Square, 16th Floor
Harrisburg, PA 17120
(717) 787-3391

RHODE ISLAND ATTORNEY GENERAL OFFICE

150 S. Main Street
Providence, RI 02903
(401) 274-4400

SOUTH CAROLINA ATTORNEY GENERAL OFFICE

1000 Assembly Street
Columbia, SC 29201
(803) 734-3970

SOUTH DAKOTA ATTORNEY GENERAL OFFICE

1302 E. Highway 14
Pierre, SD 57501
(605) 773-3215

TENNESSEE ATTORNEY GENERAL OFFICE

P.O. Box 20207
Nashville, TN 37202
(615) 741-3491

TEXAS ATTORNEY GENERAL OFFICE

P.O. Box 12548
Austin, TX 78711
(512) 463-2191

UTAH ATTORNEY GENERAL OFFICE

P.O. Box 142320
Salt Lake City, UT 84114
(801) 538-9600

APPENDIX B— *STATE ATTORNEYS GENERAL OFFICES*

VERMONT ATTORNEY GENERAL OFFICE

109 State Street
Montpellier, VT 05609
(802) 828-3171

VIRGINIA ATTORNEY GENERAL OFFICE

900 E. Main Street
Richmond, VA 23219
(804) 786-2071

WASHINGTON ATTORNEY GENERAL OFFICE

P.O. Box 40100
Olympia, WA 98504
(360) 753-6200

WEST VIRGINIA ATTORNEY GENERAL OFFICE

1900 Kanawha Boulevard E, Building 1, Room 26-E
Charleston, WV 25305
(304) 558-2021

WISCONSIN ATTORNEY GENERAL OFFICE

P.O. Box 7857
Madison, WI 53707
(608) 266-2121

WYOMING ATTORNEY GENERAL OFFICE

123 Capitol
200 W. 24th Street
Cheyenne, WY 82002
(307) 777-7841

UNITED STATES ATTORNEYS' OFFICES

MIDDLE DISTRICT OF ALABAMA

131 Clayton Street
Montgomery, AL 36104
(334) 223-7280

NORTHERN DISTRICT OF ALABAMA

1801 4th Avenue North
Birmingham, AL 35203
(205) 244-2001

400 Meridian Street, Suite 304
Huntsville, AL 35801
(256) 534-8285

SOUTHERN DISTRICT OF ALABAMA

63 South Royal Street, Suite 600
Mobile, AL 36602
(251) 441-5845

DISTRICT OF ALASKA

222 West 7th Avenue, Room 253, #9
Anchorage, AK 99513
(907) 271-5071

101 12th Avenue, Room 310
Fairbanks, AK 99701
(907) 456-0245

709 West 9th Street, Room 937
Juneau, AK 99802
(907) 796-0400

DISTRICT OF ARIZONA

Phoenix
Two Renaissance Square
40 N. Central Avenue, Suite 1200
Phoenix, AZ 85004
(602) 514-7500

Flagstaff
123 N. San Francisco Street, Suite 410
Flagstaff, AZ 86001
(928) 556-0833

Tucson
405 W. Congress Street, Suite 4800
Tucson, AZ 85701
(520) 620-7300

Yuma
7102 E. 30th Street, Suite 101
Yuma, AZ 85365
(928) 314-6410

EASTERN DISTRICT OF ARKANSAS

425 West Capitol Avenue, Suite 500
Little Rock, AR 72201
(501) 340-2600

Mailing Address
P.O. Box 1229
Little Rock, AR 72203

WESTERN DISTRICT OF ARKANSAS

414 Parker Avenue
Fort Smith, AR 72901
(479) 783-5125

CENTRAL DISTRICT OF CALIFORNIA

312 North Spring Street
Suite 1200
Los Angeles, CA 90012
(213) 894-2400

EASTERN DISTRICT OF CALIFORNIA

501 I Street, Suite 10-100
Sacramento, CA 95814
(916) 554-2700

2500 Tulare Street, Suite 4401
Fresno, CA 93721
(559) 497-4000

NORTHERN DISTRICT OF CALIFORNIA

Federal Courthouse
1301 Clay Street
Oakland, CA 94612
(510) 637-3680

Federal Courthouse
450 Golden Gate Avenue
San Francisco, CA 94102
(415) 436-7200

U.S. Attorney's Office
Heritage Bank Building
150 Almaden Boulevard, Suite 900
San Jose, CA 95113
(408) 535-5061

SOUTHERN DISTRICT OF CALIFORNIA

880 Front Street, Room 6293
San Diego, CA 92101
(619) 557-5610

Imperial County Office
516 Industry Way, Suite C
Imperial, CA 92251
(760) 370-0893

DISTRICT OF COLORADO

Main Office
1225 17th Street, Suite 700
Denver, CO 80202
(303) 454-0100

Durango Branch Office
103 Sheppard Drive, No. 215
Durango, CO 81303
(970) 247-1514

Grand Junction Office
205 North 4th Street, Suite 400
Grand Junction, CO 81501
(970) 257-7113

DISTRICT OF COLUMBIA

Judiciary Center Building
555 Fourth Street, NW
Washington, DC 20530
(202) 252-7566

DISTRICT OF CONNECTICUT

New Haven Office
Connecticut Financial Center
157 Church Street, Floor 25
New Haven, CT 06510
(203) 821-3700

Bridgeport Office
1000 Lafayette Boulevard, 10th Floor
Bridgeport, CT 06604
(203) 696-3000

Hartford Office
450 Main Street, Room 328
Hartford, CT 06103
(860) 947-1101

APPENDIX B— *UNITED STATES ATTORNEYS' OFFICES*

DISTRICT OF DELAWARE

Nemours Building
U.S. Attorney's Office
1007 Orange Street, Suite 700
Wilmington, DE 19801
(302) 573-6277

MIDDLE DISTRICT OF FLORIDA

Ft. Myers Office
2110 First Street, Suite 3-137
Ft. Myers, FL 32902
(239) 461-2200

Jacksonville Office
300 N. Hogan Street, Suite 700
Jacksonville, FL 32202
(904) 301-6300

Ocala Office
35 S.E. 1st Avenue, Suite 300
Ocala, FL 34471
(352) 547-3600

Orlando Office
400 W. Washington Street, Suite 3100
Orlando, FL 32801
(407) 648-7500

Tampa Office
400 North Tampa Street, Suite 3200
Tampa, FL 33602
(813) 274-6000

NORTHERN DISTRICT OF FLORIDA

Gainesville Division
300 East University Avenue, Suite 310
Gainesville, FL 32601
(352) 378-0996

Panama City Division
1001 East Business Highway 98, 2nd Floor
Panama City, FL 32401
(850) 785-3495

APPENDIX B— *UNITED STATES ATTORNEYS' OFFICES*

NORTHERN DISTRICT OF FLORIDA (cont.)

Pensacola Division
21 East Garden Street, Suite 400
Pensacola, FL 32502
(850) 444-4000

Tallahassee Headquarters
U.S. Courthouse
111 North Adams Street, 4th Floor
Tallahassee, FL 32301
(850) 942-8430

SOUTHERN DISTRICT OF FLORIDA

Fort Pierce
101 South U.S. 1, Suite 3100
Ft. Pierce, FL 34950
(772) 466-0899

Ft. Lauderdale
500 E. Broward Boulevard
Ft. Lauderdale, FL 33394
(954) 356-7255

Key West
301 Simonton Street
Key West, FL 33040
(305) 294-7070

Miami
99 N.E. 4th Street
Miami, FL 33132
(305) 961-9001

West Palm Beach
500 S. Australian Avenue, Suite 400
W. Palm Beach, FL 33401
(561) 820-8711

MIDDLE DISTRICT OF GEORGIA

C.B. King United States Courthouse
201 W. Broad Avenue, 2nd Floor
Albany, GA 31701

P.O. Box 2568
Columbus, GA 31902
(706) 649-7700

P.O. Box 1702
Macon, GA 31202
(478) 752-3511

NORTHERN DISTRICT OF GEORGIA

Richard B. Russell Federal Building
75 Spring Street, S.W., Suite 600
Atlanta, GA 30303
(404) 581-6000

SOUTHERN DISTRICT GEORGIA

Augusta
600 James Brown Boulevard, Suite 200
Augusta, GA 30901
(706) 724-0517

Savannah
22 Barnard Street, Suite 300
Savannah, GA 31401
(912) 652-4422

DISTRICTS OF GUAM AND NORTHERN MARIANA ISLANDS

Hagatna Office
Sirena Plaza
108 Herman Cortez, Suite 500
Hagatna, GU 96910
(671) 472-7332

Saipan Office
P.O. Box 500377
Saipan, Northern Mariana Island 96950
(670) 236-2980

DISTRICT OF HAWAII

300 Ala Moana Boulevard, #6-100
Honolulu, HI 96850
(808) 541-2850

DISTRICT OF IDAHO

Boise
Washington Group IV
800 Park Boulevard, Suite 600
Boise, ID 83712
(208) 334-1211

Coeur d' Alene
6450 Mineral Drive, Suite 210
Coeur d' Alene, ID 83815
(208) 667-6568

Pocatello
801 E. Sherman, Suite 192
Pocatello, ID 83201
(208) 478-4166

CENTRAL DISTRICT OF ILLINOIS

Peoria
One Technology Plaza
211 Fulton Street, Suite 400
Peoria, IL 61602
(309) 671-7050

Rock Island
211 19th Street, Second Floor
Rock Island, IL 61201
(309) 793-7760

Springfield
318 S. Sixth Street,
Springfield, IL 62701
(217) 492-4450

Urbana
201 South Vine Street, Suite 226
Urbana, IL 61802
(217) 373-5875

NORTHERN DISTRICT OF ILLINOIS

219 S. Dearborn Street, 5th Floor
Chicago, IL 60604
(312) 353-5300

327 S. Church Street, Room 3300
Rockford, IL 61101
(815) 987-4444

SOUTHERN DISTRICT OF ILLINOIS

Benton
402 West Main Street, Suite 2A
Benton, IL 62812
(618) 439-3808

East St. Louis
750 Missouri Avenue, 3rd Floor
East St. Louis, IL 62201
(618) 482-9361

Fairview Heights
9 Executive Drive
Fairview Heights, IL 62208
(618) 628-3700

NORTHERN DISTRICT OF INDIANA

Fort Wayne Office
3128 Federal Building
1300 South Harrison Street
Fort Wayne, IN 46802
(260) 422-2595

Hammond Office
5400 Federal Plaza, Suite 1500
Hammond, IN 46320
(219) 937-5500

South Bend Office
204 South Main Street, Room MO-1
South Bend, IN 46601
(574) 236-8287

SOUTHERN DISTRICT OF INDIANA

101 NW MLK Boulevard, Suite 250
Evansville, IN 47708
(812) 465-6475

10 W. Market Street, Suite 2100
Indianapolis, IN 46204
(317) 226-6333

NORTHERN DISTRICT OF IOWA

Cedar Rapids
111 7th Avenue, SE
Box #1
Cedar Rapids, IA 52401
(319) 363-6333

Sioux City
Ho-Chunk Building, Suite 670
600 4th Street
Sioux City, IA 51101
(712) 255-6011

SOUTHERN DISTRICT OF IOWA

Council Bluffs Office
United States Attorney's Office
P.O. Box 1887
Council Bluffs, IA 51502
(712) 256-5009

Davenport Office
U.S. Courthouse
131 East 4th Street, Suite #310
Davenport, IA 52801
(563) 449-5432

Des Moines Office
U.S. Courthouse Annex
110 East Court Avenue, Suite #286
Des Moines, IA 50309
(515) 473-9300

DISTRICT OF KANSAS

500 State Avenue, Suite 360
Kansas City, KS 66101
(913) 551-6730

444 S.E. Quincy, Suite 290
Topeka, KS 66683
(785) 295-2850

1200 Epic Center
301 N. Main
Wichita, KS 67202
(316) 269-6481

EASTERN DISTRICT OF KENTUCKY

207 Grandview Drive, Suite 400
Ft. Mitchell, KY 41017
(859) 655-3200

260 W. Vine Street, Suite 300
Lexington, KY 40507
(859) 233-2661

601 Meyers Baker Road, Suite 200
London, KY 40741
(606) 864-5523

WESTERN DISTRICT OF KENTUCKY

Louisville
717 West Broadway
Louisville, KY 40202
(502) 582-5911

Paducah
501 Broadway, Room 29
Paducah, KY 42001
(270) 442-7104

EASTERN DISTRICT OF LOUISIANA

650 Poydras Street, Suite 1600
New Orleans, LA 70130
(504) 680-3000

APPENDIX B— *UNITED STATES ATTORNEYS' OFFICES*

MIDDLE DISTRICT OF LOUISIANA

Russel B. Long Federal Courthouse
777 Florida Street, Suite 208
Baton Rouge, LA 70801
(225) 389-0443

WESTERN DISTRICT OF LOUISIANA

Alexandria Office
515 Murray Street, Room 320
Alexandria, LA 71301
(318) 473-7440

Lafayette Office
800 Lafayette Street, Suite 2200
Lafayette, LA 70501
(337) 262-6618

Monroe Office
201 Jackson Street, Room B-107
Monroe, LA 71201
(318) 322-0766

Shreveport Office
300 Fannin Street, Suite 3201
Shreveport, LA 71101
(318) 676-3600

DISTRICT OF MAINE

Bangor
202 Harlow Street, Room 111
Bangor, ME 04401
(207) 945-0373

Portland
100 Middle Street, East Tower, 6th Floor
Portland, ME 04101
(207) 780-3257

DISTRICT OF MARYLAND

36 S. Charles Street, 4th Floor
Baltimore, MD 21201
(410) 209-4800

6406 Ivy Lane, Suite 800
Greenbelt, MD 20770
(301) 344-4433

DISTRICT OF MASSACHUSETTS

Boston
John Joseph Moakley
United States Federal Courthouse
1 Courthouse Way, Suite 9200
Boston, MA 02210
(617) 748-3100

Springfield
Federal Building and Courthouse
300 State Street, Suite 230
Springfield, MA 01105
(413) 785-0235

Worcester
Donohue Federal Building
595 Main Street, Room #206
Worcester, MA 01608
(508) 368-0100

EASTERN DISTRICT OF MICHIGAN

Bay City Branch Office
101 First Street, Suite 200
Bay City, MI 48708
(989) 895-5712

Detroit Main Office
211 W. Fort Street, Suite 2001
Detroit, MI 48226
(313) 226-9100

APPENDIX B— *UNITED STATES ATTORNEYS' OFFICES*

EASTERN DISTRICT OF MICHIGAN *(cont.)*

Flint Branch Office
210 Federal Building
600 Church Street
Flint, MI 48502
(810) 766-5177

WESTERN DISTRICT OF MICHIGAN

Grand Rapids Office
330 Ionia Avenue, N.W., Suite 501
Grand Rapids, MI 49503
(616) 456-2404

Lansing Office
315 W. Allegan, Room 252
Lansing, MI 48933
(517) 377-1577

Marquette Office
First Merit Bank, 2nd Floor
1930 US 41 West
Marquette, MI 49855
(906) 226-2500

DISTRICT OF MINNESOTA

300 S. 4th Street, Suite 600
Minneapolis, MN 55415
(612) 664-5600

316 N. Robert Street, Suite 404
St. Paul, MN 55101
(651) 848-1950

NORTHERN DISTRICT OF MISSISSIPPI

Ethridge Building
900 Jefferson Avenue
Oxford, MS 38655
(662) 234-3351

APPENDIX B— *UNITED STATES ATTORNEYS' OFFICES*

SOUTHERN DISTRICT OF MISSISSIPPI

1575 20th Avenue, 2nd Floor
Gulfport, MS 39501
(228) 563-1560

501 East Court Street, Suite 4.430
Jackson, MS 39201
(601) 965-4480

EASTERN DISTRICT OF MISSOURI

Rush H. Limbaugh, Sr. U.S. Courthouse
555 Independence Street
Cape Girardeau, MO 63703
(573) 334-3736

Thomas Eagleton U.S. Courthouse
111 S. 10th Street, 20th Floor
St. Louis, MO 63102
(314) 539-2200

WESTERN DISTRICT OF MISSOURI

80 Lafayette Street, Suite 2100
Jefferson City, MO 65101
(573) 634-8214

Charles Evans Whittaker Courthouse
400 East 9th Street, Room 5510
Kansas City, MO 64106
(816) 426-3122

Hammons Tower
901 St. Louis, Suite 500
Springfield, MO 65806
(417) 831-4406

APPENDIX B— *UNITED STATES ATTORNEYS' OFFICES*

DISTRICT OF MONTANA

Billings Office
2601 Second Avenue N., Suite 3200
Billings, MT 59101
(406) 657-6101

Great Falls Office
119 1st Avenue N., Suite #300
Great Falls, MT 59401
(406) 761-7715

Helena Office
901 Front Street, Suite 1100
Helena, MT 59626
(406) 457-5120

Missoula Office
P.O. Box 8329
Missoula, MT 59807
(406) 542-8851

DISTRICT OF NEBRASKA

Lincoln
487 Federal Building
100 Centennial Mall North
Lincoln, NE 68508
(402) 437-5241

Omaha
1620 Dodge Street, Suite 1400
Omaha, NE 68102
(402) 661-3700

DISTRICT OF NEVADA

Headquarters—Las Vegas Office
501 Las Vegas Boulevard South, Suite 1100
Las Vegas, NV 89101
(702) 388-6336

Reno Branch Office
100 West Liberty, Suite 600
Reno, NV 89501
(775) 784-5438

DISTRICT OF NEW HAMPSHIRE

53 Pleasant Street, 4th Floor
Concord, NH 03301
(603) 225-1552

DISTRICT OF NEW JERSEY

Camden Branch Office
Camden Federal Building & U.S. Courthouse
401 Market Street, 4th Floor
Camden, NJ 08101
(856) 757-5026

Newark Main Office
970 Broad Street, 7th Floor
Newark, NJ 07102
(973) 645-2700

Trenton Branch Office
402 East State Street, Room 430
Trenton, NJ 08608
(609) 989-2190

DISTRICT OF NEW MEXICO

Albuquerque
P.O. Box 607
Albuquerque, NM 87102
(505) 346-7274

Las Cruces
555 S. Telshor, Suite 300
Las Cruces, NM 88011
(575) 522-2304

EASTERN DISTRICT OF NEW YORK

271 Cadman Plaza East
Brooklyn, NY 11201
(718) 254-7000

610 Federal Plaza
Central Islip, NY 11722
(631) 715-7900

APPENDIX B— *UNITED STATES ATTORNEYS' OFFICES*

NORTHERN DISTRICT OF NEW YORK

Albany Office
James Foley Building
445 Broadway, Room 218
Albany, NY 12207
(518) 431-0247

Binghamton Office
319 Federal Building
15 Henry Street
Binghamton, NY 13901
(607) 773-2887

Plattsburgh Office
Gateway Building
14 Durkee Street, Suite 340
Plattsburgh, NY 12901
(518) 314-7800

Headquarters—Syracuse Office
P.O. Box 7198
100 South Clinton Street
Syracuse, NY 13261
(315) 448-0672

SOUTHERN DISTRICT OF NEW YORK

Main Office & Criminal Division
One Street St. Andrew's Plaza
New York, NY 10007
(212) 637-2200

Civil Division
86 Chambers Street
New York, NY 10007
(212) 637-2800

White Plains Division
300 Quarropas Street
White Plains, NY 10601
(914) 993-1900

APPENDIX B— *UNITED STATES ATTORNEYS' OFFICES*

WESTERN DISTRICT OF NEW YORK

Buffalo, NY Main Office
138 Delaware Avenue
Buffalo, NY 14202
(716) 843-5700

Rochester, NY Branch Office
100 State Street
Rochester, NY 14614
(585) 263-6760

EASTERN DISTRICT OF NORTH CAROLINA

Federal Building
310 New Bern Avenue, Suite 800
Raleigh, NC 27601
(919) 856-4530

MIDDLE DISTRICT OF NORTH CAROLINA

Greensboro Headquarters Office
101 South Edgeworth Street, 4th Floor
Greensboro, NC 27401
(336) 333-5351

Winston-Salem Branch Office
251 North Main Street, Suite 726
Winston-Salem, NC 27101
(336) 631-5268

WESTERN DISTRICT OF NORTH CAROLINA

U.S. Courthouse
100 Otis Street, Room 233
Asheville, NC 28801
(828) 271-4661

227 West Trade Street, Suite 1650
Charlotte, NC 28202
(704) 344-6222

DISTRICT OF NORTH DAKOTA

William L. Guy Federal Building
220 East Rosser Avenue, Room 372
Bismarck, ND 58502
(701) 530-2420

655 First Avenue North, Suite 250
Fargo, ND 58102
(701) 297-7400

NORTHERN DISTRICT OF OHIO

Akron
2 South Main Street
Akron, OH 44308
(330) 375-5716

Headquarters—Cleveland Office
801 West Superior Avenue, Suite 400
Cleveland, OH 44113
(216) 622-3600

Toledo
Four Seagate, Third Floor
Toledo, OH 43604
(419) 259-6376

Youngstown
100 E. Federal Plaza, Suite 325
Youngstown, OH 44503
(330) 746-7974

SOUTHERN DISTRICT OF OHIO

Cincinnati Branch Office
221 East 4th Street, Suite 400
Cincinnati, OH 45202
(513) 684-3711

Columbus Main Office
303 Marconi Boulevard, Suite 200
Columbus, OH 43215
(614) 469-5715

SOUTHERN DISTRICT OF OHIO *(cont.)*

Dayton Branch Office
Federal Building
200 W. Second Street, Suite 600
Dayton, OH 45402
(937) 225-2910

EASTERN DISTRICT OF OKLAHOMA

520 Denison
Muskogee, OK 74401
(918) 684-5100

NORTHERN DISTRICT OF OKLAHOMA

110 West 7th Street, Suite 300
Tulsa, OK 74119
(918) 382-2700

WESTERN DISTRICT OF OKLAHOMA

210 West Park Avenue, Suite 400
Oklahoma City, OK 73102
(405) 553-8700

DISTRICT OF OREGON

Eugene Branch Office
405 E 8th Avenue, Suite 400
Eugene, OR 97401
(541) 465-6771

Medford Branch Office
310 West Sixth
Medford, OR 97501
(541) 776-3364

Portland District Office
1000 SW Third Avenue, Suite 600
Portland, OR 97204
(503) 727-1000

EASTERN DISTRICT OF PENNSYLVANIA

504 W. Hamilton Street, Suite #3701
Allentown, PA 18101
(215) 861-8540

615 Chestnut, Suite 1250
Philadelphia, PA 19106
(215) 861-8200

MIDDLE DISTRICT OF PENNSYLVANIA

Harrisburg Office
Harrisburg Federal Building and Courthouse
228 Walnut Street, Suite 220
P.O. Box 11754
Harrisburg, PA 17108
(717) 221-4482

Williamsport Office
240 W. Third Street, Suite 316
Williamsport, PA 17701
(570) 326-1935

WESTERN DISTRICT OF PENNSYLVANIA

Erie
Federal Courthouse
17 South Park Row, Room A330
Erie, PA 16501
(814) 452-2906

Johnstown
Penn Traffic Building
319 Washington Street, Suite 200
Johnstown, PA 15901
(814) 533-4547

Pittsburg
U.S. Post Office & Courthouse
700 Grant Street, Suite 4000
Pittsburg, PA 15219
(412) 644-3500

APPENDIX B— *UNITED STATES ATTORNEYS' OFFICES*

DISTRICT OF PUERTO RICO

Torre Chardon
350 Carlos Chardon Street, Suite 1201
San Juan, PR 00918
(787) 766-5656

DISTRICT OF RHODE ISLAND

Fleet Center
50 Kennedy Plaza, 8th Floor
Providence, RI 02903
(401) 708-5000

DISTRICT OF SOUTH CAROLINA

Liberty Center
151 Meeting Street, Suite 200
Charleston, SC 29402
(843) 727-4381

McMillian Federal Building
401 West Evans Street, Room 222
Florence, SC 29501
(843) 665-6688

One Liberty Square Building
55 Beattie Place, Suite 700
Greenville, SC 29601
(864) 282-2100

Wells Fargo Building
1441 Main Street, Suite 500
Columbia, SC 29201
(803) 929-3000

DISTRICT OF SOUTH DAKOTA

102 SE 4th, Room 312
Aberdeen, SD 57402
(605) 226-7264

P.O. Box 7240
Pierre, SD 57501
(605) 224-5402

APPENDIX B— *UNITED STATES ATTORNEYS' OFFICES*

DISTRICT OF SOUTH DAKOTA *(cont.)*

201 Federal Building
515 Ninth Street
Rapid City, SD 57701
(605) 342-7822

P.O. Box 2638
Sioux Falls, SD 57101
(605) 330-4400

EASTERN DISTRICT OF TENNESSEE

Chattanooga Winchester
1110 Market Street, Suite 515
Chattanooga, TN 37402
(423) 752-5140

Greenfield/ Johnson City
220 West Depot Street
Greenfield, TN 37743
(423) 639-6759

Knoxville—Headquarters
800 Market Street, Suite 211
Knoxville, TN 37902
(865) 545-4167

MIDDLE DISTRICT OF TENNESSEE

817 S. Gorden Street, Room 205
Columbia, TN 37083
(931) 388-6030

Post Office & Courthouse
9 East Brood Street
Cookeville, TN 38503
(931) 528-2709

110 Ninth Avenue South, Suite A961
Nashville, TN 37203
(615) 736-5151

WESTERN DISTRICT OF TENNESSEE

Jackson Branch Office
109 S. Highland, Suite 300
Jackson, TN 39301
(731) 422-6220

Memphis Branch Office
167 North Main Street, Suite 800
Memphis, TN 38103
(901) 544-4231

EASTERN DISTRICT OF TEXAS

Beaumont Office
350 Magnolia Avenue, Suite 150
Beaumont, TX 77701
(409) 839-2538

Lufkin Office
Bank of America Building
414 S. 1st Street
Lufkin, TX 75901
(409) 839-2538

Sherman Office
One Grand Centre
600 East Taylor Street, Suite 2000
Sherman, TX 75090
(903) 868-9454

NORTHERN DISTRICT OF TEXAS

Amarillo Office
Amarillo National Plaza Two
500 South Taylor Street
Amarillo, TX 79101
(806) 324-2356

Dallas Office
1100 Commerce Street, Third Floor
Dallas, TX 75242
(214) 659-8806

APPENDIX B— *UNITED STATES ATTORNEYS' OFFICES*

NORTHERN DISTRICT OF TEXAS *(cont.)*

Fort Worth Office
801 Cherry Street, Unit 4
Burnett Plaza, Suite 1700
Fort Worth, TX 76102
(817) 252-5200

Lubbock Office
1205 Texas Avenue, Suite 700
Lubbock, TX 79401
(806) 472-7351

SOUTHERN DISTRICT OF TEXAS

Brownsville
U.S. Courthouse
600 East Harrison, Suite 201
Brownsville, TX 78520
(956) 548-2554

Corpus Christi
One Shoreline Plaza South Tower
800 N. Shoreline Boulevard, Suite 500
Corpus Christi, TX 78401
(361) 888-3111

Houston
1000 Louisiana Street, Suite 2300
Houston, TX 77002
(713) 567-9000

McAllen
Bentson Tower
1701 West Highway 83, Suite 600
McAllen, TX 78501
(956) 618-8010

WESTERN DISTRICT OF TEXAS

Alpine Division Office
2500 N. Highway 118, Suite A200
Alpine, TX 79830
(432) 837-7332

Austin Division Office
816 Congress Avenue, Suite 1000
Austin, TX 78701
(512) 916-5858

Del Rio Division Office
U.S. Courthouse
111 East Broodway, Room A300
Del Rio, TX 78840
(830) 703-2025

San Antonio Division Office
Headquarters
601 NW Loop 410, Suite 600
San Antonio, TX 78216
(210) 384-7100

El Paso Division Office
700 East San Antonio Avenue, Suite 200
El Paso, TX 79901
(915) 534-6884

Midland Division Office
400 W. Illinois Street, Suite 1200
Midland, TX 79701
(432) 686-4110

Unstaffed Pecos Office
U.S. Courthouse
410 S. Cedar, Room 255
Pecos, TX 79772
(432) 445-4343

Waco Division Office
800 Franklin, Suite 280
Waco, TX 76701
(254) 750-1580

DISTRICT OF UTAH

Salt Lake Office
185 South State Street, Suite 300
Salt Lake City, UT 84111
(801) 524-5682

St. George Office
20 North Main Street, Suite 208
St. George, UT 84770
(435) 634-4270

DISTRICT OF VERMONT

Burlington
P.O. Box 570
Burlington, VT 05402
(802) 951-6725

Rutland
P.O. Box 10
Rutland, VT 05702
(802) 773-0231

DISTRICT OF VIRGIN ISLAND

Christiansted
1108 King Street, Suite 201
St. Croix, VI 00820
(340) 773-3920

St. Thomas
Federal Building & U.S. Courthouse
5500 Veterans Drive, Room 260
St. Thomas, VI 00802
(340) 774-5757

APPENDIX B— *UNITED STATES ATTORNEYS' OFFICES*

EASTERN DISTRICT OF VIRGINIA

2100 Jamieson Avenue
Alexandra, VA 22314
(703) 299-3700

World Trade Center
101 W. Main Street, Suite 8000
Norfolk, VA 23510
(757) 441-6689

Fountain Plaza Three, Suite 300
721 Lakefront Commons
Newport News, VA 23606
(757) 591-4000

919 E. Main Street, Suite 1900
Richmond, VA 23219
(804) 819-5400

WESTERN DISTRICT OF VIRGINIA

Abingdon
180 W. Main Street
Abingdon, VA 24210
(276) 628-4161

Charlottesville
255 W. Main Street, Room 130
Charlottesville, VA 22902
(434) 293-4283

Harrisonburg
Federal Courthouse Building
116 North Main Street, Room 130
Harrisonburg, VA 22802
(540) 432-6636

Roanoke
P.O. Box 1709
Roanoke, VA 24008
(540) 857-2250

APPENDIX B— *UNITED STATES ATTORNEYS' OFFICES*

EASTERN DISTRICT OF WASHINGTON

Spokane
P.O. Box 1494
Spokane, WA 99210
(509) 353-2767

Yakima
402 E. Yakima Avenue, Suite 210
Yakima, WA 98901
(509) 454-4425

WESTERN DISTRICT OF WASHINGTON

Seattle Main Office
700 Stewart Street, Suite 5220
Seattle, WA 98101
(206) 553-0882

Tacoma Branch Office
1201 Pacific Avenue, Suite 700
Tacoma, WA 98402
(253) 428-3800

NORTHERN DISTRICT OF WEST VIRGINIA

Clarksburg Branch
Clarksburg Federal Building
320 West Pike Street, Suite 300
Clarksburg, WV 26301
(304) 623-7030

Martinsburg Branch
U.S. Courthouse & Post Office Building
217 West King Street, Suite 400
Martinsburg, WV 25401
(304) 262-0590

Wheeling
1125 Chapline Street
Wheeling, WV 26003
(304) 234-0100

SOUTHERN DISTRICT OF WEST VIRGINIA

Beckley Branch
United States Courthouse
110 North Herber Street, Room 257
Beckley, WV 25801
(304) 253-6722

Charleston
Robert C. Byrd U.S. Courthouse
300 Virginia Street, Suite 4000
Charleston, WV 25301
(304) 345-2200

Huntington Branch
Sydney L. Christie Building
845 Fifth Avenue, Room 209
Huntington, WV 25701
(304) 529-5799

EASTERN DISTRICT OF WISCONSIN

205 Doty Street, Suite 301
Greenbay, WI 54301
(920) 884-1066

530 Federal Building
517 East Wisconsin Avenue
Milwaukee, WI 53202
(414) 297-1700

WESTERN DISTRICT OF WISCONSIN

222 West Washington Avenue, Suite 700
Madison, WI 53703
(608) 264-5158

DISTRICT OF WYOMING

Cheyenne—Headquarters
P.O. Box 668
Cheyenne, WY 82003
(307) 772-2124

Casper Branch Office
P.O. Box 22211
Casper, WY 82602
(307) 261-5434

Lander Branch Office
P.O. Box 449
Lander, WY 82520
(307) 332-8195

Yellowstone National Park Branch Office
P.O. Box 703
Yellowstone National Park, WY 82190
(307) 690-7394

APPENDIX B— *UNITED STATES ATTORNEYS' OFFICES*

APPENDIX C
BLANK APPLICATION FORM

Motion Under 28 U.S.C. § 2244 for Order Authorizing District Court to Consider Second or Successive Application for Relief Under 28 U.S.C. § 2254 or § 2255

MOTION UNDER 28 U.S.C. § 2244 FOR ORDER AUTHORIZING DISTRICT COURT TO CONSIDER SECOND OR SUCCESSIVE APPLICATION FOR RELIEF UNDER 28 U.S.C. § 2254 OR § 2255

United States Court of Appeals for the ___ Circuit		
Name of Movant	Prisoner Number	Case Number (leave blank)
Place of Confinement		

IN RE: _____, **MOVANT**

1. Name and location of court which entered the judgment of conviction from which relief is sought: _____
_____

2. Parties' Names: _____ vs. _____

3. Docket Number: _____ 4. Date Filed: _____ 5. Date of judgment of conviction: _____ 6. Length of sentence: _____ 7. Nature of offense(s) involved (all counts): _____
_____

_____

_____

_____

8. What was your plea? (Check one) ☐ Not Guilty ☐ Guilty ☐ Nolo Contendere

9. If you pleaded not guilty, what kind of trial did you have? (Check one) ☐ Jury ☐ Judge only

10. Did you testify at your trial? (Check one) ☐ Yes ☐ No

11. Did you appeal from the judgment of conviction? (Check one) ☐ Yes ☐ No

12. If you did appeal, what was the

    Name of court appealed to: _____

    Parties' names on appeal: _____ vs. _____

    Docket number of appeal: _____ Date of decision: _____

    Result of appeal: _____ _____

_____

_____

_____

_____

13. Other than a direct appeal from the judgment of conviction and sentence, have you filed any other petitions, applications for relief, or other motions regarding this judgment in any federal court? ☐ Yes ☐ No

14. If you answered "yes" to question 13, answer the following questions:
    A. FIRST PETITION, APPLICATION, OR MOTION
    (1) In what court did you file the petition, application, or motion? _____

    (2) What were the parties' names? _____ vs. _____

    (3) What was the docket number of the case? _____

    (4) What relief did you seek? _____

    (5) What grounds for relief did you state in your petition, application, or motion? _____
    _____
    _____
    _____

    (6) Did the court hold an evidentiary hearing on your petition, application or motion? ☐ Yes ☐ No

    (7) What was the result?   ☐ Relief granted   ☐ Relief denied on the merits

    ☐ Relief denied for failure to exhaust   ☐ Relief denied for procedural default

    (8) Date of court's decision: _____

    B. SECOND PETITION, APPLICATION, OR MOTION

    (1) In what court did you file the petition, application, or motion? _____ (2) What were the parties' names? _____ vs. _____ (3) What was the docket number of the case? _____ (4) What relief did you seek? _____
    _____
    _____
    _____
    _____

C. THIRD AND SUBSEQUENT PETITIONS, APPLICATIONS, OR MOTIONS

For any third or subsequent petition, application, or motion, attach a separate page providing the information required in items (1) through (8) above for first and second petitions, applications, or motions.

D. PRIOR APPELLATE REVIEW(S)

Did you appeal any order regarding your petitions, applications, or motions to a federal court of appeals having jurisdiction over your case? If so, list the docket numbers and dates of final disposition for all subsequent petitions, applications, or motions filed in a federal court of appeals.

First petition, application, or motion	☐ Yes Appeal No. _____	Date _____	☐ No
Second petition, application, or motion	☐ Yes Appeal No. _____	Date _____	☐ No
Subsequent petitions, applications or motions	☐ Yes Appeal No. _____	Date _____	☐ No
Subsequent petitions, applications or motions	☐ Yes Appeal No. _____	Date _____	☐ No
Subsequent petitions, applications or motions	☐ Yes Appeal No. _____	Date _____	☐ No
Subsequent petitions, applications or motions	☐ Yes Appeal No. _____	Date _____	☐ No

If you did not appeal from the denial of relief on any of your prior petitions, applications, or motions, state which denials you did not appeal and explain why you did not.

_____ _____

_____

_____

15. Did you present any of the claims in this application in any previous petition, application, or motion for relief under 28 U.S.C. § 2254 or § 2255? (Check one)   ☐ Yes   ☐ No

16. If your answer to question 15 is "yes," give the docket number(s) and court(s) in which such claims were raised and state the basis on which relief was denied.

_____ _____

_____

_____ 17. If your answer to question

15 is "No," answer the following questions:

   A. State the claims which you did not present in any previous petition, application, or motion for relief under 28 U.S.C. § 2254 or § 2255: _____ _____

_____

   B. State the reasons why you did not present the above claims in any previous petition, application or   motion for relief under 28 U.S.C. § 2254 or § 2255:* _____

_____

_____

*NOTE: This Court will grant you authority to file in the district court only if you show that you could not have presented your present claims in your previous § 2254 or § 2255 application because . . .

  A. (For § 2255 motions only) the claims involve "newly discovered evidence that, if proven and viewed in light of the evidence as a whole, would be sufficient to establish by clear and convincing evidence that no reasonable factfinder would have found [you] guilty"; or,

  B. (For § 2254 petitions only) "the factual predicate for the claim could not have been discovered previously through the exercise of due diligence" and "the facts underlying the claim, if proven and viewed in light of the evidence as a whole, would be sufficient to establish by clear and convincing evidence that, but for constitutional error, no reasonable factfinder would have found [you] guilty of the offense"; or,

  C. (For both § 2254 and § 2255 applicants) the claims involve "a new rule of constitutional law, made retroactive to cases on collateral review by the Supreme Court [of the United States], that was previously unavailable."

State how you meet the above requirements:

_____
_____
_____
_____
_____

If it has been more than one year since either (1) your conviction became final; (2) you discovered the new evidence on which you rely; or (3) the United States Supreme Court case on which you rely was decided, state why you could not file your petition earlier:

_____
_____
_____
_____
_____

  Movant prays that the United States Court of Appeals for the _____ Circuit grant an Order Authorizing the District Court to Consider Movant's Second or Successive Application for Relief Under 28 U.S.C. §§ 2254 or 2255.

_____
Movant's Signature

I declare under Penalty of Perjury that my answers to all questions in this Motion are true and correct.

Executed on _____
                    [date]

_____
Movant's Signature

PROOF OF SERVICE

A copy of this motion and all attachments must be sent to the state attorney general (§ 2254 cases) or the United States Attorney for the United States judicial district in which you were convicted (§ 2255 cases).

I certify that on _____ I mailed a copy of this motion and all attachments
                    [date]

to _____ at the following address:

_____

Rev. 2/99

                                                                         Movant's Signature

APPENDIX D
GLOSSARY OF TERMS

Actual innocence: evidence that proves the accused could not have committed a certain crime (e.g., DNA evidence, videotape showing the accused was elsewhere at time of crime, etc.).

Adjudicate: render a decision after consideration of the facts and applicable law.

Administrative segregation: temporary confinement, within prison, to an isolation cell, often called "the hole."

Affidavit: written statement sworn to under oath before a notary public.

Affirmative defense: legal defense that ends a disputed claim in a court case.

Annual term: yearly period during which a court hears and decides cases.

Appendix: additional, supplementary information or documents at the end of a book or legal pleading.

Applicable: legally appropriate or relevant.

Ban: block, prohibit, or make illegal.

Bedrock procedural element: foundational legal principle on which a law or procedural rule originates from.

Brady violation: prosecution's suppression of evidence favorable to the accused, so named for Brady v. Maryland, 373 U.S. 83 (1963).

Case law: rules and principles of law established by appellate court decisions.

Category of punishment: broadly grouped set of punishments to be served for a certain criminal offense, such as murder, robbery, rape, etc.

Cite: support a legal position or argument by quoting or directing a court to a specific legal authority, case law, statute, etc.

Class of defendants: group of defendants belonging to a specific category (e.g., juvenile offenders, mentally retarded offenders, etc.).

Clear and convincing evidence: evidence showing that something required to be proven is highly probable or reasonably certain. (This standard is higher than the preponderance of evidence standard.)

Collateral proceeding: proceeding in which the convicted can present a challenge to conviction, raising postconviction claims such as ineffective assistance, newly discovered evidence, Brady violation, etc.

Collateral review: process in which postconviction claims are reviewed by the courts.

Comity: a court's respect for another court outside of its jurisdiction, shown by abiding by the second court's laws when not legally required to do so.

Constitutional error: error that violates and affects rights guaranteed by the United States Constitution.

Constitutional guarantee: right provided by the United States Constitution such as the First Amendment right to access to the courts, or the Fourteenth Amendment right to not be deprived of life, liberty or property without due process of law, nor denied the equal protection of the law.

Countervailing need: need to assure that any criminal punishment is only imposed when authorized by law, offsetting the effect of a case's finality.

Culpability: degree of a person's criminal liability or guilt.

Direct review: first appeal to immediately follow a criminal conviction.

Discretionary review: review by an appellate or supreme court, conducted not as a legal right but at a court's discretion.

Due diligence: continual actions taken by a prisoner to satisfy a legal requirement and obtain relief.

E.g.: abbreviation of Latin exempli gratia ("for the sake of an example").

En banc: entire panel of judges, for appellate or supreme court, hearing a case due to the importance of an issue being decided.

Equitable tolling: allowance for a prisoner's failure to seek relief in court within the time allotted by rule or statute, based on a reasonable excuse by the prisoner.

Exhaustion: use of every available remedy for relief provided by state or federal rule or statute.

Expedient: (of a court's decision) reasonably speedy.

Extraordinary circumstances: circumstances beyond a prisoner's control, which made the timely filing of a court pleading impossible.

Factual predicate of claim: material facts that comprise the support for a legal conclusion and establish a violation of a constitutional right or privilege.

Finality: end of legal challenges and opportunity to be heard by the United States Supreme Court, after a period of time, in order to enforce a judgment and mandate in accordance with the law.

Forensic evidence: evidence that proves a fact through the method of scientific tests or techniques.

Germane: important to a subject under consideration.

Habeas corpus: Latin ("you shall have the body" in court) name for a writ requiring a prisoner to be brought before a judge or court to ensure the detention is lawful.

Ibid. (also ib.): abbreviation of Latin ibidem ("in the same place"), in the same source as a previously quoted reference.

Impediment: obstruction, bar, or block to information, evidence, or the court.

Infringement: violation of, or encroachment upon, a right or privilege.

In re: Latin phrase ("in the matter of") referencing a legal case.

Judgment and mandate: a court's final decision and directive disposing of a case.

Leave of court: permission (granted by a court) to perform, or proceed with, an action.

Legal standard: criteria that must be met before one may be entitled to relief based upon a right or privilege.

Mandatory exhaustion: requirement by rule or statute that a prisoner seek relief through all available state-court remedies before proceeding to a federal court.

Merits: factual claims, as opposed to technical matters, for a court's consideration (e,g., procedural rules, exhaustion, or jurisdiction).

Newly discovered evidence: evidence, neither cumulative nor impeaching, discovered after trial, which could not have been earlier discovered through due diligence, and which is relevant to an issue from trial.

New rule of constitutional law: rule announced by the United States Supreme Court that defines a right and establishes new constitutional law to be imposed upon the state or the federal government to follow.

One full round of appeals: direct appeal and all available postconviction remedies, from the highest state court or United States Supreme Court through a writ of certiorari.

Perjury: false statement willfully made regarding a material fact, while under oath, at a trial or deposition.

Precedent: legal decision that acts as established legal authority in an area of law.

Preponderance of evidence: evidence that is more convincing then the evidence offered in opposition to it.

Prima facie: Latin term ("first showing") for that which is accepted as fact until proved otherwise.

Principle: fundamental rule or legal doctrine that other rules or case law may evolve from.

Procedural default: principle that denies a federal court jurisdiction to review the merits of a prisoner's habeas corpus petition before a state court's opportunity to do so, in accordance with a state procedural rule or statute. See also exhaustion.

Procedural rule: a rule dictating that something be done before certain actions are taken or a judgment rendered and enforced.

Prosecutorial misconduct: failure by the State to disclose Brady material, knowingly offering false testimony or false evidence, etc.

Reasonable fact-finder: jurors or a judge in a trial.

Recant: change or correct one's prior false or misleading trial testimony.

Retroactivity: principle requiring a new rule or law to be applied to past cases with equal force as to those in the future.

State-court remedies: rules and statutes that provide a prisoner an opportunity to attack a conviction in a collateral proceeding.

Statute of limitations: time limit, set by rule or statute, for filing a petition, motion, or application.

Sua sponte: Latin term ("of [one's] own accord") denoting action taken by a court upon its own motion.

Substantive rule: rule that forbids the criminal punishment of certain conduct or prohibits a certain category of punishment for a class of defendants due to their status or the type of crime committed, because it violates certain inalienable rights guaranteed by the United States Constitution.

Watershed procedural rule: rule that implicates the fundamental fairness and accuracy of a criminal proceeding (e.g., denying a defendant the right to counsel).

Writ of certiorari: writ issued by the United States Supreme Court that directs a lower court to either reverse or affirm a previous decision.

ACKNOWLEDGMENTS

First, thank you, Kristin Summers, my publisher at redbat books, for all the many talents used to make this fifth *Smith's Guide* a reality.

Thank you to my mother, Barbara Bristor, for searching for every address of the United States attorney general, mailed in to the prison five pages at a time. Without them, I wouldn't have been able to provide you with Appendix B.

Thank you, Byron Case, for superb editing of another invaluable tool in the pro se litigator's arsenal.

I'm also grateful to all the court clerks who accepted my phone calls and provided example applications and information about their circuits application processes.

WISDOM IS THE KEY TO SUCCESS
Get Wise; Get a Smith's Guide™

Let Smith guide you step-by-step through the courts
and do it right the first time—every time.

All Smith's Guides are designed for the beginning pro se prisoner
and the practicing pro se litigator alike and are complete
with example pleadings from successful cases.

    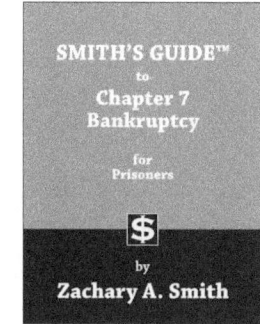

NEW! *SMITH'S GUIDE*™ to State Habeas Corpus Relief for State Prisoners

Provides detailed information and instructions for seeking relief via state habeas petition and for exhausting state-court remedies before proceeding to federal court to file a §2254 petition or an application to file a second or successive habeas petition. Includes state habeas rules and statutes for all 50 states. [±540 pages]

SMITH'S GUIDE™ to Habeas Corpus Relief for State Prisoners Under 28 U.S.C. §2254

This book covers the entire process for filing the initial §2254 habeas petition to the final petition for a writ of certiorari in the U.S. Supreme Court. [380 pages]

NEW! *SMITH'S GUIDE*™ to Second or Successive Federal Habeas Corpus Relief for State and Federal Prisoners

For those seeking to file a second or successive habeas petition under §2244 or §2255, based on newly discovered evidence or retroactive effect of a U.S. Supreme Court case, this book provides detailed instructions for preparing the application. [352 pages]

SMITH'S GUIDE™ to Executive Clemency for State and Federal Prisoners

For those who have exhausted all legal remedies or have sentences that are too long to serve, this book lays out every aspect of the clemency process, self-development and personal transformation, communication skills, clemency campaign and promotional strategies, and much more. It is also applicable for parole hearings and could make the difference between freedom or additional incarceration. [288 pages]

SMITH'S GUIDE™ to Chapter 7 Bankruptcy for Prisoners

Get immediate freedom from liens against offender account (including from incarceration reimbursement judgment, halfway house costs, probation/parole intervention fees, and other debt) by filing chapter 7 bankruptcy. Includes blank bankruptcy forms and filing instructions. [256 pages]

All titles available online at Amazon.com

WISDOM IS THE KEY TO SUCCESS
Get Wise; Get a Smith's Guide™

Let Smith guide you step-by-step through the courts
and do it right the first time—every time.

All Smith's Guides are designed for the beginning pro se prisoner
and the practicing pro se litigator alike and are complete
with example pleadings from successful cases.

NEW! SMITH'S GUIDE™ to State Habeas Corpus Relief for State Prisoners

Provides detailed information and instructions for seeking relief via state habeas petition and for exhausting state-court remedies before proceeding to federal court to file a §2254 petition or an application to file a second or successive habeas petition. Includes state habeas rules and statutes for all 50 states. [±540 pages]

SMITH'S GUIDE™ to Habeas Corpus Relief for State Prisoners Under 28 U.S.C. §2254

This book covers the entire process for filing the initial §2254 habeas petition to the final petition for a writ of certiorari in the U.S. Supreme Court. [380 pages]

NEW! SMITH'S GUIDE™ to Second or Successive Federal Habeas Corpus Relief for State and Federal Prisoners

For those seeking to file a second or successive habeas petition under §2244 or §2255, based on newly discovered evidence or retroactive effect of a U.S. Supreme Court case, this book provides detailed instructions for preparing the application. [352 pages]

SMITH'S GUIDE™ to Executive Clemency for State and Federal Prisoners

For those who have exhausted all legal remedies or have sentences that are too long to serve, this book lays out every aspect of the clemency process, self-development and personal transformation, communication skills, clemency campaign and promotional strategies, and much more. It is also applicable for parole hearings and could make the difference between freedom or additional incarceration. [288 pages]

SMITH'S GUIDE™ to Chapter 7 Bankruptcy for Prisoners

Get immediate freedom from liens against offender account (including from incarceration reimbursement judgment, halfway house costs, probation/parole intervention fees, and other debt) by filing chapter 7 bankruptcy. Includes blank bankruptcy forms and filing instructions. [256 pages]

All titles available online at Amazon.com

www.ingramcontent.com/pod-product-compliance
Lightning Source LLC
Chambersburg PA
CBHW080724230426

43665CB00020B/2613